People who have a common interest in a collective good do not necessarily find it easy to act collectively in pursuit of that interest. There is usually some mismatch between individual and group interests. There may be an *efficacy problem*, when no individual is able to provide enough common benefit to make acting worthwhile, or a *free-rider problem*, when most or all individuals hope that someone else will provide the good. Any attempt to overcome these problems through coordination and collaboration entails costs and problems of its own.

This book is a formal mathematical analysis of some of the processes whereby groups solve the problems of collective action. The authors break new ground in showing that the problem of collective action requires a model of group process and group heterogeneity and cannot be deduced from simple models of individual behavior. They emphasize the role of small subgroups of especially motivated and resourceful individuals who form the "critical mass" that sets collective action in motion.

The book will be read with special interest by sociologists, social psychologists, economists, and political scientists. It will also be of concern to those in industrial relations, communications research, and other fields who are working on issues in collective action and rational choice.

THE CRITICAL MASS IN COLLECTIVE ACTION

A MICRO-SOCIAL THEORY

Gerald Marwell and Pamela Oliver

University of Wisconsin-Madison

THE CRITICAL MASS IN COLLECTIVE ACTION

A Micro-Social Theory

CAMBRIDGE
UNIVERSITY PRESS

Published by the Press Syndicate of the University of Cambridge
The Pitt Building, Trumpington Street, Cambridge CB2 1RP
40 West 20th Street, New York, NY 10011-4211, USA
10 Stamford Road, Oakleigh, Victoria 3166, Australia

© Cambridge University Press 1993

First published 1993

Printed in the United States of America

Library of Congress Cataloging-in-Publication Data
Marwell, Gerald, 1937–
The critical mass in collective action : a micro-social theory /
Gerald Marwell & Pamela Oliver.
p.   cm. – (Studies in rationality and social change)
ISBN 0-521-30839-9 (hc)
1. Social action.   2. Collective behavior.   3. Microsociology.
I. Oliver, Pamela.   II. Title.   III. Series.
HM291.M376   1993
302'.14 – dc20   92-23162
                                                        CIP

A catalog record for this book is available from the British Library.

ISBN 0-521-30839-9 hardback

Contents

Preface

First separately and then together, we have been writing about collective action since the mid-1970s. The work that forms the basis for this book began in the early 1980s, and most of the formal results presented here have previously appeared in published articles. But because our ideas and assumptions changed over time, differences among the articles in models, notation, and approach have made it difficult for scholars to evaluate and use our published work. Thus, although the formal mathematical results in most chapters of this book stand largely intact from prior publication, their presentation has been completely revised. We have developed one overarching general model (explicated in Chapter 2) and explain in detail how the specific models in later chapters are special cases of the general model. We explicitly discuss the similarities and differences in the assumptions of the different analyses. We have also revised the exposition to use one consistent example throughout the book, in another attempt to provide the reader with a more unified point of reference for evaluating our results. Finally, the analysis of selectivity and information cost in Chapter 6 is wholly new.

We have several audiences in mind for this book, and their requirements are not entirely compatible. We want to speak not only to experts in collective action theory, but to scholars who study social movements and other empirical instances of collective action and to graduate students studying collective action or mathematical models. We have added to this volume extended expositions of the underlying logic of our models and of the considerations involved in creating a model of a collective action process. We realize that these expositions will seem unnecessary or irritating to the experts and to the mathematically sophisticated, and we realize that those who are comfortable with mathematics will find our mathematical tools elementary. We ask these readers to bear with us. We feel that there is too little appreciation in our discipline of the value of mathematical models and too little understanding of how to think about them. Unsophisticated readers often feel unable to evaluate mathematized models critically and must either accept or reject them with little more to go on than faith or prejudice. Although people who are not used to thinking mathematically will find parts of our work tough sledding, we have tried to put into words the assumptions about process embodied in our math so that the reader can think about the plausibility of those assumptions. We also try to persuade the reader to think of assumptions not as true or false, but as applicable or inapplicable to particular empirical instances.

Our work is driven by two intellectual imperatives. The first is to set up plausible assumptions and then work out the deductive consequences of those assumptions. We believe that one of the most important jobs of theorists is to push theories to the limit, to figure out just where you have to go if you follow the logic of your premises. In this, we agree with the small cadre of formal theorists in our discipline, but disagree with the majority who seem to believe that the central stuff of theory is trying to list exactly the "right" set of initial premises. In particular, although we employ simplistic instrumentalist or rationalist *assumptions* about individuals in our work, we do *not* claim that these assumptions are "true" about real people, and certainly do *not* "prove" that collective actors are rational or instrumentalist.

We think the major contribution of our work is to explore the consequences of group heterogeneity and interdependent action for collective action. What we find interesting and important is that group outcomes cannot be determined from models about individuals, but must include specific information about the distributions of important properties among group members and specific information about how group members communicate and interact. Our understanding of how our models behave leads us to conclude that the assumptions we make about individual psychology play almost no role in determining the outcomes. Throughout the book, we return to this issue, illuminating the underlying mechanisms in each result and reflecting on the work each assumption does or does not do in producing the outcome. We try to guide the reader to thinking about the kinds of situations to which each result might apply. We are confident that any thoughtful reader will be able to think of counterexamples to every one of our results. Nothing we say in this book is true in any absolute empirical sense. The question is whether it helps to illuminate some of the processes in complex empirical cases.

Our second intellectual imperative is to understand at least some of the empirical phenomena known as collective action and to use theory to create a cognitive map of the different kinds of collective action, a map that can help us and others improve our ability to theorize meaningfully about collective action. We draw extensively, if unsystematically, on our wide experience in and reading about social movements and voluntary action. All theories, no matter how abstractly written, are created by people who have specific empirical cases in mind when they write. As we have talked with other scholars about our ideas, we have found it helpful to acknowledge that our ideas are rooted in our experiences in a wide variety of voluntary associations, and that they draw culturally more on the ethos of the 1970s and 1980s than on the ethos of the 1960s. For example, the central insight of Chapter 4 on production functions – the difference between accelerating and decelerating functions – arose directly from our observation of the dynamics of neighborhood associations. The organizer-centered model employed in later chapters similarly comes from our own experiences as activists and our observations of and conversations with activists in the field. Turning these experiences into abstract mathematical models necessarily divorces them from their empirical base, and it is easy for us to get so interested in the abstract deductive consequences of our models that we lose sight sometimes of the complex empirical reality that gave rise to them. But because both of us also read and write about social movements and voluntary action in other, more substantive forms, we hope that we have been able to maintain enough contact with empirical cases to provide at least a partial reality check on our theorizing.

Throughout this project, we have experienced the pleasure and pain of receiving thoughtful critical commentary on our work from some of the finest intellects in social science, many of them disguised as anonymous reviewers. We have had enough time to incorporate at least some of this commentary into our thinking and hope that we have used this occasion to improve our work in light of it. Where we think the critics had a point, we have tried to deal with the issue, although perhaps too often with a patch instead of a whole new part. Of course, we still find some of the criticism wrongheaded. In these cases, we have tried in this volume to explain more carefully why we believe we are right.

Acknowledgments

Without the support, advice, and assistance of numerous people, this book would have been completed anyway, but certainly not this year or next, and probably with some reduction in quality.

Ralph Prahl deserves special mention. As coauthor of Chapter 7 and the first author of the article on which that chapter was based, he made major contributions to conceptualizing the problem and theory, performed most of the analyses, and wrote the first draft. A draft of this material became his master's thesis in sociology at the University of Wisconsin-Madison. Ralph also served as our assistant and programmer for other parts of this project and was a junior coauthor of a second paper.

While they were graduate students, Ruy Teixeira and David Weakliem also worked as programmers and assistants. Ruy was a junior coauthor of one article from the project. All three of these assistants were enormously helpful, skilled, reliable, and professional. We were lucky to have them work with us.

We have also been lucky to be in a department that is enormously supportive of intellectual work – both materially and affectively. We thank all of our colleagues for making this a positive environment. A few were particularly helpful on this project, reading drafts and giving advice: Charles Halaby, Robert Mare, Elizabeth Thomson, and Erik O. Wright.

John Lemke aided the project in many ways over the years – always as a supportive spouse and coparent for Pam, and from time to time as a mathematical editor and programming consultant. Pam would also like to acknowledge Elizabeth and Robert, who were major impediments to the completion of the project, but who created more than enough joy to make it all worthwhile. Jerry's kids were launched and caused no problems. Bobbie has survived thirty-five years of collective effort, and survived this book too.

Karen Bloom, Karina Davenport, Jinkuk Hong, and John Lemke helped us produce the manuscript. Robert Racine did a wonderful job of copy-editing.

Most of this work was supported by the National Science Foundation through grant NSF SES–8408131. Supplementary support was provided by the Wisconsin Alumni Research Foundation.

Finally, we would like to thank the reviewers for and editors of the journals and edited volume in which earlier versions of parts of this book appeared. Although the material in the book has been extensively revised, the reviewers and editors gave us substantial advice and assistance. The relevant previous publications are the following:

Chapter 3: Pamela Oliver and Gerald Marwell. 1988. ''The Paradox of Group Size in Collective Action: A Theory of the Critical Mass. II.'' *American Sociological Review* 53:1–8.

Chapter 4: Pamela E. Oliver, Gerald Marwell, and Ruy Teixeira. 1985. ''A Theory of the Critical Mass. I. Interdependence, Heterogeneity and the Production of Collective Action.'' *American Journal of Sociology* 91:522–56.

Chapter 5: Gerald Marwell, Pamela Oliver, and Ralph Prahl. 1988. ''Social Networks and Collective Action: A Theory of the Critical Mass. III.'' *American Journal of Sociology* 94:502–34.

Chapter 5: Gerald Marwell and Pamela E. Oliver. 1991. ''A Theory of the Critical Mass. VI. Cliques and Collective Action.'' In *Disciplin und Kreativitat,* ed. Henrik Kreutz and Johann Bacher, pp. 49–62. Opladen: Leske and Burdich, 1991.

Chapter 7: Ralph Prahl, Gerald Marwell, and Pamela Oliver. 1991. ''Selectivity as Strategies of Recruitment for Collective Action: A Theory of the Critical Mass, V.'' *Journal of Mathematical Sociology* 16:137–64.

1. The critical mass and the problem of collective action

An atomic pile "goes critical" when a chain reaction of nuclear fission becomes self-sustaining; for an atomic pile, or an atomic bomb, there is some minimum amount of fissionable material that has to be compacted together to keep the reaction from petering out. . . . The principle of critical mass is so simple that it is no wonder that it shows up in epidemiology, fashion, survival and extinction of species, language systems, racial integration, jaywalking, panic behavior, and political movements.

Thomas C. Schelling (1978, p. 89)

The idea of the *critical mass* is central to many understandings of collective action. Social movement activists, community leaders, and fund-raisers use the term when they talk about getting together enough resources to accomplish some goal. They express the understanding that it takes some minimum number of people or some minimum accumulation of seed money to draw in the participation and contributions of others. The phenomenon can also be seen in other, less intentional forms of collective action. Lynchings, wildcat strikes, and riots proceed when people become convinced that enough others are participating. Detailed observational studies of spontaneous collective action show incipient "organizers" calling to others to join their action, and they show potential participants talking to each other and reaching a common agreement about who will act (see McPhail 1971; Berk 1974; Fantasia 1988). The riot was the archetypal phenomenon of interest for early analysts of collective action. Had more been known about nuclear fission when Gustav LeBon was writing *The Crowd* (1895), for example, he would undoubtedly have found the metaphor of the chain reaction very attractive.

The term *collective action* is understood by most social scientists today to be an abstraction that encompasses a staggeringly broad array of empirical phenomena: from raising an army to raising a barn; from building a bridge across a gulf separating states to building a faith community that spans the gulf between races; from organizing a business cartel to organizing a small partnership to compete in a crowded market; from the food riots of revolutionary France to the progressive dinners of charitable New York. As we will explain more carefully, the elements common to these disparate phenomena are mutual interests and the possibility of benefits from coordinated action. Given this variety, it is no surprise that over the past two decades most of the social sciences have shown an accelerating interest in understanding the process by which collective action comes to occur.[1]

Our theory of the critical mass is a contribution to the tradition of studying collective action in the abstract. It differs from previous theory primarily in its focus on interdependence among actors, heterogeneity within groups, and the role of mobilizing agents. We assume that in most instances collective action is produced by a relatively small cadre of highly interested and resourceful individuals, rather than by the efforts of the "average" group member. Our major objective is to delineate the structural conditions under which such a "critical mass" of individuals and resources will be accumulated and directed toward the achievement of a collective goal.

We offer a general framework and a series of specific theoretical analyses. Our specific analyses address only a subset of the possibilities suggested by our general framework. We do not provide a comprehensive, "one size fits all" theory of collective action. To the contrary, we will

---

[1] Although the sociological literature on formal collective action theory is relatively small (see Obserschall 1973, 1980; Coleman 1973, 1986, 1988, 1989; Smith 1976; Fireman and Gamson 1979; Marwell and Ames 1979; Oliver 1980; Marwell and Oliver 1984; Oliver, Marwell, and Teixeira 1985; Heckathorn 1988, 1989, 1990, 1991, 1992; Macy 1989, 1990, 1991a, 1991b; Oliver and Marwell 1992), the literatures in economics, political science, and psychology are much too large to review adequately here. The "public goods problem" is longstanding in economics, although Samuelson (1954) and Bator (1958) are usually seen as the classic statements; Head (1974) provides a clear treatment of the fundamental economic issues; Schelling (1973) ties public goods to the more general issue of externalities; Brubaker (1982) examines some empirical evidence in experimental economics. Olson (1965) is important for having exported the economic ideas to other social sciences, but does not provide a definitive formal statement of the problem. Political scientists who have refined these ideas and applied them to collective action dilemmas include Chamberlin (1974); Frohlich and Oppenheimer (1970) and Frohlich et al. (1975); Hardin (1971); Schofield (1975); Van de Kragt, Orbell, and Dawes (1983); and Chung (1991). Perhaps the most thorough and wide-ranging treatment of the issues of collective action is Hardin (1982). Psychologists generally explore experimentally the dynamics of social dilemmas in relatively small groups (Kelley and Grzelak 1972; Bonacich et al. 1976; Dawes, McTarish, and Shaklee, 1977; Dawes 1980; Dawes and Orbell 1982; Messick and McClelland 1983; Messick et al. 1983; Brewer 1985).

show that there is no unitary phenomenon of "collective action" that can be described by a simple set of theoretical propositions. We will attempt to show the futility of posing general questions such as "Is collective action rational?" or "Do people free-ride?" Instead, we will lay out the dimensions of the field of collective action, then focus in on small parts of the field and provide detailed analysis of what we find in those small plots. There won't be any readers who walk away from this book feeling that they have learned everything there is to know about collective action.

But we hope that most will realize how many interesting questions there are to pursue and why there are real benefits to be gained from pursuing them, at least in part, through formal mathematical representations.

Background

Beginnings: free riding and The Logic of Collective Action

For us, as for most social scientists (Turner 1981), Mancur Olson's treatise *The Logic of Collective Action* (1965) served as an exciting introduction to the field of public goods and to the problem of collective action. Much of Olson's impact results from his strongly worded three-page introduction, in which he asserts that "rational, self-interested individuals will not act to achieve their common or group interests" (1965, p. 2). The reason for this claim is that, when interests are shared, rational actors should prefer to free-ride, that is, let others pay the costs of goods that will benefit everyone. The rationale for this assertion is explicated in the first, widely cited part of Olson's book. The rest of the book surveys the history of labor unions, classes and the state, interest groups, and pressure groups, defending Olson's thesis that collective action is always accompanied by private (selective) incentives to reward contributors or to punish noncontributors; this material is only rarely cited or discussed (an exception being Fireman and Gamson 1979).

Economists had long argued that economically rational individuals will not voluntarily contribute money to pay for public goods such as armies, legislatures, parks, public schools, or sewage systems. Olson's important contribution was to argue that all group goals or group interests were subject to the same dilemma. For Olson, the central issue was *nonexcludability* (also called "impossibility of exclusion" [Hardin 1982, p. 16] or "infeasibility of exclusion'' [Head 1974]).[2] Olson defined a *collective good* as any good in which a group of individuals is *interested* (i.e., from which each thinks he will benefit) and which, if provided to one member of the group, cannot be withheld from any other member. For example, a park is a collective good for the ''group'' of park-loving city residents if none of them can be prevented from enjoying it. This is true even if the park were wholly purchased and built through private contributions to a park fund or, in the extreme, by a single private benefactor. If its use cannot be – or in practice is not – restricted to contributors, the park is a collective good.

In this conception, any and all activity aimed at the provision of a collective good is defined as *collective action*. By this definition, a single person providing a collective good is engaging in collective action, and the individual provision of collective goods is an important phenomenon that should not be overlooked. Nevertheless, most scholars in this tradition also implicitly restrict their attention to actions that are collective in an older sense as well, so that the working definition of collective action is *actions taken by two or more people in pursuit of the same collective good.*

Olson argues that because of the ''free-rider problem,'' collective goods such as parks will generally *not* be provided through voluntary contributions. ''Free riders,'' in this context, are people who do not contribute to the provision of a good but consume it (or, in the case of parks, use it) anyway. Unfortunately, according to Olson, the logic of collective goods is such that free riding is usually the *only* ''rational'' economic response for all members of the group. Since I will be able to use the park whether I contribute to the park fund or not, I will be best off if I keep my money in my pocket and let everyone else pay for it. Moreover, since everyone else in the city is rational (Olson's initial assumption), and makes the same calculation as I do, no one should contribute to the park fund, and the park will never be built. Olson further argues that this dilemma will be greater the larger the group; we will engage this argument in Chapter 3.

The free-rider problem is a classic expression of the conflict that often arises between individual and group ''rationality.'' The emergence of col-

---

[2] In the early work of Samuelson (1954), Head (1974), and others ''pure'' public goods are defined by *both* nonexcludability and ''jointness of supply.'' In later work jointness of supply tends to actually be treated as a variable, regardless of the formal definition used. For a good summary of this issue, see Hardin (1982, pp. 17–20). We discuss jointness of supply extensively in Chapter 2.

lective action in groups is not simply a matter of the group "realizing" its collective needs and therefore acting to meet them. Groups cannot be reified. In Olson's formulation, they simply consist of a number of individuals who share an interest in a good. They do not have explicit organization or institutions. They are *interest groups,* such as social classes ("in themselves" in Marx's [1963] terms), or occupational categories, or parents whose children share a similar disease. Any "collective action" by such a group must be understood as the aggregated behavior of its individual members.

For each individual member, the group and its needs are usually only part of his life. He has a broader array of interests that he is attempting to realize through his activities. For any specific activity, his interests may or may not coincide with the interests of the group; in fact, we have reasons to suppose that they frequently do not. For the people of a city, taken as a whole, the expenditure of $10,000 for a park might bring $40,000 worth of pleasure and be completely "rational." For Sam Citizen, the $10 he is asked to contribute for a park that he would enjoy once in a while might bring much more pleasure if spent on an evening at the movies or on his children's clothes. Besides, he will get to use the park in any case. The problem of collective action is thus the conflict between individual group members' pursuit of their own interests and the needs of the group as a whole. This problem is everywhere in social life.

Notice that, contrary to a common misunderstanding, Olson does *not* argue or prove that individuals participate in collective action out of self-interest. Rather, he argues that self-interest implies that individuals will not participate in collective action. One perfectly reasonable conclusion to deduce from Olson's logic is that only *irrational* motives can explain collective action. The argument readily supports scholars who claim that solidarity or altruism or some other motive besides self-interest is particularly important for collective action. Olson himself does not go in this direction and instead sticks with the usual assumption of economists that all behavior is motivated only by self-interest. He therefore invokes selective incentives, but other scholars should not neglect the import of Olson's logic.

Although we are ultimately critical of some of Olson's theorizing, the importance of Olson's argument to the history of social science cannot be underestimated. Before Olson, almost all social scientists assumed that people would instinctively or naturally act on common interests, and that *inaction* needed to be explained. After Olson, most social scientists treat collective action as problematic. But what scholars who pursue the field learn very quickly is that Olson is neither the first nor the last economist to write on the subject, and that understanding the details of Olson's argument is not all there is to understanding the logic of collective action. A great deal of economic literature, particularly in public finance, addresses an enormous number of distinct issues and complexities that arise around what very generally are called "externalities," "market failures," and "nonlinearities." It would take several books to do justice to this literature, and we will not be using it much in our work. What we do use to some extent are very general insights from economics and the collective action literatures in sociology, political science, and psychology to show how Olson's claims are an important special case of a much larger multidimensional problem. As we write, we focus on those issues and dimensions that seem to us to be central from the vantage point of sociologists who study social movements and voluntary action.

Providing collective goods: theories and research

Free riding is a real problem. And yet collective goods are everywhere provided. Most real societies have armies, parks, and some form of public works. More important, voluntary action is widespread. People often make large personal sacrifices for social movements for diffuse collective goods such as freedom for everyone. Unions are organized. Ordinary people are brave in the face of repression. Charities are funded, sometimes by rich donors, but sometimes by the small gifts of thousands of individual donors responding in their own homes to appeals received through the mail. Any reasonable theory must account for these phenomena, as well as for the equally obvious fact that many collective goods ardently desired by some group, or even a whole population, never come to pass.

Of course, the obvious source of many collective goods is coercion by government. The classic analysis of the reason for government is precisely that armies, parks, and sewer systems require taxation, impressment, and the right to back up these processes with force. To Olson, however, coercion is only one instance, albeit possibly the most important, of a broader class of phenomena he calls "selective incentives." These include "social status and social acceptance" (p. 61) and monetary incentives that are privately delivered for participation in the collective action. The fundamental example of the latter is the salaries paid some individuals to work for organizations engaged in collective action. Examples cited by Olson are insurance plans, price discounts, and other services offered by organizations like unions, or the AARP for joining their "social movement." In a footnote, Olson adds "erotic incentives, psychological incentives, moral incentives, and so on" (p. 61) to his list of selective incentives.

As it has been reinterpreted by other scholars, Olson's selective incentives thesis is quite consistent with the emphasis on solidarity and morality found in other theoretical perspectives. Following Clark and Wilson (1961) and James Wilson (1973), the concept of selective incentives is now understood to include not only material incentives, but also solidary incentives, which arise from interaction with others, and purposive incentives, the moral feeling of self-satisfaction from doing the right thing. Thus, Olson's thesis may be reinterpreted as saying that people will not engage in collective action solely from motives of isolated *material* self-interest in the collective good, but will also have solidary ties to other collective actors, have a sense of moral purpose, stand to gain personally from the very fact of acting, or any combination of these motives.

Although we are not offering a systematic review of the empirical literature here, it is our impression that the major predictors of participation are the level of *subjective* interest in the collective good, solidary ties to other collective actors, and personal satisfaction or moral rectitude from feeling that one is accomplishing good. These subjective factors are actually consistent with the microeconomic approach, which *always* contains *subjective* preferences in its equations. Interestingly, even in experimental conditions designed to make Olson's assumptions about the irrationality of individual contributions to collective action clearly hold true, research indicates that people tend to contribute substantial amounts to the collective action, although the amount of the collective good provided is suboptimal (Marwell and Ames 1979, 1981). Selective incentives are actually Olson's "simple and sovereign" theory of collective action: "Only a *separate and 'selective' incentive* will stimulate a rational individual . . . to act in a group-oriented way. . . . The incentive must be 'selective' so that those who do not join the organization working for the group's interest . . . can be treated differently from those who do" (p. 51). Olson further argues that selective incentives are much more easily administered in small than in large groups, which accounts for the fact that most (almost all) collective action actually arises in smaller (''privileged'') groups. This position is particularly plausible when the incentives at issue are social in nature. Plausible as it may seem, Olson's argument is wrong on its own terms. Subsequent formal analysts have shown that selective incentives, particularly the material incentives stressed by Olson, cannot automatically solve the collective action dilemma (Frohlich and Oppenheimer 1970; Oliver 1980). The problem is simply that somebody has to pay for the selective incentive, and paying for a selective incentive is *also* a collective action in that it will provide a benefit to everyone interested in the collective good, not just the people who pay for the incentive. Thus, the free-rider problem adheres just as much to providing selective incentives to induce others to provide collective goods as to the original collective action problem.

Apart from this central critique, an extensive literature disputes most of the other details of Olson's analysis (Frohlich and Oppenheimer 1970; Chamberlin 1974; Frohlich, Hunt, Oppenheimer, and Wagner 1975; Scholfield 1975; Bonacich, Shure, Kahan, and Meeker 1976; Smith 1976; Hardin 1982; Oliver and Marwell 1988) and suggests other reasons for what appears to be the frequent solution of the free-rider problem in real life. Briefly summarized, many of the major critiques disagree with Olson's assertions that (1) each individual's maximum possible contribution is too small to make any noticeable difference in the provision of the collective good, (2) others' behavior makes no difference in the effect of one's contribution, and (3) coordination of action is not possible. According to his critics, these assertions are merely *assumptions,* and inspection of empirical reality suggests that one or another is unwarranted more often than not. When any one (or several) of these assumptions does not hold, the conclusion that collective action is ''irrational'' cannot be drawn. In fact, it is well established in the formal literature that *no* general conclusions about ''collective action'' can be drawn.

Because it is so important for everything that follows, let us repeat the point another way. One must *begin* with information or assumptions about the specific characteristics of the situation. Most importantly, Olson *assumes* that every individual finds that the cost of action exceeds the benefit to him of the collective good and *assumes* that individual benefits cannot be increased by coordinating actions with others. If this is true, collective action without selective incentives is ''irrational.'' But this is an *input* into the model, not a derivation from it. If the premise is false, so is the conclusion. Thus, the central question of collective action theory is *not* whether collective action is rational, but rather *when* it is rational, that is, under what circumstances individuals find that the benefit of participation exceeds their personal cost.

Development

Interdependence and the theory of the critical mass

Taking these criticisms to heart, we begin the development of the theory of the critical mass by assuming that although it may often prevent collective action or lead to suboptimal provision of collective goods, free riding does not automatically prohibit collective action in large groups. Our task, therefore, is to elaborate a theory that distinguishes those variables – including, but not limited to, group size – that affect the occurrence and amount of collective action.

Our key difference with Olson's formulation (although not our only difference) is that we do not assume that the individuals in an interest group are acting in total isolation. Instead, we assume *interdependence* among actors, where interdependence may be defined most generally as behavior that takes account of the effect of one's participation in collective action on the participation of others. The structural conditions for interdependent behavior are that the effect on the collective good of one actor's choice varies depending on the choices of others, and that actors have at least some information about each other's actions.

Interdependence is certainly common in the empirical world of collective action. An urbanite considering joining in a riot may assume that the risk of any one individual being arrested declines with larger numbers of rioters; an office worker may consider the possibility that her contribution to United Way will increase the social pressures on others to contribute as well; a participant in a wildcat strike may also expect his presence on the line to embolden others to participate. People join groups involved in collective pursuits not only out of perceived common interests, but also because they regard the groups or individuals organizing the action as in some sense efficacious. Belief in the efficacy of a group may be based on a record of previous successes at stated goals, on the endorsement of a friend or relative who is already involved in the group, or even on lip service by authorities to the goals of the group. For most people, however, the most prominent and convincing evidence of a group's efficacy is probably the group's size and command over resources. Groups that are large and rich are likely to be seen as powerful. Growth itself is often seen as further evidence of potency and tends to attract still more contributions; groups that are stagnant or shrinking are likely to be seen as ineffective, accelerating their loss of membership. In this simple fashion, the decisions of individuals who come into contact with a group or its organizer are clearly interdependent with the decisions of others.

It is important to note that although assumptions of interdependence complicate formal models of collective campaigns, they in no way invalidate a basic decision-theoretic approach. Nor are we the first social scientists to employ interdependence assumptions in formally analyzing various problems of collective action (e.g., Frolich and Oppenheimer 1970; Oberschall 1973, 1979, 1980; Frohlich et al. 1975; Granovetter 1978, 1980). Together with these scholars, we believe that the assumption of isolated actors is the weakest feature of the rather pessimistic appearance of previous theory. Deserting it seems a good place to start.

Group heterogeneity and the critical mass

In line with almost everyone who has taken the task of analyzing interdependent action seriously, we rapidly realized that assumptions must be made about the distributions of key variables across group members, and that the results are always affected by these distributions. Homogeneous groups yield very different results from heterogeneous groups. As our work has developed, we have pursued the implications of group heterogeneity and the complex ways it interacts with other features of collective action situations. Early on, we began to realize that "large contributors" – those who are highly interested and highly resourceful – play special roles in collective action, and we also realized that *what* role they play varies from situation to situation. Sometimes they provide the collective good themselves, and other times they play a central role in mobilizing others. (This argument is developed in Chapter 4.)

Having realized the importance of the critical mass in mobilizing others, we turned a great deal of our attention to developing an explicit theory of organizing. We developed a model of organizer-centered mobilizations and discovered that there were very interesting results that followed from this model concerning the effects of social networks, information levels, and recruitment strategies. These are the subjects of Chapters 5, 6, and 7.

Models of decisions and models of information

We develop our theory using an instrumentalist cost–benefit metatheory. We use this metatheory not as true believers who think that all decisions are or should be made "rationally," but because it gives us a fairly simple set of assumptions about individuals that permit us to gain a great deal of purchase in our understanding of groups. However, we do find this to be a plausible metatheory for collective action when collective action is *resource constrained*. Economics is often referred to as the science of behavior under conditions of scarcity. While we certainly do not think that our sociological theories can be reduced to economics, we do think that people contemplating collective action are usually operating in conditions of scarcity. If they are not, our theory will not apply. But when they have limited time and money, as most people do, they have to make choices about how they will allocate their time and money, and we believe they will somehow attempt to weigh costs and benefits. We do *not* assume that only material costs and benefits matter, but we do assume that subjective concerns are somehow balanced by people in a way that can be captured as a comparison of costs and benefits. To the extent that our assumption fits a particular situation, our models ought to apply. When the assumption is simply wrong, then the situation falls outside the scope of our theory.

Our models are all within the school of bounded rationality. That is, we assume that people are weighing not the universe of all logically possible actions, but the very limited set of cognitively available choices. At some points in the analysis, we assume perfect information about these limited choices, not because we believe information is ever perfect, but to provide a solid baseline for analysis. Later in the analysis, the degree of information itself becomes a variable.

As our work has developed, we have found it less and less necessary to make strong assumptions about the decision rules for most actors in our models. In general, all we need is the assumption that each individual has some fixed "contribution level" that is exogenously determined. This is still a significant assumption, because it means that we do *not* have models for how organizers persuade people to contribute more, and because we have no alternate theory for what causes those contribution levels. But it does let us get a great deal of purchase on the constraints on organizing in a heterogeneous group.

The nature of the enterprise

In each chapter we pose a theoretical problem, set up a model of the process, make a set of simplifying assumptions, and explore the deductive implications of our model. Sometimes we use Monte Carlo simulations or extensive numerical explorations to aid our understanding. We end up seeing patterns and relationships that were not obvious at the beginning. Then we try to figure out why the model behaves the way it does and what that would imply for the generality of the result.

Every conclusion in this book should begin with the words, ''Given our assumptions, our model predicts that . . . '' This makes for very ugly prose and a lot of subordinate clauses. For the sake of style, we prefer the active voice and unqualified assertions. But no sentence in this book expresses an empirical generalization or a claim to universal truth. We are not proved wrong by counterexamples any more than we are proved right by examples we offer. The long-range test of our theory will be the extent to which it can successfully point to significant patterns of differences among groups and among collective actions, and to the extent that the differences illuminated by our models turn out to make a difference in empirical cases.

Structure of the book

The remainder of this book describes the model we call the theory of the critical mass and attempts to derive from the model a series of assertions about the way collective action should come to pass (or not) in the empirical world. Because our model rests on a formal base, Chapter 2 is devoted to describing the elements and assumptions of the model in some detail. In Chapter 3, we consider the factor to which Olson himself paid the most attention, group size, and show how the cost function for the good and the degree of group heterogeneity condition the relation between group size and the possibility of collective action. In Chapter 4, we turn our attention to the way in which certain characteristics of the collective good at issue, particularly its production function, affect its provision. For reasons explained in Chapter 4, the balance of the book focuses on problems of simultaneous coordinated collective action with accelerating production functions. Chapter 5 is devoted to what emerges as the key characteristic of the process of organizing collective action, the choices organizers make in selecting the group members they mobilize. Chapter 6 is directly concerned with perhaps the most imminent aspect of interdependence, social networks within the group, and how their form and size affect collective action. The last analytic chapter, Chapter 7, uses the concept of selectivity to address the problem of choices among recruitment strategies. Finally, Chapter 8 is devoted to a summary and to concluding ruminations.

2. Building blocks: goods, groups, and processes

In this chapter we describe the "building blocks" of our analytic strategy – the major concepts and simplifying assumptions that we use for modeling collective action – and discuss many of the scope conditions that circumscribe the applicability of the models. The real world of collective action is obviously much too complex to be captured by any single theoretical model. Real events are always the result of the conjunction of many processes and accidental occurrences. We make drastic simplifying assumptions in our models not because we believe they are "true," but as a way of isolating a tractable part of a complex phenomenon.

It will be helpful to ground our often technical discussion in an example (used throughout the book) drawn from our experience with voluntary action and social protest. Imagine that there are several cities that have just passed identical ordinances requiring their employees to be city residents, effective next year. (Such ordinances are, in fact, quite common.) Each of the cities currently employs some workers who will be directly affected. None of these ordinances now exempts current employees from the requirement, but an amendment providing such an exemption (a "grandfather clause") is possible.

In Olson's terms, the grandfather clause amendment is a clear example of a collective good for suburban-dwelling city employees: all such employees will benefit from the amendment, whether or not they help to get it passed. However, a simplistic "Olson model" would predict that every rational employee will try to free-ride (assuming a large group), that no collective action will take place, and that the amendment will not be passed. Each affected employee should hope that her similarly affected colleagues will contribute time or money toward passing the amendment, while she watches movies on her new VCR. Since everyone will have the same hope, no one will campaign (and everyone will see a lot of movies).

Our thesis is that this oversimplified prediction is useless. It does not fit the existing empirical data, and it is not consistent with the extensive theoretical literature on collective action that has been produced in the past twenty-five years. In the real world of city politics, employees in situations like the one we describe will sometimes mount a campaign and other times will not. This does not mean that we should throw up our hands and declare the problem indeterminate. Instead, we should try to determine which factors will promote collective action, and which will hinder it. Obviously, we cannot provide a comprehensive inventory of relevant factors in this book. Instead, we hope to identify some of the key factors and to provide an agenda for future theorizing. To help organize the presentation, we discuss separately the characteristics of four key components of our theory: (1) the individuals who constitute the groups, (2) the group as a collectivity, (3) the collective good at issue, (4) the process by which collective action is organized.

Characteristics of individuals

Our theory is concerned with groups, but we must make some assumptions about the individuals within those groups. We treat individuals as characterized primarily by their *interest* in the collective good, v, and the *resources* they have available to contribute. In the equations that follow, we generally represent individual-level factors with lowercase symbols. Thus, r is an individual's resource contribution, and t is the total amount of resources held by the individual. (These unstandardized terms are in roman type; later we will use italics to denote their standardized counterparts.)

Interests and resources are always defined with respect to a particular process for achieving a particular collective good. These terms may summarize a variety of subjective considerations, and thus individuals may have complex motivations and still stay within the scope of the theory.

We assume that each individual's interest and resources are fixed characteristics at the moment of decision about collective action. Violation of this assumption would necessitate rewriting our models. Our models cannot capture the dynamics that arise when people's understandings are changing over time. We do not believe that interests and resources are actually static, but we do believe that the patterns we can identify using static models are valuable baselines that must be constructed before we can hope to develop models that successfully capture complex dynamic processes. We assume that individuals' decisions about contributing are determined by weighing the costs and benefits of such a contribution. The benefit is a function of an actor's interest in the good and the efficacy of the action for promoting the good.

Interest

An individual's *interest* in the good is the value to her of a standard increment in the amount of the good that is provided. Interest is defined *subjectively* by each actor (see Klandermans 1984) and may be based on any of the wide array of factors that motivate human beings – including the desire for monetary gain, ideological commitment, group solidarity, a need for interpersonal support, and so on. Objective conditions do *not* define, although they may determine, membership in the group. A suburban-dwelling employee who is looking forward to being fired so that she can collect unemployment insurance while taking some time off with her kids is not a member of the group for whom a grandfather clause is a collective good. Another employee who is just too stupid to realize that she is going to be fired without the clause, and therefore is not interested in it, is also not a group member. Combining all motivational factors into a single summary term certainly oversimplifies any reasonable model of human motivation, but it allows us to concentrate our analysis on the structural variables that differentiate groups.

Interest may be only slightly positive. At points in our analysis we will include in the group individuals whose interest is so slight that it is best represented as zero. A negative interest means only that an individual would be harmed by something that benefits others, and this happens all the time. However, a model that would explicitly take negative interests into account would require us to include the possibility of countermobilizations to prevent the good from being provided. Such a complex analysis is beyond the general set of issues usually addressed in this literature and would make analysis extraordinarily difficult. Thus, we assume that there will be no countermobilizations, and that negative interests may be treated as zero.

Resources

Besides interest, the most fundamental characteristic of actors in our model is the fact that they (and, at first, they alone) possess the *resources* that are required to produce the collective good. It is their contribution of these resources that constitutes the collective action that is our basic dependent variable.

An individual's resource level is the amount of discretionary resources, such as time or money, that she could potentially contribute toward provision of the collective good.[1] We treat resources as objective and fixed. In economic terms, we assume that there is a true budget constraint and ignore the possibility that more resources could be obtained by paying interest. Our substantive concern is the world of voluntary action, where even the ability to borrow money is constrained by individual assets, and where more time is often not available at any price.

Clearly, what is discretionary is partly determined by subjective factors. An employee whose overriding ambition is to become a novelist, and who spends all of her nonworking hours trying to write, will feel that she has less discretionary time to devote to raising money for the lobbying fund than will most of her similarly affected colleagues. But that is only because of her particular preferences. Perceptions of discretion are probably themselves influenced by the extent of the individual's interest in the collective good. Given this confounding, we simplify our analysis by assuming that differences in interest levels, rather than in discretionary resources, account for variation in contribution levels among people with the same objective amounts of free time or surplus money.

Fungibility

Our most unreasonable but necessary assumption is that all of the interests and resources to be considered are *fungible,* that is, that they can be reduced to a single, quantifiable metric like money. Thus, we proceed as if a unit of a given individual's time is worth a certain amount of money (to him), and that a unit of what he gets out of the collective good can also be translated into money. We assume that a suburban-dwelling employee can calculate how much it will cost him to move, or to lose his job, and then compare those potential losses with the cost of his contribution toward paying for the lobbyist. The assumption that people can make these judgments so exactly is obviously incorrect, although it is clear that people somehow do compare the incommensurate.

[1] In this book, we generally ignore the differences between time and money as resources. See Oliver and Marwell (1992) for an extended discussion of the differences and why they are important.

By assuming fungibility we ignore a set of issues and analyses that are important for real-life collective action (as well as for decision processes in general). Fireman and Gamson (1979), for example, critique collective action by distinguishing between "hard" and "soft" incentives (or interests). Hardin (1982) considers the "asymmetries" caused by the nonfungibility of collective goods, on the one hand, and the kinds of contributions people usually make in their pursuit, on the other, to be one of the major reasons that the free-rider problem is so often "solved" in practice. Nevertheless, we will not explore these issues in the present analysis. Instead, we will use simple-minded assumptions about individuals to permit us to explore complexities about groups that have not been treated by others. It turns out that most of our results do not depend on the assumptions we make about individuals. That is, our results show what happens in groups when individuals vary in what they will contribute, and the mechanism by which these contributions get set is a black box that does not affect our results.

Characteristics of groups

We are concerned with actions that are collective in their form, not just in their consequences. Thus, we need to talk about the collective properties of groups. A *group* is defined as the aggregate of all individuals who have a positive interest in some collective good. It has often been assumed that collective action by a group can somehow be deduced from equations about one individual at a time. We shall show that this is false. Groups of actors entail important dynamics that cannot be deduced from single individuals. Groups are described not only by their size and the total (or mean) of their interest and resources, but by the way their interest and resources are distributed across the group. Group-level factors are indicated by uppercase symbols. Thus, R is the total amount of resources contributed in the group, and T is the total of all available resources.

The *total level* of interest or resources in a group (V or T) is simply the sum of that factor over all group members. For example, if there are five hundred employees who each stand to lose $2,000 from a requirement that they live in the city, the total interest level for this group is $1 million. This total value may seem exceptionally high to any reader who has not worked with collective goods equations, but it is not. Large groups will necessarily have very large total interests in collective goods. This fact has sometimes been overlooked even by experienced scholars.

Any total can always be expressed as the product of the group size and the mean. The size of the group has been a topic of intense debate in the field of collective action, and we shall treat it in detail in Chapter 3. If group size and the mean are treated as distinct concepts, explicit assumptions must be made about their relation. From Chapter 4 on, we generally assume that the mean interest is independent of group size.

The mean interest or resource level in a group is always an important predictor of collective action. Ceteris paribus, a city in which the economy is tight, and affected employees are desperate to keep their jobs without moving, is more likely to see a lobbying campaign than one in which good alternative employment is easily available to workers living in suburbs. Similarly, a city in which the affected employees are mostly well-paid bureaucrats or skilled workers can more easily generate a large pool of monetary contributions than one in which it is the lowest-paid workers who are affected because they commute into a gentrified city from economically ghettoized low-service suburbs.

Although substantively very important, the mean levels of interest and resources are theoretically uninteresting because their effects are obvious. In our analyses, we hold them constant at some moderate level that makes collective action possible but problematic. Our central analytic focus is on the effects of group heterogeneity.

Group heterogeneity

Although all members of the group have some positive interest in the good, some may be more interested than others. We permit interest and resources to vary from negligible to very high. A city employee who owns her suburban home might want the grandfather clause more than does her neighbor who rents. She may lose money if forced to sell her home. Similarly, a mother of three may have less free time for picketing and demonstrating than does her childless fellow employee. In that sense, she has fewer resources available to contribute.

The likelihood that interest heterogeneity affects collective action has not escaped the attention of previous scholars. For example, Olson describes the "exploitation of the great by the small" (1965, p. 29), by which he means the difference in participation in collective action by those individuals who have a very large interest in the good, and those whose interest, although positive, is relatively small. Since the former are so interested, he argues, they will provide the good themselves, regardless of the actions of the less interested parties. The latter exploit the "great" by not contributing at all: they know they will get the good anyway, because the "great" will provide it. Hardin (1982, pp. 72–5) also discusses interest heterogeneity, focusing on the question of whether intensely interested persons can be satisfied with private alternatives to the public good, and arguing that collective action is more probable when they cannot.

On the other hand, heterogeneity of resources has received scant attention in the literature (an exception being Marwell and Ames 1979). As we shall show, the mean level of resources is generally more important for collective action than its heterogeneity (which is not the case for interest). Beyond that generality, however, the distribution of resources can play an important role, particularly regarding the predictability of outcomes for specific groups.

Thinking about heterogeneity

Everything we do in this book turns on an understanding of the significance of group heterogeneity and how it interacts with other determinants of collective aciton. Thus, it is useful to develop an understanding of heterogeneity per se before proceeding into our more complex analyses. The concept of the critical mass rests on the assumption that a collective good can at least sometimes be provided through the efforts of only some members of an interest group. If such is the case, it should be apparent that the significant determinants of collective action occur in the upper tail of the distribution. That is, collective action is affected by the size and other characteristics of that *subset* of the interest group who are most interested or resourceful or otherwise willing or able to contribute to collective action.

To illustrate simply, let us assume that all of our employees are drawn from the population of Americans who our newspapers tell us are the contemporary norm – those concerned only with their immediate profits. Suppose further that 499 of the 500 affected employees in a particular city rent their suburban homes, would each have to pay about $2,000 a year more to live in the city, but would be saddled with no other costs by the new requirement. The 500th employee, however, has a particular problem. He is a high-paid executive with the city, but his wife is a high-paid executive in another city, and their suburban residence splits the commuting distance between them. They believe that the requirement, which would force one or both of them to change jobs, or force them to maintain two homes, will cost them at least $20,000 a year, no matter what they do. We do not need formal analysis to conclude that this couple would find it profitable to support hiring a lobbyist for $10,000, even if they personally pay the entire fee. If they could be sure the lobbyist would succeed, they would net a profit of $10,000 in the first year. Of course, they would have even greater preference for some process in which others bear the cost, but if forced to choose between paying the whole cost themselves and doing nothing, they would unambiguously prefer to pay everything than to let nothing happen. (In Chapter 4, we discuss predictions about behavior in this situation, which we formally define as involving a "surplus" of contributors.)

In this example, the total interest (potential annual loss) for all 500 employees is $1,018,000; it is distributed very heterogeneously. Suppose instead that this same total potential annual loss were distributed *homogeneously* across the group so that each of the 500 affected employees has the same interest level of $2,036. In this situation, none of the employees comparing the cost of the lobbyist to their one-year loss will be willing to pay the entire $10,000 cost alone, even though the expected loss to the whole group is well over $1 million. If this group is to find any solution, it must be collective, in contrast with the prior case in which an individual solution is possible. Of course, interesting and realistic cases are more complex than this comparison. Our point is that it is always misleading to treat a heterogeneous interest group as if it were homogeneous by examining only the total (or mean) level of group interest in the collective good.

Olson (1965), Hardin (1982), and our own following analyses all treat cases in which heterogeneity improves the prospects for collective action. But this is because we make assumptions that ensure positive heterogeneity effects. It is possible to be more specific about the conditions under which more heterogeneity is beneficial and when it is not. What heterogeneity does to a distribution with a given mean is to push a higher proportion of group members farther out into the tails. This is beneficial for collective action if at least some level of the collective good can be provided with less than unanimous action and if the individuals in the tails are more likely to contribute to collective action. To keep the discussion as clear as possible, we will talk about variables for which higher values of the factor are better for collective action, as is true for interest and resources. These principles also apply to costs and number of network ties, which we shall discuss later. Of course, costs are more favorable if they are lower; all the foregoing discussions apply to costs if the word *lower* is substituted for *higher*.

To think about this issue, imagine that groups have fixed means but can change their dispersion around that mean. This is not possible, of course, but makes for a much clearer exposition than trying to talk about different groups.

Heterogeneity is beneficial or harmful for collective action only when there are thresholds, that is, when people above or below a given value are more (or less) likely to contribute to collective action. If there are no thresholds to action, every individual in the group contributes whatever value he has, so that only the mean determines the total contribution; heterogeneity is irrelevant.

When there are thresholds, there are two conditions that determine whether greater heterogeneity is beneficial or harmful for collective action. The first and most important is the *mean level* of the distribution. If the mean of the distribution is too low, so that individuals with the mean value are unwilling to participate, greater heterogeneity will force a higher proportion of people into the upper tail of willing participants, and so promote collective action. In contrast, if the mean is already high enough to favor collective action, greater heterogeneity would put a greater proportion of cases into the lower tail of the distribution where people are unwilling to participate, and thus would not be helpful. Olson and Hardin found positive effects of heterogeneity because they implicitly assume that the mean level is unfavorable for collective action; this is the assumption we generally use, as well.

The second, and more complex, effect of heterogeneity is a *conjunction of probabilities* effect. Unless they are perfectly correlated, the probability of two random variables being within the "favorable" range is always less than the probability for either one taken individually. When several factors are all heterogeneous across a group, increasing the heterogeneity of all of them can create the problem that there is a point at which the negative conjunction of probabilities effect outweighs the positive heterogeneity effect of each variable one at a time. Some proportion of the people who are high enough on one criterion will not be high enough on the others. For example, when groups are very heterogeneous, there is the risk that the people who have enough resources to provide the good will not be the ones who have enough interest in the good to be willing to contribute. The suburban dwellers with plenty of time may also be the ones who care least about losing their jobs.

The conjunction of probabilities issue obviously depends on whether the factors are correlated. Our abstract discussion to this point fits those cases when factors are independent, or when the departure from independence is small. A positive correlation between interest and resources (or among other factors) is always beneficial for collective action, for it ensures that those who are high enough on one factor will also be in the most favorable range on the other factor. By contrast, a negative correlation between interest and resources is extremely unfavorable for collective action, as it ensures that those who have the interest do not have the resources, and vice versa. In short, there is always a problem for collective action when the people who care the most about the issue do not have a lot of resources, and it is always beneficial for collective action when the people who care the most also have the most money or time. This statement is presumably obvious, and we do not claim to have discovered it; we are simply showing how this falls within the larger matter of the conjunction of probabilities when we have to consider the joint distributions of a number of factors affecting the prospects for collective action.

Characteristics of the good

One problem with trying to derive useful predictions from Olson's book is that he assumes that all collective goods are theoretically interchangeable. But this is clearly not true. Collective goods (and all goods, for that matter) can differ from one another in many theoretically significant ways, some of which should affect the likelihood of collective action. For example, some collective goods, such as office microwaves, are cheap. Others, such as office fitness centers, are expensive. Some goods come in (almost) continuously divisible increments; consider library books and air pollution as examples. In contrast, library buildings, bridges, and other such goods are available only in large, ''lumpy'' units; part of a bridge is worth no more than no bridge at all. Some goods are or can be controlled by a very small number of people – government officials, the CEOs of large polluting industries, and their ilk. Other goods, such as pollution from fireplace emissions, are controlled by the aggregate actions of very many people. Some goods, like defense from foreign attack, may affect everyone in a group almost equally. Other goods, such as the suppression of revolutions, may have vastly different effects on different people.

All these factors, and many others, particularly those involving the cost functions of goods, affect the prospects for collective action. Many of these factors have been treated extensively by others. We focus on a relatively small number of differences that are of central importance and that divide collective goods into fundamentally distinct sets with very different dynamics.

Production functions

Many of these differences are reflected in the production function $P(R)$, which specifies the relationship between how many resources R are "contributed" to (or invested in) "purchasing" the collective good by the group, and the amount of the collective good P that is realized or "provided" by that level of contribution. That is, $P(R)$ is the relationship between inputs and outputs. Unnoticeably embedded in many analyses of collective action is the assumption that the collective good at issue has a given *price,* and that the group either gets none of the good until that price is met, or that the group must pay some specific, unchanging price per unit of the good. An example of the former might be a bridge that costs $10 million. Any less buys nothing worth having. At the same time, no group in its right mind would allocate *more* than $10 million to the bridge project because more money won't buy any more bridge. Such goods are often called "lumpy" in the literature. An example of a more (but not completely) continuous good might be defense, where, say, $20,000 "buys" one soldier, $40,000 "buys" two soldiers, and so on. Hardin (1982, p. 51) distinguishes "step" or binary goods (the bridge) and "continuous" goods (the soldiers). More generally, they constitute two extreme examples of a broad range of possible production functions.

Any discussion of a specific collective action must make a commitment to a particular production function. The (usually) naive assumption that each unit of cost provides a given unit of value is a *linear* production function, actually a very special case that, when true, produces unexpectedly extreme behavior. In contrast, politics involves winning and losing elections and is properly described with discontinuous *step* functions. These also have a variety of peculiar properties. Standard economic models of market behavior and optimization require a third production function – one that assumes *diminishing marginal returns,* that is, that there is some point at which additional resource expenditures produce proportionately less. A contested school of economic thought argues that some industries such as electronics have yet a fourth kind of production function, one with *increasing* marginal returns. We will discuss issues related to production functions more fully in Chapter 4. We will not engage the debates in economics, but we will show that increasing marginal returns are an important element of many collective actions and will devote a great deal of attention to this case in Chapters 5 and 6.

In our analyses, the nature of the production function emerges as the most important determinant of the outcome of a potential collective action. *None of our other general results transcend the effects of production functions.* From our perspective, therefore, Olson's implicit but constant assumption of linear production functions and U-shaped marginal cost functions – both invariant with group size (1965, p. 22; also see Chapter 3) – yields results that are peculiar to those specifications and cannot be generalized. This is not to say that general theoretical predictions are impossible using our perspective, only that they cannot be simple and global. Instead, the predictions that we can validly generate must be complex, interactive, and conditional.

In its complete form, the production function for a collective good is

$$g_i(R) = v_i[P(R)] - c_i(r). \tag{1}$$

The term $g_i(R)$ is the net value to an individual of a collective action consisting of a total of R resources contributed by the group as a whole. The value to that individual of a given level of provision P of the collective good to the group is v_i. $P(R)$ is the provision level of the collective good as a function of the total resource contribution. The cost to the individual of contributing r resource units is $c_i(r)$. All three of these functional relations can take on any form and, in general, are not linear.

The total production function captures the relation between the costs borne by individuals and the benefits they obtain from collective action. There are three links in this chain: (1) the relation between costs borne and resources contributed by the individual, $c_i(r)$; (2) the relation between resources contributed and the level of collective good produced, $P(R)$; and (3) the relation between the level of good produced and the benefit or value experienced, $v_i(P)$. We are required to assume that, for each individual, there is some common metric for costs and values, so that the two may be compared.

Of the three links, only the middle one, $P(R)$, is a property of the production process itself and does not involve individual tastes or preferences. It relates objective levels of group contributions to objective levels of provided collective good. In the real world, this relation is generally *not* linear, that is, the amount of the good provided by a contribution of a given size varies, depending on how many resources have already been contributed by other group members.

The first and last links combine objective factors with subjective factors that may vary among individuals. For example, the cost of contributing five hours or five dollars, $c_i(r)$, may entail not only the contribution itself, but the objective ancillary costs of making the contribution, such as transportation time, babysitters, postage, the time spent looking for the checkbook, and bank service charges. Additionally, individuals surely differ in the subjective cost they experience from a given expenditure of money or time; they differ not only in the magnitude of subjective cost, but in the shape of the relation between objective and subjective cost. Rich, busy people may rather give $60 than sixty minutes. Poor people may not.

The last link, $v_i(P)$, is similarly complex. A change of one unit in the provision level of the good may have a different value to the individual depending on whether it occurs at a low or high total provision level, or near some critical threshold. For example, for a good that is lumpy, P may represent the *probability* of receiving the good, such as getting the grandfather clause. Here, the subjective assessment of the risk of losing the vote in the city council may well mean that the perceived value of spending more money for lobbying is not linearly related to the perceived probability of winning. The subjective gain in value of changing the chance of winning from .2 to .4 is probably much smaller than the subjective gain of changing it from .8 to 1.0. As with costs, a dollar realized from a collective good is generally worth more to those members of the group who begin with fewer dollars.

Each one of these three links or subfunctions can have its own peculiar functional form or shape, and the composite production function can be mathematically intractable. We do not propose to deal with the intractable. Instead, our analysis explores those situations in which the overall input–output relation can be approximated by various simple forms. We do this mathematically by treating two of the links as linear or constant, and putting all the variation in the third link. Although which link dominates the empirical production function varies greatly from case to case, we assume that the fundamental dynamics of collective action are determined by the overall form of the production function, not which link dominates it. There are, of course, some very complex cases in which the chain of links does not resolve to a simple composite form, and we will not be able to illuminate these in the present work.

In Chapter 3, we focus on cost, examining the issue of jointness of supply, which is the extent to which the cost of a good varies with the number of people who share it. This analysis implicitly treats the production and value functions as unproblematic. In Chapter 4, we examine the effect of the overall "shape" of the production function on the forms of collective action, contrasting accelerating and decelerating production functions. We do this by treating $c_i(R)$ and $v_i(P)$ as linear, and putting all the mathematical action into $P(R)$. We further simplify our equations by permitting only value to have a subjective element and treating the cost as constant across individuals. Our rationale for this is the plausible assumption that the subjective costs of action are largely influenced by the perceived value of the collective good. In Chapters 5 and 6, we explore the problems of organizing interdependence when the production functions are accelerating, again treating the value and cost functions as linear.

Standardization

We will generally standardize P to fall between 0 and 1. We assume that $P(0) = 0$, that is, that the provision level will be 0 if there is no collective action.[2] The maximum provision level of 1 has two interpretations. The first interpretation is that the collective good is a lumpy dichotomy (the grandfather amendment is either passed or not), and the "level" of the good is the probability that it is provided. The second interpretation is that the metric of a continuous collective good (e.g., dollars in a compensation fund) has been standardized so that 0 is its minimum and 1 is the maximum amount that can possibly be provided. Many of our mathematical analyses require an upper bound on the range of the production function. For con-

[2] If there is a nonzero baseline provision level that will occur without collective action, we simply reparameterize around zero by subtracting this baseline level from the provision level. Thus, this simplifying assumption is unproblematic.

tinuous distributions with no necessary upper bound, standardization may still be accomplished by assigning some particular high provision level the value 1, even though it is logically possible for this value to be exceeded. Notice that our assumption that there is an upper bound, which we require for many of our analyses, seems perfectly natural when the good is lumpy, but seems arbitrary when the good is continuous. This should reinforce our central argument that no one set of mathematical assumptions can ever capture all collective action situations. There is no "general" logic of collective action; there are different logics for different situations.

When we simplify the production function in our analyses by treating value and costs as linear, the functional relations v_i and c resolve to constants. In this situation, we may further standardize the constant value v_i as the value an individual would experience from a provision level of 1, and the constant cost of contributing one unit of resources as c. If we let M stand for the total resource contribution that produces the maximum provision level of the collective good, that is, $P(M) = 1$, then the total cost of the collective good is cM. We always work with situations in which $\Sigma v_i > cM$; this simply ensures that there is a collective good for which the collective benefit exceeds the collective cost. It does not ensure that there are individuals who will be willing to contribute.

Production choices in collective action

There is a common tendency, even in our own work, to speak as if the production function is inherent in the collective good itself. But in reality, and certainly in theory, any and every good can be produced in more than one way, and some of these alternatives have quite different production functions. This is true even of seemingly obvious goods like bridges. Here, the collective good is really a transportation linkage across some obstacle; this linkage might be provided by a ferry, a tunnel, or a bridge. Even if a bridge is the only feasible alternative, there are always choices about size and construction technology. Only after these choices have been made can we relate dollars of contributions to bridge building.

In the real worlds of voluntary action and social movements, the situation is typically less well defined than the bridge problem. Activists are often oriented to very vague global principles such as ending world hunger, goals that can be pursued by way of a wide variety of more proximate goals. Our city employees actually have a wide range of options for dealing with the city ordinance requiring them to live in town. We have narrowed their options by fiat in declaring repeal of the ordinance impossible, and that only a grandfather clause is feasible. Even so, the employees have many choices left. They could lobby the council as individuals, stage some kind of collective protest, hire a professional lobbyist, threaten a costly lawsuit, or seek charitable donations from the community to compensate them for their costs. Each one of these choices would have a different production function. Of course, actors never choose from the full range of all logical possibilities that could be invented. Only a very small number of choices are ever actually considered, often only one. But to the extent that people are aware of alternatives, they are choosing among different production functions. We will show the consequences of different production functions but will not treat the matter of how people choose between them.

Homogeneity of the good

Using a diverse set of examples, Hardin (1982, pp. 76–81) argues that goods themselves may be heterogeneous, and that this heterogeneity may serve to increase the likelihood of collective action. Translating his distinction into our own example, consider the possibility that several of the affected employees of a given city know a young lawyer on a personal basis and would very much like to see him have a decent first job. Hiring him as their lobbyist would then produce more than just the increased probability of the amendment. As Hardin puts it, hiring the young lawyer would be like raising sheep – the group gets both meat and wool, in what is called "jointness of production" (as distinct from jointness of supply). Movement activists often view campaigns around specific issues not just as ends in themselves, but as a means to raising consciousness or promoting mobilization around some larger principle. Hardin points out that such heterogeneity allows different kinds of people, with different priorities, to join together in collective action, thereby increasing the total amount of interest and resources available for the action.

But such heterogeneity can work the other way, too, as actors who share an interest in a common goal may have competing interests about which mode of action should be used to obtain it. A second set of employees may have a needy lawyer of their own. Although these problems are worth considerable attention, we will not address them in this book. Instead, we will assume that all such factors can be captured by individual differences in the value of a given level of the collective good obtained through a given production function.

Characteristics of the process

If it is assumed that individuals act in isolation, and if the production function makes the net value of contributing independent of how many others contribute, simple individual decision-making models may be used without attending to the process of action. If we explore the consequences of permitting actors to coordinate their actions, however, we need more complex models. Even if we are not going to permit actors to coordinate their actions, we need some model for interaction and information when the marginal value of a contribution depends on how many others contribute.

Any model of collective action requires some process by which the activities of individual group members are aggregated into actions that may be attributed to the group. Sometimes this process is minimal, as when one or two individuals take it upon themselves to provide the group with the good. Five different people might call the police to complain about a car whose broken alarm system is keeping everyone in the neighborhood awake. No coordination of effort is necessary. Each individual can be assumed to weigh the cost against the benefit of acting and the likelihood that someone else is acting, and make some decision. Even in these simple situations, actors' behavior would change if they knew the behavior of others. If they don't like talking to the police, no one would call once they knew someone else had called. However, because the cost of action is so low relative to the benefit, we do not worry very much theoretically about whether they would try to coordinate their efforts. In our discussion of group size in Chapter 3, we stay at this simple level of analysis, counting potential contributors without worrying how they would coordinate their actions.

But it is clear that more complex analyses of collective action do require an explicit model of interdependence. When the marginal value of a contribution changes markedly depending on how much others contribute, we know that anyone who understands her situation will be very interested in information about the behavior of others, and thus we must have some model about how decisions are collectively patterned and how information is conveyed. The model we choose is not content-free; it will interact with the other parameters of a situation and have significant effects on the outcome. It is well established, for example, that the simplest collective action situation, an experimental prisoner's dilemma, has very different outcomes depending on whether subjects are isolated or permitted to talk to each other (Howard 1971; Caldwell 1976; Dawes et al. 1977; Fox and Guyer 1978).

If choices are isolated and independent, most subjects defect, although some cooperate; if subjects are permitted to talk to each other, mutual cooperation is nearly always the outcome, especially if they watch each other while the choices are made.

Different real-life situations obviously have different characteristics in terms of the physical and social connections among the actors and the ability of the actors to communicate, as well as in terms of the intrinsic nature of the action itself. For example, some actions require an instantaneous irrevocable commitment, while others may be done slowly and reversibly, so that others' actions can be monitored as the behavior progresses. In some situations people can discuss and bargain about who will do what. Other times the required action does not permit such leeway.

We will employ several different approaches to interdependence and coordination. In Chapter 3, we ignore the problem or, rather, assume that it is solved without asking how. In Chapter 4, we work with a model of sequential decision making. At the end of Chapter 4, we also discuss a model of simultaneous coordinated action. This model becomes central to Chapters 5, 6, and 7, where we add an explicit organizer of the coordinated action.

Each of our models for the relation among group members leads to a different model for how individuals make their decisions. To permit the reader to compare these models, we describe them all here. We also point to a great many possibilities and complexities that we do not treat in this book. Readers who are impatient with the details of this exposition may wish to get on with the book, returning to this section as needed.

Independent decisions

If decisions are made independently (by an actor in isolation), we may write a simple decision equation for the individual's net gain from contributing, $g = P(r)v - cr$. If we assume that $c = 1$, that is, that the "cost" of contributing resources is simply the loss of those resources, we may further simplify the gain equation to $g = P(r)v - r$. This equation says that an individual decides what to do assuming that only she will make a contribution. An individual acting independently finds that her individual contribution produces a profit if $g > 0$, that is, if $P(r)v > r$, meaning that the individual's interest times the probability of obtaining the good exceeds the size of her contribution. An algebraically equivalent expression for this condition is $P(r) > r/v$. There are many situations in which the cost of action r is low enough relative to its benefit $P(r)$ that individuals are perfectly willing to act in independent isolation. (The possibility that they will engage in gaming behavior and hope to free-ride on the efforts of others requires an explicit model for the interdependence of the situation and will be treated in Chapter 4 after appropriate theory has been developed.)

Sequential interdependence

In this model, individuals make independent decisions one at a time, but the past decisions of others are known. We imagine that our workers do not directly coordinate their actions, but that whenever one of them does something, everyone else is aware of the action. Our formal model is pure sequential decision making, where each person goes "to bat" one at a time in strict rotation. Even though real-world situations usually permit more than one person to choose at a time and impose no particular order on who chooses next, the sequential model gives a plausible approximation to reality when contributions are made over time and people are aware of others' actions. The sequential model also suggests the possibility that early actors can consider the effects of their choices on the subsequent choices of others; this issue is also explored in Chapter 4.

If decisions are made sequentially, P depends not only on r but on R, the total contribution previously made by others. In this case, our more complex decision equation is $g = v[P(r + R) - P(R)] - r$. This implies that a profit will result from contributing when $P(r + R) - P(R) > r/v$. In Chapter 4, we show that collective action varies tremendously depending on how P varies with R.

Simultaneous coordinated actions (all-or-none contracts)

For this model, we assume that negotiation and discussion are possible, that tentative choices are revocable, and that these and other features of the situation prohibit isolated defection from coordinated action. The consequence of these assumptions can be characterized as a formal or informal all-or-none contract. Formally, the model assumes that either *all* parties to the agreement will do what they agreed to, or no one will. People do not have to agree to participate, but duplicity is impossible. No one acts (or incurs costs) until there are enough who have agreed to act to ensure that everyone who acts will experience a profitable outcome, and once a jointly profitable action has been agreed to, no one will defect from it, because no one will contribute what he has promised unless everyone does.

This is another extreme model that is often unrealistic but is a good approximation of some situations. It is an excellent model for real-world processes like the provision of office microwaves. In the example of our employees, they could quite readily use this model to create a collective subscription for hiring a lawyer, where it was agreed that the fund would be spent only if it exceeded a certain threshold. It applies quite well to situations in which the actors are in intense face-to-face interaction and the collective action happens slowly and revocably. Perhaps our employees might sit in at city hall, where they could watch each other go in and know if they were accompanied by enough others to make the action safe. Anyone who considered backing out at the last minute would realize that everyone else would see him leave, and follow him out the door. The model of the formal contract is a reasonable approximation to many informal processes relying on convention (Hardin 1982, pp. 155–230), normative pressure, or solidarity (Fireman and Gamson 1979).

The individual decision rule for contributing to a simultaneous coordinated action modeled by the all-or-none contract makes one crucial change in the previous equation. The *total* contribution by all parties to the contract, $r + R$, replaces r, the *individual's* contribution level, in the production function. The rationale for this substitution is that the actor's defection will lead everyone else to defect, so she must compare the payoff of contributing when everyone else does to not contributing when no one does; not contributing but having others contribute is precluded as an option. This gives us the revised decision equation $g = P(r + R)v - r$. Contributing to the contract produces a profit if $P(r + R) > r/v$, that is, if the total payoff from *all* contributions to the contract exceeds the individual's r/v ratio. Obviously, this is much more conducive to a positive decision than either of the previous decision rules.

Organizers

Common as formal or informal contracts are, they rarely happen spontaneously. They entail communication and enforcement costs that are never uniformly distributed across parties to the contract. Empirically, these kinds of contracts generally have well-defined points of origin, that is, some specific person (or small cadre) who incurs costs in organizing the contract. In short, they have organizers. In Chapters 5 and 6, we extend this model of simultaneous coordinated action by assuming that the action is *not* spontaneous, but rather that some individual absorbs the cost of organizing and coordinating the concerted action. In this analysis, we assume that some form of coordinated action is possible and focus on the question of how it will be structured and paid for. For our employees, this model says that one employee develops a plan for a collective action that will involve others and absorbs the communication and enforcement costs of locating enough other employees to make the action successful. In Chapter 5, there is full information and the organizer takes no risk. The question is simply whether the organizer is able to pull together a critical mass of other employees to make a simultaneous coordinated action successful. In Chapter 6, we explore the organizer's problem of incomplete information in trying to organize such an action. In Chapter 7, the organizer is present only by implication, and emphasis is on determining the total contribution to be expected from subgroups with various characteristics.

Organizers, just like everyone else, have available resources and an interest in the collective good. They are different in that they use their resources to organize a contract that will make others willing to contribute to the collective good. It is not always clear who will do the organizing. In our example, it might be a union representative, if the city employees are organized. Or it might simply be an enthusiastic self-starter. For the purposes of our model, any group member is permitted to organize, although for reasons to be detailed later, some may be more likely to be successful than others.

Organizing (transaction) costs

Organizing requires communication, but organizers may be able to communicate with all other group members only under those circumstances in which communication costs are very low (and social networks, which we will discuss in Chapter 5, are very extensive). Organizing requires the expenditure of resources (transaction costs) that could otherwise be allocated directly toward the collective action. Face-to-face contacts take a certain amount of time per contact. Letters and telephone calls usually require less time per contact, but more money. Local telephone calls cost less than long-distance calls. Mass media (television, radio, newspapers) or diffuse media (posters, leaflets) have certain costs, which include the "waste" of communicating with people who are not potential contributors, such as workers who already live in the city. It is much less expensive for employees to contact each other if they all work in the same building than if they are dispersed all over town, and less expensive if they all live in the same suburb than if they are spread thinly across the countryside. Interdepartmental mail is much cheaper to use than the U.S. mail. The surveillance or enforcement mechanisms for the contract may also have some material or social cost.

The effects of different kinds of organizing costs are complex enough to require separate analysis. In the present work, we make the very simple assumption that organizing costs are exactly proportional to the number of parties to the all-or-none agreement, and that this constant cost per participant is a characteristic of the interest group that does not vary with the organizer or the particular individuals involved. Thus, average organizing costs may be higher in one city than another because of telephone cost differences, but Fred Jones and Ann Smith, who are both employed by the same city, are assumed to face identical costs for each member they recruit.

Organizers' decisions

A group member's decision to organize is more complex than the decision to contribute. Although other models are possible, we assume that organizers organize simultaneous coordinated actions that are captured by the model of the all-or-none contract. Organizing will be profitable if the $P(R)$ produced by the contributions of the *other* group members exceeds the *organizer's* r_o/v. A group member's interest v is the same regardless of whether she is organizing or contributing. To find the cost of organizing, we make the simplifying assumption that organizing costs are linear with the number of contributors. If c is the cost per contrbutor, and k is the number of contributors, then the *organizer's* cost or contribution, $r_o =$

kc. If we let R_k represent the total contributions of the k individuals the organizer contacts, then the organizer's gain from organizing is $g_o = P(R_k)v - kc$. The payoff will be greater than zero, and organizing will be profitable, if the potential organizer knows and can afford to contact a group of k individuals, such that $P(R_k) > kc/v$.

The process of forming a contract

We simplify our model of organizing greatly by assuming that every group member has at least some information about everyone else's interest and resource levels, and that everyone's behavior is a perfectly determinate function of their own interest and resources. In the extreme, this means that when social worker Fred Jones, organizer, approaches patrolwoman Ann Smith, group member, with the proposition ''Will you agree to spend five hours fighting for an exemption if you are guaranteed that a total of fifty hours will be contributed to this project?'' Fred knows the answer before he asks. He can mentally review a list of his acquaintances and determine whether he knows and can afford to contact a critical mass who are interested and resourceful enough that their combined contributions would produce a big enough impact to make everyone willing to contribute. He spends his resources to pay the organizing costs only if he is sure he will be successful. In this simplified world, there are no unsuccessful organizing drives. At times we make the less extreme assumption that organizers know only that people in certain subgroups have given probabilities of contributing and only know the ''average costs'' per successful contact. But we still assume that they know whether their campaign will be unsuccessful beforehand and never waste resources on doomed attempts.

Group outcomes and multiple organizers

Two (or more) organizing campaigns going at the same time could reinforce each other, but they could also hurt each other if they compete for the same contributors. The complexities of multiple mobilizations are beyond the scope of our analyses. Here we will only identify the *best* contract possible in a given group. This implies that mobilization is preemptive, that is, that one organizer's efforts preclude another's. This is often a realistic assumption, as few people will attempt to organize a separate collective action if they know someone is already on the way to providing the good (see Oliver 1984). It would not make sense for two of our employees to compete to hire different lobbyists. They are much more likely to join forces. Preemption is especially common when the interest group already has some official representative (such as a city employees' union). In real life, the preemptive organizer is not necessarily the one who would organize the *best* possible contract, but we will assume that decision rule.

The probability that an interest group will contain at least one successful organizer is much higher than the probability that any particular individual can be a successful organizer. When preemption is assumed the probability that at least one of N potential organizers will be successful is given by $1 - (1 - q)^N$, where q is the probability that any particular organizer will be successful. Very small probabilities of success for individual organizers produce very large probabilities of at least one success in a group. For example, in a 400-person group, if the probability of any individual being a successful organizer is .01, the probability of there being at least one successful organizer is over .98. For there to be a better than even chance of the group having at least one success (i.e., the group probability is greater than .5), the individual probability can be as low as .002. Once again, we find that we cannot jump from predictions about individuals to predictions about groups without explicit models for the interdependence among individuals.

A final word

Common interests are the occasion for collective action. But the mere fact of common interest does not define or determine behavior. To understand the possibilities for action, we must understand the characteristics of the group of people who share the interest, the characteristics of the interest that they share, the characteristics of the action possibilities available to them, and the nature of the social relations among group members. Our task as theorists is not to make universal claims about all forms of collective action, but to identify salient kinds of action and illuminate the dynamics within them. In the remaining chapters, we undertake this task.

3. The paradox of group size

We begin our redefinition of the problem of collective action with what has become an almost classic debate over Mancur Olson's "group-size" thesis. Hardin summarizes the thesis succinctly as "large groups will fail [to provide collective goods]; small groups may succeed" (1982, p. 38). Olson's argument seems to be intuitively compelling for many observers of everyday life and has convinced a large number of scholars, as well. It also articulates well with a major set of research findings in social psychology regarding the "diffusion of responsibility." These findings suggest that the presence of other people who might also assist someone in need reduces an individual's propensity to help that person (Latane and Nida 1981; Piliavin, Dovidia, Gaetner, and Clark 1981, pp. 120–32).

Applying his argument to our example, Olson would predict that a small group of city employees might be able to obtain the grandfather clause, while a large group of employees would not. In the larger group each employee would hope to free-ride on the efforts of others, so none would act and all would suffer. In the smaller group interpersonal dynamics and the "noticeability" of contributions (addressed later) might overcome the tendency to free-ride.

In contrast to this intuitively appealing prediction stands a significant body of empirical research that argues just the contrary, that is, it finds that the size of a group is *positively* related to its level of collective action. For example, Spilerman (1970, p. 654) summarized his analysis of the black riots of the 1960s by saying: "The larger the Negro population, the greater the likelihood of the disorder. Nothing else appears to matter." Scott and El-Assal (1969) found that size of the student body was the only significant predictor of demonstrations and other disturbances on college campuses. Interpreting their results, Marwell argued that the simplest theory would assume that a given proportion of students [at all schools] are ready to stage a demonstration in response to certain types of events but this proportion is small. Given that a demonstration is a collective event, it takes some minimum number of such students to get a demonstration off the ground. The larger the university, the greater the chance it has to get a minimum number. (1970, p. 916)

Very large constituencies, such as African Americans or women, have given rise to much larger social movements in the United States than small constituencies like Armenian Americans or paraplegics. These empirical findings make a great deal of sense, since larger groups have more resources and more people who might contribute them for collective action.

When theory conflicts with empirical research, the problem usually lies with the theory. Thus, we start this chapter by reexamining the theory, beginning with a critical examination of just how little Olson actually proved. We then provide a brief review of other critics, who have identified important factors that affect the relation between group size and collective action. Out of these we select one issue we consider most important, the extent to which the collective good has jointness of supply.

Our own increment to this theoretical literature is in one sense rather modest. We show the paradoxical result that providing a collective good to a larger interest group may require *fewer* individual contributors. But we argue from this result that the whole problem of collective action has been misrepresented in formulations derived from Olson, and that we need to start over with new premises if we are to develop useful theory that might actually illuminate collective action processes.

Olson's argument and the empirical problem

For Olson, groups come in three theoretically different sizes:

1. "small" or "privileged," in which some individual may have enough interest in the collective good to provide some level of it himself;
2. "moderate," in which no individual can provide a significant portion of the good himself, but some individuals can make a "noticeable" difference in the level of provision of the collective good, that is, affect it enough that it seems to have increased a small amount; and

3. "large," in which no individual can make even a noticeable difference (p. 44).

Olson seems to *define* a large group as one in which no contribution is noticeable, and thus makes the group-size thesis vacuous. Olson himself notes that this would be tautological (pp. 48–9n) and recasts his position as "the (surely reasonable) empirical hypothesis that the total costs of the collective goods wanted by large groups are large enough to exceed the value of the small fraction of the total benefit that an individual in a large group would get" (p. 49n). Hence, Olson argues, no rational individual in a large group would ever contribute toward the provision of a public good.

It is actually not necessary to invoke any additional evidence to show the flaw in Olson's size argument. His claim fails to stand on its own terms. Olson's verbal arguments have a persuasive ring, and his mathematical equations seem to imply that the size argument has been "proved," but careful inspection of his original equations reveals that they are actually *independent of group size.*[1] To make this point as forcefully as we can, we will use Olson's original notation in this discussion. (Note that Olson's notation differs substantially from our own.)

Olson defines the "size" of a group S_g not as persons but as the total group interest. He assumes a linear relation between the value of the good to an actor, V_i, and the level T at which it is provided with the equation $V_i = F_i S_g T$ (p. 23), where F_i is the fraction an individual's value is of total group value, that is, $F_i = V_i/V_g$. Olson takes derivatives and solves for the point at which the marginal cost equals the marginal value. He gives two versions of his result, $dC/dT = F_i S_g$ (p. 23) and $dC/dT = F_i(dV_g/dT)$ (p. 24); the latter he interprets by saying, "The rate of gain to the group (dV_g/dT) must exceed the rate of increase in cost (dC/dT) by the same multiple that the group gain exceeds the gain to the individual concerned ($1/F_i = V_g/V_i$)" (p. 24).

His implication in this passage, and in the subsequent references he makes to his results, clearly is that the likelihood of the marginal gain to the group exceeding the marginal cost by the appropriate multiple declines as the group size increases, since F_i gets small as the group size gets large. But this is not true. Notice that we have two equations involving F_i, $V_i =$

---

[1] This proof was originally published in Oliver (1980) but has never been cited in the literature, probably because a typesetting error rendered it unintelligible.

$F_i S_g T$, which implies $F_i = V_i/S_g T$ and $F_i = V_i/V_g$. Equating these two, we find $V_i/S_g T = V_i/V_g$, which implies $S_g T = V_g$, that is, that the group value is simply the group size times the level of provision. But F_i, which has V_g in the denominator, is always paired with S_g or V_g in the numerator; the "size" terms seem to cancel out.

We may nail this down formally with a simple algebraic proof. Compare a group of size S_g with a larger group of size $S_g' = S_g + d$. The linearity assumption $V_i = F_i S_g T$ implies $F_i = (V_i/S_g T)$, so the individual's fraction of the larger group is $F_i' = [V_i/(S_g+d)T]$. The level of T that should rationally be purchased in the augmented group occurs when $(dC/dT)' = F_i'S_g' = (S_g + d)[V_i/(S_g + d)T]$. Note that the augmented group size occurs in both the numerator and denominator of this expression and thus cancels out, leaving $(dC/dT)' = F_i'S_g' = V_i/T = F_i S_g = dC/dT$. That is, the solution is the same for both the original group and the larger group. It is *independent of group size*. This result also holds for the equation $dV_g/dT = 1/F_i(dC/dT)$ (p. 25), which is simply an algebraic rearrangement of the previous result.

To show that Olson's mathematics are independent of group size is not to prove that group size never has an effect. Of course it has. But the effects of group size cannot be deduced from very simple, all-purpose equations. Instead, one must begin with assumptions (or facts) regarding the effects of group size, and then derive group-size results that are direct consequences of those assumptions. This does not mean that there is nothing interesting to be learned about group size, but rather that what we need to know is more complex and interesting than simple aphorisms. Thus, various scholars have added assumptions about the elasticity of the good, or the nature of interdependence among the actors, and shown that these alter the effect of group size on collective action (Frohlich and Oppenheimer 1970; Chamberlin 1974; McGuire 1974). Among these, we believe that the interaction of group size with the degree of jointness of supply is the most important to pursue. (See Hardin 1982, pp. 38–49, for a very thorough treatment of this issue.)

Jointness of supply and the group-size argument

In his seminal discussion, Samuelson (1954) defined a *public* good as being *both* nonexcludable and "joint" in supply. By jointness of supply (generally called "jointness" for short) Samuelson meant that consumption (or use) of the good by one individual does not limit the amount of that good available to any other group member. Most (but not all) governmental laws and regulations have this characteristic, as do most useful ideas (Hardin 1982, p. 17). A commonly used concrete example of a jointly supplied good is a bridge. Regardless of how many others use it, you can still get the bridge's full value when you cross yourself.

At the other extreme are goods that have zero jointness. In this case, the amount of the good each individual receives is inversely proportional to the number who enjoy it. Most private goods have zero, or close to zero, jointness. However, so do some of the goods that we call "collective," including many of the examples used by Olson. His primary example is price setting in a competitive market. Olson's only concrete discussion of jointness appears in a footnote where he says: "at least one type of collective good considered here exhibits no jointness whatever, and few if any would have the degree of jointness needed to qualify as pure public goods. Nonetheless, most of the collective goods to be studied here do display a large measure of jointness" (1965, p. 14n). Despite this, Olson never discusses how jointness of supply would affect collective action.

As Olson's comment indicates, many, perhaps most, collective goods lie between the extremes of pure and zero jointness, and jointness is now generally viewed as a continuum. There are "crowding effects" such as the traffic jams that make many bridges less useful to individuals at certain times of day. On the other hand, there are economies of scale that might make otherwise nonjoint goods less than strictly proportionate. It is now customary to define "collective" goods solely in terms of nonexcludability (e.g., Hardin 1982), leaving jointness as a variable to be analyzed.

To appreciate the significance of jointness of supply for the group-size argument, it is crucial to recognize that the relevant cost for collective action is only the cost that is borne by the collective actors. In the realm of politics and social movements, collective action gains benefits most often by affecting government policy. Collective actors bear the cost of influencing government officials, not the cost of actually providing the good. Influencing government policy almost always has very high jointness of supply. The issue for our city employees is how much it will cost them to persuade the government to relent, not what it will cost the taxpayers if they win their clause. Those paying lobbyists for tax loopholes are concerned only with the cost of lobbying, not with the cost of the lost tax revenues. The cost of cleaning up pollution may be roughly proportional to the number of polluters, but the cost of obtaining laws requiring polluters to clean up their own messes is not. An interest group or social movement campaigns for legislation of benefit to its members, but their costs are unaffected by the existence of others who would also benefit from the legislation.

A simple model

To investigate the effect of jointness of supply, we have to consider how group size affects the relation between the total contributions from all group members and the value experienced by any one individual. Nothing in the models in Chapter 2 captures this, so we have to add it explicitly. Returning to our original notation, we can either say that v, the value experienced by the individual from a unit level of P, varies with N, the total group size, and use v_N in our equations, or say that the total contributions necessary to produce a given level of P varies with N. We will use the latter representation.

Zero jointness of supply: the negative effect of group size

Olson's group-size argument is clearly correct *only* when the good has zero jointness of supply, that is, when the cost of providing the good increases proportionately to the number who share in it, or equivalently, that the value of a given level of the collective good declines proportionately with the number who share in it. In our production function terms, this means that the total contributions R necessary to provide a given level of the good P increases proportionately with the number of people who will share in the good. This relation can be expressed alternately as saying that P has the form $P(R/N)$, that is, that the level of the collective good is a function of the total contributions divided by the group size. The latter form has seemed so natural to some scholars that they have failed to see the assumption it entails.

It is the rare nonexcludable good that has zero jointness, and our example will sound implausible for just that reason. What we will have to imagine is that the affected employees will try to obtain money for a compensation fund that will be divided up among the affected employees. We will have to assume that city populations and city finances are constant, so that the size of the pool of affected employees does not vary with the city's overall tax base or total number of employees, but only with the extent to which city employees currently live outside the city. Even so, we have to stretch our credulity to imagine that the cost of persuading a government to establish such a fund is strictly proportional to the size of the fund, so perhaps we should instead imagine that the affected employees must engage in voluntary fund-raising in the community. Let's say that it takes an hour of time to raise $100, and that the provision level P is the payment to each individual from the fund. If every affected employee will get a share of the fund, regardless of whether he helped to create it, then we will have a nonexcludable good with zero jointness of supply. If there are 10 affected employees, each hour spent fund-raising pays $10 per employee, and P(1/10) = $10. If there are 100 affected employees, P(1/100) = $1 and each hour spent fund-raising pays only $1 per employee. Turning it around, an individual would have to spend 10 hours to earn $100 for himself if there are 10 employees, but 100 hours if there are 100 employees. In this situation, there is a strict negative relation between the size of the group of affected employees and the value to the individual of a given amount of collective action.

If the cost of a nonexcludable good increases proportionately (or more) with the number who enjoy it, larger groups are much less likely to be provided with the good than smaller groups. This is clearly the situation Olson has in mind in his analysis, and there is nothing wrong with his logic. The trouble is that few collective goods meet this condition. Most goods with no jointness of supply are also quite excludable. Olson's major example is a group of businesses joining together to restrict production in a perfectly competitive market. This kind of "collective action" is hardly what we as students of social movements had in mind when we were attracted to the theory, nor is it especially representative of the broad spectrum of phenomena that comprise the class of actions that fit our definition of "collective." What this analysis does show is why groups have a strong reason to prefer strategies in which they affect government policy over self-help strategies in which they provide the good themselves.

There are situations in which Olson's logic seems compelling, and it may be helpful to look more closely at the most important one, the problem of environmental pollution or the degradation of the commons. One's instinct is that this problem gets worse, and the collective good is harder to provide, the larger the group. But notice where the problem lies. Each individual emits a given level of pollution or consumes a given amount of a finite common resource and concludes that the gain to him from doing this far outweighs the loss he would experience from restraining his individual behavior. Individually, the pollution from his car is not enough to exceed the value to him of driving; the loss of grass from another sheep does not exceed the benefit of the sheep. This individual relation is just as true for one or two people as it is for a million. Individuals and small communities residing in pristine areas do *not* typically restrain their pollution; in fact, they often dump raw sewage into streams and otherwise behave in ways that would be intolerable in an urban setting. Socially desirable environmental behavior, that is, "collective action," is *not* more common when there are fewer people around (i.e., when the "group" is small).

The problem with pollution is *externalities,* that is, the fact that when a million people behave in this way, they all suffer from the effects of *others'* actions, and the fact that one can dump one's pollution downstream or in someone else's terrain. What changes with group size is not the nature of individual choices or the prevalence of collective action, but the harmful effects of individual choices and the cost of getting *everyone else* to stop polluting. The costs of creating and enforcing individually oriented agreements to jointly reduce pollution also go up with the number of individuals involved. But that is why solutions to pollution do *not* lie in influencing individuals, but rather in laws passed through political institutions. Laws have high jointness of supply.

Pure jointness of supply: positive effect of group size

When a good has pure jointness of supply, group size has a *positive* effect on the probability that it will be provided. The value of a good is unaffected by the number of others who share it. In this case, P is a function of R and is unaffected by group size. Then, larger interest groups are much more likely to have a critical mass of people willing to provide the collective good. If, no matter how many employees are affected, it costs the same to get a city council to pass a grandfather clause, the clause has pure jointness of supply. We can provide another example. In the course of this research we had to purchase a simulation compiler. The license for the compiler is for the whole computer, but we could place the compiler in a public access file or in a private file available only to ourselves. Obviously, the fact that others can use the compiler is totally irrelevant to the benefits we obtain from it, so we opted for public access. Because this good has pure jointness of supply, we had absolutely no reason to withhold it from others. A wealthy individual who stands to make $15 million from a special tax exemption will willingly spend $100,000 in payoffs or lobbying fees to obtain it and is indifferent about whether no one or a million other citizens will also benefit.

There is at least one objection that might be raised against this argument. If many people would prefer buying the good themselves to not having it, an individual may conclude that an even greater profit can be obtained by letting someone else pay for the good. A standard economic argument says that everyone will use this reasoning and no one will provide the good. We think this argument flies in the face of both the empirical evidence and the assumption of self-interest underlying the model. It says that most people prefer to risk substantial costs rather than obtain certain profit in the often far-fetched hope that they can wait out everyone else and thus gain an even greater (but sometimes only marginally greater) profit. This is different from the prisoner's dilemma, in which individuals can profit from cooperating only if others also cooperate. Here, an individual can assure himself a profit by his own actions and prefers to cooperate if he knows no one else is cooperating. Neither choice dominates the other; instead, individuals are motivated to obtain information about the choices of others. In Chapter 4, we show that this problem arises only under certain circumstances and provide a more detailed discussion of how we think the problem is resolved. Briefly, we argue that the most interested individuals provide the good for everyone, which is exactly what Olson predicts (1965, pp. 27–30). If people are comparable, the situation is more indeterminate, and the provider is often determined accidentally. (See Cornes and Sandler 1983, 1984a, 1984b, 1985 for a comparable result in economics.) Whether or not we are correct in our predictions about this indeterminate situation, notice that *group size is not a factor in the payoff structure.*

Means and standard deviations being equal, larger groups contain more total resources and larger numbers of highly interested people. Because pure jointness of supply makes group size irrelevant to individuals' payoffs, pure jointness of supply generally creates a *positive* group-size effect for (1) the probability that *someone* in a group will provide the good and (2) the total amount of contributions from (collective action by) the group. The scope condition for this result is that the value of the good is high enough relative to its cost, and the cost low enough relative to individuals' resources, that at least some group members would profit from providing it.

If the good is too expensive for individuals to buy, or if individuals' interest in the good is too low relative to its cost, no one will provide the good. But in this case group size still is irrelevant to the outcome. *There really is a dilemma of collective action for public goods, but the dilemma adheres to the high cost of providing them, relative to individual resources and interests, not to the number who share in them.*

When the cost of the collective good is very low relative to the group's interest, the group's size will have little effect on the probability that *somebody* in the interest group will contribute, but will have a positive effect on the total number of contributors and the total amount of the contributions. Consider the problem of providing the collective good of calling the power company to report an outage. Making a phone call entails some cost and will benefit others who have not called. There are doubtless many free riders, and even a "diffusion of responsibility" effect of people assuming that someone else is making a call that they would be perfectly willing to make themselves. Nevertheless, someone nearly always calls, whether the affected group is big or small. In fact, there are almost always quite a few calls made about any particular outage, and the number of calls is usually greater the more people are affected. Although a higher *proportion* of smaller affected populations might call, there is a greater total number of calls, that is, more overall collective *action,* in a larger group. Of course, once an individual is certain that someone else has called, she will not call and will "free-ride" on the calls of others. But as long as she is uncertain whether the call has been made, its cost is low enough relative to its value that she will make the call.

What about intermediate goods, whose cost is low enough that someone might be willing and able to pay for them, but high enough that this willingness and ability is a relatively rare trait? Suppose that our employees' fate rests not on joint collective action, but on individual collective action. That is, suppose that the issue is whether one person has enough time and interest to lobby single-handedly for the grandfather clause. If a group has at least one such person, collective action will occur; if not, not.

We can model this as a large population from which random samples of various sizes are drawn. Suppose that only one person in a hundred has the capacity and interest to do this kind of lobbying. The probability that a sample (group of employees) of size N will have at least 1 person who exceeds a threshold with probability p is $1 - q^N$, where $q = 1 - p$, while the expected number who will exceed that threshold is Np. If there are 10 employees, the expected number of lobbyists when p is .01 is .1, and the probability that there is at least one lobbyist in the group rounds off to about .1. That is, only 10% of employee groups of size 10 would be expected to have a competent and interested lobbyist. If there are 100 employees, the number of expected lobbyists is 1, and the probability that a group will have at least 1 is about .6, so that 60% of all employee groups of size 100 would have a competent and interested lobbyist in their ranks. But if there are 1,000 employees, the expected number of lobbyists is 10, and it is virtually certain that there will be at least 1 person who will lobby.

Interactions: group size and economies of scale

As we have previously noted, most real cases lie between the extremes of pure and zero jointness of supply. They exhibit partial jointness of supply, or economies of scale, wherein the cost of the collective good rises less than proportionately with the number who enjoy it. In these intermediate cases, the amount of collective action as a function of group size depends on the interaction between the cost function for the collective good and the distribution of potential contribution levels among members of the group.

These interactions are always specific to a particular case, but we can identify the two important principles that govern them. First, the more the cost function for the collective good approximates jointness of supply, the more likely group size is to have a positive effect on the provision of the good. Increasing the size of the interest group promotes collective action when the good has high jointness of supply and hinders collective action when the good has low jointness of supply. A compensation fund, which has zero jointness, is more likely to be created for smaller groups of affected employees and less likely to be created for larger groups. Hiring someone to lobby for a grandfather clause, which has high jointness of supply, is more likely to happen in a larger group than in a smaller group, because there will be more total money available to pay the lobbyist in the larger group.

Second, the more heterogeneous and positively skewed the distribution of potential contribution sizes, the more likely group size will have a positive effect on the provision of the good. In a homogeneous group,

group size generally has little effect on collective action. Either the conditions are favorable or they are not. But when a group is heterogeneous, larger groups are statistically more likely to have more people in them who have high levels of interest and resources.

These two relations interact. Group size has a positive effect whenever the interest and resource distributions are skewed enough relative to the steepness of the cost function that the effect of enlarging the pool of potential contributors compensates for increased costs. If the costs increase greatly with group size (i.e., jointness of supply is close to zero), increasing the group size will always have a negative effect on collective action unless the group is very heterogeneous and the good can be provided by a very small number of very large contributors. But if costs increase only slightly with group size (i.e., jointness of supply is high), almost any heterogeneity in contribution levels is enough to make larger groups more successful than smaller ones. Using simulations, we have explored these relations extensively. However, we do not think that numerical examples do much to clarify the substantive meaning of this result. The principle of relating the cost function to the heterogeneity of the population always applies, but real-world situations differ greatly in the actual forms of the two functions and therefore differ greatly in the outcome predicted by their interaction.

The paradox of group size and the number of contributors

Our analysis has allowed us to recognize at least one important paradoxical relation that has not previously been appreciated. *When groups are heterogeneous and a good has high jointness of supply, a larger interest group can have a smaller critical mass.* That is, when a good has high jointness of supply it may be provided by fewer people in a larger group than in a smaller group.

There are precursors of this result in the literature. Both Olson, briefly (1965, p. 29), and Hardin, much more extensively (1982, pp. 67–89), argue that group heterogeneity has a positive effect on the prospects for collective action. Hardin gives several examples to show that the especially interested and resourceful members of an interest group may provide collective goods that benefit many others. He proves that what he calls the "efficacious subgroup" (what we call the "critical mass") will be smaller in a more heterogeneous group. We go one step further and demonstrate that if groups are heterogeneous and a good has jointness of supply, the critical mass will be smaller in a larger interest group.

We may illustrate the paradox with another example. Suppose someone gets the idea of asking all the affected employees to chip in to pay for a $1,250 advertisement in the local paper. This collective good has perfect jointness of supply: the cost adheres to the size of the ad, not to the number of people for whom it speaks. For the moment, ignore the social process problem of coordinating contributions. It happens that the "average" employee can afford to contribute $50. If the group is homogeneous, it therefore takes 25 people to provide the good, a result that is invariant with group size.

In contrast, consider three groups of 100, 1,000, and 10,000 affected employees in which the distributions of resources are *heterogeneous*. Table 3.1 shows the proportions and actual numbers of employees within each of these groups expected to have each whole number of resource units for two arbitrary distributions.[2] The first is a normal distribution (which is, of course, symmetric), and the second is a lognormal distribution; both have a mean of $50 and a standard deviation of $10; this is a very slight degree of heterogeneity.

The data in Table 3.1 show that, regardless of group size, the simple fact of heterogeneity (around the same mean) reduces the minimum size of the critical mass. Even in the symmetric distribution, the smallest heterogeneous group (100) contains a minimum critical mass of size 20 (1 person contributing $8, 6 contributing $7, and 13 contributing $6), 5 less than the 25 contributors needed under homogeneity. This minimum number declines slightly with group size: to 17 for the group of 1,000 employees, and to 16 for the largest group of 10,000 employees.

This pattern is more pronounced when the resource distribution is more skewed. For the moderately skewed distribution in this example, the minimum number of contributors is 15 for the smallest group, 9 for the medium-sized group, and 7 for the largest group. Extremely skewed distributions, in which some members might be willing and able to contribute 100 times more than the mean of all others, would show even more pronounced

---

[2] This example is not strictly correct mathematically, since it treats continuous distributions as if they were discrete, and expected frequencies as if they were determinate; but it shows clearly and concretely how the group-size paradox arises.

Table 3.1. *Computation of critical mass for two distributions and three group sizes*

A. Expected number of individuals willing to make each size contribution (rounded to integers)

	Normal[a]				Lognormal[a]			
Value	Probability	$E(100)$	$E(1,000)$	$E(10,000)$	Probability	$E(100)$	$E(1,000)$	$E(10,000)$
0	.0000	0	0	0	.0000	0	0	0
1	.0002	0	0	2	.0046	0	5	46
2	.0060	1	6	60	.0747	7	75	747
3	.0606	6	61	606	.1877	19	188	1,877
4	.2417	24	242	2,417	.2197	22	220	2,197
5	.3829	38	383	3,829	.1821	18	182	1,821
6	.2417	24	242	2,417	.1273	13	127	1,273
7	.0606	6	61	606	.0815	8	81	815
8	.0060	1	6	60	.0497	5	50	497
9	.0002	0	0	2	.0296	3	30	296
10	.0000	0	0	0	.0175	2	17	175
11					.0103	1	10	103
12					.0061	1	6	61
13					.0036	0	4	36
14					.0022	0	2	22
15					.0013	0	1	13
16					.0008	0	1	8
17					.0005	0	1	5
18					.0003	0	0	3
19					.0002	0	0	2
20					.0001	0	0	1
21					.00008	0	0	1
22					.00005	0	0	1
23					.00003	0	0	0
24					.00002	0	0	0
25					.00001	0	0	0

B. Computation of size of critical mass

Distribution	Group size (N)	Size of critical mass (N)	Detail[b]
Normal	100	20	1 @ 8; 6 @ 7; 12 @ 6; 1 @ 3
Normal	1,000	17	6 @ 8; 11 @ 7
Normal	10,000	16	2 @ 9; 13 @ 8; 1 @ 3
Lognormal	100	15	1 @ 12; 1 @ 11; 2 @ 10; 3 @ 9; 5 @ 8; 2 @ 7; 1 @ 1
Lognormal	1,000	9	1 @ 17; 1 @ 16; 1 @ 15; 2 @ 14; 3 @ 13; 1 @ 10
Lognormal	10,000	7	1 @ 22; 1 @ 21; 1 @ 20; 2 @ 19; 2 @ 18

[a]Mean 5; standard deviation 1.
[b]The figures indicate number of people at a particular dollar value of contribution.

effects, so that 1 or 2 people might be able to provide the good for the whole group.

It should be clear that this pattern is not dependent on any particular distribution, but rather may arise whenever a group is heterogeneous in the sizes of its members' potential contributions. The mechanism causing the paradox is really very simple: the expected number of individuals who are willing and able to give at any specific contribution level will always be higher for a larger group. Since collective goods with pure jointness of supply have a fixed cost that does not vary with the size of the group enjoying the good, the greater expected number of large contributors in a larger group means that in general fewer people will be needed to achieve a given *total contribution* size than in a smaller group.

Group size and the social process for collective action

Olson is right, of course: most public goods will never be provided by individuals acting in independent isolation, and the importance of this claim cannot be underestimated. We do not expect spontaneous action in pursuit of collective goals to arise from an unorganized undifferentiated population. Interdependence, communication, organizations, and social process are central to collective action, and Olson has played a key intellectual role in making this clear.

However, Olson argues that even if we allow for social processes, the group-size effect would obtain, since such social processes, as well as feelings of group solidarity, are more likely to overcome the collective dilemma in moderate-sized groups than in large ones (p. 48). This argument is seriously flawed by a floating conception of what the "group" is. When a good has jointness of supply, it is irrelevant to the payoffs of those who contribute how many others there are "out there" in the interest group who might benefit. When a "social" solution to the collective dilemma is required, what matters is the pattern of relations among the possible contributors *in the critical mass,* not the relations among everyone in the interest group. Paradoxically, if a collective good has jointness of supply, the size of the critical mass can be smaller when the size of the interest group is larger, and social processes may be *more* beneficial in larger interest groups.

Because larger interest groups have more total resources, they are generally more likely to have the *possibility* for a successful collective action. Especially when goods have high and lumpy costs (i.e., where a large minimum amount is needed to provide any of the good, such as a bridge), smaller interest groups may simply be unable to supply enough resources, no matter how well they organize. Where a larger group might need to mobilize only 5% of its potentially available resources to provide a good, a smaller group might require 100% of its resources, or more.

There are some small interest groups with the kind of social structure that would permit them to mobilize 100% of their members to action, and it is a very exciting process to watch when it happens. But it is a much more common event to see a critical mass coalesce within a larger interest group. There are costs to organizing and coordinating contributions by a number of people, and those costs are usually higher when more contributors are involved. Thus, it will generally be much easier and cheaper to organize a collective action that involves a small number of contributors within a large interest group than one involving a larger number of contributors within a small interest group.

Of course, it may be especially difficult and costly for the small number of potential contributors in a very large interest group to find one another and coordinate their actions. If society were organized randomly, this would always be a serious problem for collective actors. If social ties were distributed randomly across a large city, it would be unlikely that the five people who would be willing to contribute $1 million each to a geology museum, or the ten people who would be willing to devote six months of their lives to organizing a nuclear freeze campaign, or the six city employees willing to pay for an ad, would ever meet. In fact, the real world surely contains many interests whose distributions are essentially random and about which collective action is very unlikely. But randomness is *not* the rule. Very wealthy people know many of the other very wealthy people. Potential political activists associate themselves with events and organizations expressing their political concerns. City residents who would be most harmed by a proposed expressway live near each other, in its path. City employees who are suburban residents may be members of the same union, or attend the same churches, or ride in car pools together; at a minimum they see each other at work.

Thus, the problem of collective action is not whether it is possible to mobilize every single person who would benefit from a collective good.

It is not whether it is possible to mobilize everyone who would be willing to be mobilized. It is not even whether all the members of some organization or social network can be mobilized. Rather, the issue is whether there is some social mechanism that connects enough people who have the appropriate interests and resources so that they can act. It is whether there is an organization or social network that has a *subset* of individuals who are interested and resourceful enough to provide the good when they act in concert and whether they have sufficient social organization among themselves to act together.

In one sense, our argument is that Olson's "large-group" problem is often resolved by a "small-group" solution. Olson is absolutely correct to say that collective action rarely takes the form of small, unnoticeable contributions from thousands or millions of isolated individuals. If everybody's interest or resources are equally small, collective action will generally not happen, no matter how big or small the interest group. Collective action arises around those interests for which there are groups of especially interested and resourceful individuals who are socially connected to one another.[3]

A small number of wealthy people are able to act collectively to get what they want not because there are few of them, but because they are wealthy. Resources and interests being equal, movements on behalf of very large constituencies often are more successful than movements on behalf of tiny minorities. Large interest groups sustain more collective action than do smaller ones, when costs are equal and the individuals in the groups have comparable interest and resource levels. Resources and social organization are the problem, *not* group size. If a group is heterogeneous enough that it contains a critical mass who can make large contributions, and if those members are socially connected to one another so that they can act in concert, collective action for jointly supplied collective goods *is* possible and *more* likely in larger groups.

Our theoretical analysis is consistent with the thrust of a great deal of recent empirical scholarship on social movements. It is never the case that all women (J. Freeman 1973), all blacks (Morris 1981, 1984), everyone opposed to the reopening of the Three Mile Island reactor (Walsh and Warland 1983), everyone for a clean environment (Mitchell 1979), or all northern whites concerned about voting rights in the South (McAdam 1986)

---

[3] For a much fuller analysis of the effects of social ties within groups, see Chapter 6.

are mobilized, nor is the existence of a large mass of "free riders" any particular hindrance to the mobilization or success of a movement. In fact, public opinion polls identifying large pools of nonactivist adherents to a cause tend to help the cause, not hurt it. What matters for successful mobilization is that there be enough people who *are* willing to participate and who can also be reached through social influence networks. Empirical accounts of actual social movements and movement organizations show again and again that most of the action originates from a relatively small number of extremely active participants.

The dilemma of collective action, correctly analyzed, is the problem of not being able to make a big enough difference in the outcome to compensate for the costs one bears. Thus understood, the theory of collective action does *not* predict that collective action will *never* occur, but rather that it will not take the form of small isolated contributions. Collective action theory as articulated by Olson does fit some empirical circumstances. It successfully predicts that most individuals will not voluntarily incur the costs of reducing energy consumption or avoiding pollution, because the benefit they can produce individually by their self-restraint is far smaller than its cost. But it is not the group-size problem that is working here; it is the noticeability problem and the ability to transfer pollution costs to others through dumping downstream or living in the suburbs. Smaller populations do not pollute less on a per capita basis; its members just experience less harm from others' actions. In fact, environmental pollution is essentially caused by the continuation of small-population manners when populations grow large. It is larger populations that pay for sewage treatment plants.

Correctly understood, the theory of collective action explains why most action comes from a relatively small number of participants who make such big contributions to the cause that they know (or think they know) they can "make a difference" or who, like the radicals of the sixties portrayed by Gitlin (1987), decide to suspend their evaluation of reality and act *as if* they could make a difference.

Theory and empirical research on social movements also agree in tending to discount the causal significance of the size of the aggrieved population as a direct determinant of collective action. Current research stresses the importance of social networks and organizational resources among some interested subset of the population, coupled with "political opportunities" created through party politics (e.g., McAdam 1982; Jenkins 1987). Full-time professional activists (McCarthy and Zald 1973, 1977) are also seen as important, although less important than they were viewed several years ago.

Let us not, however, conclude that the "masses" are irrelevant for collective action. We have shown theoretically that larger groups *should be* more likely to give rise to collective action than should smaller ones (given the jointness of supply of so many collective goods), and it is empirically true that very large social movements tend to arise from very large mass bases. However, undifferentiated impoverished masses do not usually support social movements. What seems to be critical is the presence of a minority of the aggrieved population who are well educated or especially politically conscious, who have substantial discretionary time, or who are economically independent of their oppressors.[4] Larger populations are likely to have larger numbers of these unusual members, and their potential contribution sizes are likely to be larger.

The more obvious effect of interest group size is also important: larger populations generally have more *total* resources than do smaller ones. This has tended to be ignored by those who are theoretically sophisticated, because it is understood that those resources do not automatically or easily turn into contributions. But one thing the small critical mass of large contributors can do is invest time, energy, and money in organizing and coordinating events that draw in and make use of small contributions. They can use preexisting organizations and networks to create the social conditions under which small contributors will participate in a march or demonstration. They can pay the overhead for large mass mailings to solicit small monetary contributions under circumstances that make the donors' costs low relative to their psychic benefits. (For more discussion, see Oliver and Furman 1989.) The larger the total size of the interest group, the larger the potential gain from either of these strategies.

In short, our investigation of the group-size problem leads us to conclude that we must move away from simplistic images of "collective action" as a unitary phenomenon and toward theory that identifies the important dimensions along which interest groups and collective actions vary. We

---

[4] Perhaps we should cite Lenin on this point, as well as the social movements literature. We should stress that we are emphasizing the theoretical importance of differentiation *within* the aggrieved population; this is very different from an "external resources" argument, which has fared badly in empirical research (e.g., McAdam 1982; Jenkins and Eckert 1986).

see that we must pay attention to exactly how contributions or actions affect the collective good. We also see that we must start from the assumption that interest groups are heterogeneous and give special attention to the effects of heterogeneity on collective action.

4. The dynamics of production functions

Assume that the probability of success . . . of [a] collective action is . . .
a function of the number of demonstrators. . . . This function is assumed
S-shaped because a small demonstration is expected to have little impact
up to a certain size, and again large numbers beyond a certain size would
not make much difference either, whereas in the middle range, additional
numbers increase visibility and impact.

Anthony Oberschall (1980, p. 48)

With this paragraph, Oberschall sought to move the analysis of social
movements beyond the generally implicit assumption of a linear relationship between effort and effect that pervaded the previous literature. However, Oberschall gave us only this brief glimpse of a fundamental theoretical
issue. He did not pursue further the relationship between the form of the
production function and the probability of collective action. In this chapter,
we take up this unfinished task.

Production functions can take many exotic forms, but the important
dynamics of collective action can be captured with the five types sketched
in Figure 4.1. Each of the figure's curves is intended to capture the entire
production relation between individual costs borne and value received from
the collective good. As discussed in Chapter 2, the overall shape is a
composite of the relations between costs borne and resources contributed,
between resources contributed and the level of the collective good, and
between the level of the collective good and the value experienced. As
our examples indicate, in different situations the overall shape of the
production function is dominated by different links in the chain. In our
equations, we will assume that two links are linear – the relation between
costs borne and resources contributed, and the relation between level of
the good and the value obtained. This puts all the mathematical "action"

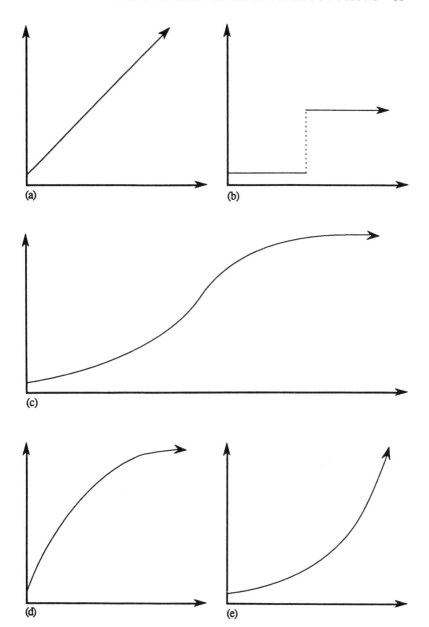

Figure 4.1. General types of production function. (a) Linear; (b) discontinuous, or step; (c) general third order; (d) decelerating; (e) accelerating.

in the middle link, which simplifies the exposition without changing the substance of our conclusions.

In all of our discussion, we assume that all production functions are monotonic increasing, up to the maximum where $P = 1$. That is, an additional contribution always adds to the provision level of the collective good, although this addition may be so small as to be negligible. We do not treat cases in which additional contributions might be counterproductive and lower the level of the collective good. Our analysis also will assume that the production functions are continuous and twice differentiable, so that we can talk about rates of acceleration and deceleration in terms of the second derivative. The substantive logic of our discussion does not, however, depend on these two assumptions.

If each added unit of contribution produces about the same amount of the collective good regardless of how much has already been contributed, the production function is linear and looks like Curve 1a. Much naive theorizing has used this model, but we will show that it has surprisingly extreme consequences.

Curve 1b is a step function: no benefit is obtained if contributions are below the threshold, and full benefit is obtained if they are above the threshold. Step functions arise when collective goods are lumpy, like bridges. Because voting, a central process in the democratic provision of collective goods through governments, is generally presumed to follow step functions, they have been of particular interest in political science. When a simple majority wins an election, the one vote that changes a minority to a majority is of crucial importance. (See Hardin 1982, pp. 52–61, for an extended discussion.) However, step functions are neither general nor tractable for formal analyses of collective action and tend to be relegated to the status of "special cases." We will not be working with step functions in this book. For some purposes, step functions may be approximated by S-shaped curves (Curve 1c) with very very flat regions of low returns and very very steep regions of high returns, so our discussion will provide some illumination of these cases, although it will not deal with the peculiar properties of discontinuous functions.

Curve 1c is Oberschall's "general case," a monotonic increasing third-order curve with an S shape. The curve begins with a period of start-up costs or other sources of low initial returns for contribution, followed by a period of higher returns, and finally by a saturation effect and lower returns. Mathematically, this assumption implies that there are first increasing and then diminishing marginal returns from resource contributions to the collective action. In general, an S-shaped curve implies that people will find it most worthwhile to contribute to a collective good in the middle of the curve, after some have already made contributions but before participation approaches unanimity. It is there that they make the most difference.

The assumption of a third-order curve is quite reasonable but so general that it obscures the very important questions of how large the start-up costs are and how quickly the marginal returns decline. We will explore these issues with two extreme cases. The *decelerating* production function (1d) is a general third-order curve with no start-up costs, so that the initial period of low but increasing returns is reduced to zero, and returns are highest for initial contributions and decline thereafter. By contrast, the *accelerating* production function (1e) is a third-order curve with especially high start-up costs and a long initial period of low returns, followed by a period of high returns extending to the edge of the range of feasible contributions. We show that these two extreme cases produce very different dynamics for collective action. Having done this, we put the general third-order curve back together in the last section and discuss what our analysis implies about collective action in general.

Types of Production Functions

Decelerating production functions

Marginal returns decrease in the decelerating case. Each additional contribution always adds to the provision level, but the size of this addition declines. The first few units of resources contributed have the biggest impact on the collective good, and subsequent contributions have progressively less impact. For this reason, a decelerating production function leads to *negative interdependence:* each contribution makes others' subsequent contributions less worthwhile, and thus less likely. Our analysis assumes what we term *uniform* deceleration, meaning that the second derivative is negative, that is, the curve is always convex. More precisely, we assume that the second derivative is always nonpositive; the second derivative may sometimes be zero but may never be positive and must be at least sometimes negative.

A simple example of a decelerating production function might be calling about a pothole in a middle-class urban area where politicians are sensitive to complaints from the public: the first person who takes the time to call makes the probability .4 that the hole will be fixed, the second raises it to .7 (an increase of .3), the third to .8 (an increase of .1), the fourth to .85 (an increase of .05), the fifth to .88 (an increase of .03), the sixth to .90 (an increase of .02), and so forth, with each subsequent call adding a smaller and smaller increment to the probability. Another example might be organizing a picnic. Half of the fun of a picnic is assured if someone arranges for a good location and adequately publicizes the time and place. Another good-sized increment comes from making some definite arrangement about food. From then on, each additional contribution of game equipment or food adds to the picnic's likely success, but each of these increments is smaller than the previous ones.

Returning to our employees fighting for a grandfather clause, a decelerating production function would arise if simply paying the first several hundred dollars to a lawyer to talk to a few influential council members makes the probability quite high that the council will change its position and pass the amendment without the expense of an extensive campaign of testimony, legal briefs, and political negotiation (although certain success can be assured only by doing all of these). This might be the case if the city has historically been a stronghold of support for unions or the council members are worried about finding replacements for the workers if they choose not to move into the city.

A wide variety of forms of collective action have the general character of a largely decelerating production function, although not the extreme form we model. These include lobbying, publicity, organizational maintenance, newsletter publication, and all the other common activities in which a few people can provide the good for all, and once action reaches a basic level, additional contributions add little.

Accelerating production functions

By contrast, marginal returns increase in the *accelerating* case. Again, any contribution always produces an increase in the provision level of the good, but in the accelerating case, early contributions produce very small increases, while later contributions produce much larger ones. There are large start-up costs, but there is no point of diminishing marginal returns within the feasible range of contributions. Successive contributions generate progressively larger payoffs. An unbounded accelerating function goes to infinity, which is impossible, so we always assume that the interest group and its resources are finite and put an upper bound on the function. Again, we assume *uniform* acceleration, in that the second derivative is everywhere nonnegative. Regions of constant slope are permitted (zero second derivative), but the slopes are generally increasing and never decrease.

Accelerating production functions are characterized by *positive interdependence:* each contribution makes the next one more worthwhile and, thus, more likely. Since initial contributions of resources have only negligible effects on the collective good, it is only after long start-up costs have been borne that contributions start to make a big difference in the collective good. This will prove to be an important feature of accelerating production functions.

An example of an accelerating production function might be calling about a pothole from a poor minority urban area with little political clout: it takes twenty calls before the probability reaches even .01 and another twenty to reach .1, but then the next twenty calls worry city hall and make the probability .9. A second example might be creating a community center: hours and dollars have to be spent buying the land and materials and building the structure before the last few hours of painting it and furnishing it produce big payoffs in having a place to meet.

Our employees would face an accelerating production function if paying for a lawyer's initial work has only a negligible impact on the city council, while raising the money to cover an extensive lobbying effort makes the probability of victory accelerate to certainty. This case might arise if voting with the employees were considered ethically correct but a political liability, so that council members would only vote for the amendment if they could be assured that most of the other council members would do the same.

Collective actions characterized by the dynamics of the accelerative production function are mass actions whose effect increases with the number of participants, such as strikes, boycotts, collective defiance, and some kinds of demonstrations. Lumpy collective goods with high costs also generally exhibit the dynamics characteristic of accelerating curves, up to the threshold.

Some simplifying assumptions

Several of the simplifying assumptions presented in Chapter 2 are of particular importance for this analysis, and therefore bear brief review. We also introduce a few additional assumptions that facilitate comparisons among production functions.

Standardized production functions

As described in Chapter 2, the general form of a production function is $g_i(r) = v_i[P(R)] - c_i(r)$, where g is the net gain to an individual of a contribution of size r, c is the cost to the individual of contributing r, P is the provision level of the collective good as a function of the total contribution level R, and v is the value to the individual of the provision level P.

Let us begin by summarizing our simplifying assumptions and standardizations. First, we assume that P, the provision level of the good, ranges continuously from 0 to 1 and is dependent only on R, the total contributions. We define M as the amount of total contributions that yields the maximum provision level, that is, $P(M) = 1$. Second, we assume that the value v_i experienced from the collective good is a constant multiple of the provision level, so the value experienced is linear with the total contributions but may vary across group members. We will vary the "shape" of the production function by varying $P(R)$. Third, we choose a *standarized* metric for cost, contribution, and value that expresses the standardized contributions r and R and value v_i as multiples of the total cost of the maximum provision level, cM. This gives us the simpler production function $g_i(R) = v_i P(R) - r$, where R, r, and P range from 0 to 1, and v_i is expressed as a fraction of the total cost (cM) of the maximum provision level.

There is no range constraint on the standardized value v_i, which may be 1 if the value to the individual exactly equals the total cost of the good, greater than 1 if the value to the individual is greater than the total cost of the collective good, and less than 1 if the individual's value is less than the total cost of the good. As we have argued in Chapter 3, there are many collective goods with jointness of supply whose total cost is less than the value experienced by a single individual, so there is nothing impossible or paradoxical about standardized values of v_i greater than 1, although there are obviously many other cases in which v_i is smaller than 1.

We assume that the whole interest group has a total standardized resource level T of at least 1; this total may exceed 1, sometimes by a great deal. All groups have the capacity to achieve the maximum provision level of the collective good. The question is whether this collective capacity can be realized.

It is possible for the total contributions from the group to exceed 1, that is, for the group to contribute more than is needed to achieve certainty or the maximum level of the collective good. This would simply mean that the group expends more than necessary for the provision of a collective good with an upper bound, something that happens fairly often in real life when people have incomplete information about others' contributions. When we impose assumptions of full information, we assume that contributions stop after a total of 1 is reached and are largely concerned with whether that level can be reached or not.

Sequentiality, full information, and group hetrogeneity

In this chapter, we assume that decisions are made sequentially. In our formal model, group members take turns deciding one at a time in a strict rotation. Each member has full information about all prior contributions, but makes her own decision independently, without coordinating actions with others or considering the effects of her actions on others' subsequent actions. If everyone were the same, the order of their decisions would not matter. But because we assume groups are heterogeneous in how much members might contribute, we must consider the order of their contributions. We explicitly investigate the effects of different orders of decision making, and thus are able to say how the order of choices affects the outcome and what would happen if people were offered repeated chances to choose. Our analysis thus may be readily generalized to situations in which actors make their choices over time with full information about others' prior actions, but with everybody able to make a choice whenever they want to.

Besides looking at the process of decision making when groups are heterogeneous, we give particular attention to how the degree of group heterogeneity affects collective action. We find that the effects of the degree and kind of heterogeneity interact substantially with the production functions. Resource heterogeneity has a much greater effect on collective action with accelerating production functions. Interest heterogeneity always affects collective action, but in different ways for different production functions.

Results I: differences among production functions

In this section we present the initial steps of our formal analysis. We begin by setting up an individual decision model, first for the most simplified case where there is only one actor, and then for the slightly more complex case where the group is homogeneous. We then show the effect of varying forms of production functions for these two simple cases. We show that the production function makes a big difference, and that, for some production functions but not others, the homogeneous group is very different from the one-actor case.

The one-actor case

We can get a clearer understanding of the effect of the production function if we begin by assuming that the *only* affected employee is our high-paid executive from Chapter 2. That is, we will assume that the grandfather clause is really a private good – a good whose benefits accrue to only one actor. Recall that it will cost this executive $20,000 a year to be forced to choose between his job or his wife's, or to maintain two homes; this is his unstandardized v_i. If we know the total cost of producing the grandfather clause, cM, we may represent the executive's decision with the simple standardized decision equation

$$g(R) = vP(R) - R. \tag{1}$$

This equation says that the gain or net standardized payoff $g(R)$ to the individual from spending R units of resource equals the expected payoff of the expenditure minus its cost. The net gain will be positive whenever $vP(R) > R$.

Our next step is to solve for the optimum value of R, that is, the size contribution our single actor should make to maximize his profit. To find this optimum contribution, we take the derivative of (1) with respect to R, set the derivative denoted by $g'(r)$ equal to zero, and solve for the derivative of the production function $P'(R)$, yielding

$$P'(R) = 1/v. \tag{2}$$

The term $P'(R)$ is the derivative or slope of the production function, that is, the change in the probability of obtaining the collective good produced by a contribution of one resource unit at the point R. Except when the production function is linear, the slope $P'(R)$ varies with R, the total amount contributed. The steeper the slope, the greater the impact of a unit contribution. The term $1/v$ is the reciprocal of the value the actor attaches to the maximum provision level, expressed in standardized terms as a fraction of the cost of the maximum provision level. When $P'(R)$ is greater than $1/v$, each unit contributed produces a profit for the individual; $P'(R)$ is less than $1/v$, further contribution produces a loss. When $P'(R)$ equals $1/v$, we are at the turning point between profit and loss. The maximum net payoff, if any, will occur at such a turning point.

Linear production functions. If the production function is linear, that is, if each unit of resources produces the same change in the provision level, the slope of the production function, $P'(R)$, is a constant that is invariant with R and is always greater than, less than, or equal to $1/v$. In this case, our executive will pay either nothing, if $P'(R) < 1/v$, or as much as he can afford, up to M, if $P'(R) > 1/v$. When P is linear with R, our standardization implies $P(R) = R$, and the net gain g will be positive whenever $v > 1$, that is, whenever the value of the maximum provision level exceeds the total cost of the maximum provision level. For example, if the total cost of the maximum provision level is cM = \$30,000, then a linear production function will yield a positive gain whenever the unstandardized value of the maximum provision level exceeds v_i = \$30,000. Turning this around, our executive whose unstandardized value for the collective good is v_i = \$20,000 will pay for any strategy with a linear production function whose total cost is less than cM = \$20,000.

Notice that, when the production function is linear, our executive will do everything he can or nothing at all. Linear production functions must yield dichotomous behavior. The extremity of this assumption is seen more clearly when we consider a homogeneous group.

It is also worth stressing that even if the production function is nonlinear, it is linear in its consequences if its slope is everywhere greater or everywhere less than $1/v$. It is only when the range of variation in the slopes of the standardized production function is both above and below the standardized value of the good that the shape of the production function has any effect. For this reason, we assume in all subsequent discussions that the slope of the production function is *not* always greater or always less than $1/v$.

Decelerating production functions. Since contributions never reduce the probability of the collective good, the slope $P'(R)$ is always positive. In the uniformly decelerative case, this positive slope begins at its maximum and then consistently decreases toward zero. This means that the point where $P'(R) = 1/v$ is a maximum. Our executive should invest to this point, thereby investing an optimum amount of resources to produce a high (but not maximum) provision level of the collective good. This predicted behavior is the same regardless of whether or not the executive would be willing to pay for the maximum provision level if that were his alternative to doing nothing.

Consider first the case in which the executive would prefer paying the maximum to doing nothing, that is, in which the standardized $v > 1$. Suppose, for example, the executive is considering a strategy that would have a maximum cost of $15,000, and continue to assume he stands to lose $20,000. He would make a profit of $5,000 if he paid the maximum. But if the production function is decelerating, there will be a lower contribution level that will produce even greater profit. In this example, his standardized $v = \$20,000/\$15,000 = 1.33$, and $1/v = .75$. Suppose that the slope of the production function is .75 for $R = .4$ and that $P(.4) = .8$. In this case, a contribution of $6,000 = .4(\$15,000)$ will yield a provision level of $16,000 = .8(\$20,000)$, for a profit of $10,000. If this is the point where the standardized slope equals the reciprocal of the standardized value, this is the greatest profit the executive can realize. Even though he would make some profit from doing the maximum, he will make more profit from the optimum.

The decelerating production function may also lead to contributions even when the executive is unwilling to pay the maximum. (This case falls outside the scope of our assumption that the collective good is worth more than its cost, but provides worthwhile illumination of the dynamics of production functions.) Still leaving his unstandardized value at $20,000, let us now consider a strategy whose maximum cost is $30,000. In this case, the standardized $v = \$20,000/\$30,000 = .67$, and $1/v = 1.5$. It is clear that our executive will not pay the maximum, as this would produce a net loss of $10,000. But if the production function is decelerating, there may be some initial regions of small contributions with steep enough slopes to make contributing worthwhile. Suppose that $P'(.3)$

= 1.5 and that P(.3) = .7. At this point, an investment of $9,000 = .3($30,000) will yield a provision level worth $14,000 = .7($20,000), for a profit of $5,000. Again, this is the maximum profit the executive could realize in this example, and we would predict that he would spend the $9,000, even though he would not be willing to spend $30,000 to buy the maximum provision level. Whenever he is not willing to pay the maximum, however, we do need to check that the optimum produces a profit, not a loss, that is, that G > 0, which is true in this case.

Accelerating production functions. Although the slope of a uniformly accelerative production function is positive, it starts at its minimum (near zero) and consistently increases (or, more generally, never decreases). This means that the point where $P'(R) = 1/v$ is a *minimum,* not a maximum. As long as R is below this point, each additional unit contributed produces another unit of loss for the executive. For larger Rs, each additional unit invested produces a profit, but the initial losses still have to be compensated for, so R must be quite a bit greater than the turning point before the net payoff is greater than zero. From that point on, things get better and better, and the actor should, rationally, contribute everything available to the collective action.

It will be helpful to show how this works with an example. Suppose our executive whose unstandardized v is $20,000 considers a strategy whose maximum cost is $15,000, making the standardized $v = \$20,000/\$15,000 = 1.3333$, and $1/v = .75$. Imagine a production function with the following reference points: P(.2) = .01, P(.4) = .1, P(.6) = .3, P(.8) = .6, and P(1) = 1; these points trace an accelerating production function where early contributions have little impact, but the provision level soars as contributions approach the maximum. Further suppose that we have solved for the derivative and that the production function's slope equals $1/v$ at R = .4, that is, P'(.4) = .75. A contribution of $3,000 yields a value of $200 = 1.333(.01)$15,000, for a loss of $2,800. A contribution of $6,000 yields $2,000 = 1.333(.1)$15,000 for a loss of $4,000. This is the turning point that, for an accelerative production function, is the minimum, the point of greatest loss. Contributions larger than this yield better payoffs, but only in the sense that they are smaller losses. A contribution of $9,000 yields $6,000 = 1.3333(.3)$15,000, for a loss of $3,000. Only at the highest contribution levels is there a net profit. A contribution of $12,000 yields $12,000 = 1.3333(.6)$15,000 and is the break-even point between profit and loss. But the maximum contribution of $15,000 yields $20,000, for a net profit of $5,000. This is true for all accelerative production functions: the greatest profit is achieved from the largest possible contribution.

This is a somewhat paradoxical result: if the production function is accelerating, the "optimum" is to provide the maximum level of the good, if one has the resources to do so. If one is interested enough to be willing to make some investment in the good and resourceful enough to "buy" the whole thing, one should buy all of it, and any less would be irrational. Thus, for our single actor buying a private good, the accelerative production function is like the linear production function, in that it predicts dichotomous behavior: do nothing, or do the maximum.

The difference between the linear and accelerative cases is also instructive. In both cases, if $T > cM$, that is, if the actor can afford to pay for the maximum provision level, he will. They differ in the prediction for actors with modest resources. In the linear case, an actor who would be willing to contribute the maximum if he had the resources to do so will also be willing to contribute lesser amounts, that is, to contribute whatever he can. If a production function is linear, its standardized slope is 1, and the provision level equals the contribution level. If the standardized value v exceeds 1, each contribution will produce a profit. In the example we have been working with where $v = 1.333$, a contribution of $3,000 toward the linear production function yields a value of $4,000, for a profit of $1,000. Larger contributions will earn proportionately more, so a person will want to contribute as much as he can, but if he has only $3,000 to invest, he will still find it profitable to do so. Not so in the accelerative case. If our executive has only $3,000 available to invest and the production function is accelerative, he can only produce a gain of $200 and will lose $2,800. Only if the executive has more than $12,000 to invest can he make a profit.

General third-order production function. In the general case, the production function is first accelerating and then decelerating. The dynamics of the general case can be seen to be a simple composite of the two. In the initial accelerating portion of the curve, returns are low. Our executive will not spend anything on trying to get a grandfather clause unless he has enough resources to put him far enough over on the curve to produce a net profit. If he can get that far, he will contribute everything he can as long as the curve remains accelerative. If he has enough resources to reach into the decelerating portion of the curve, he will keep contributing until he reaches the optimum, where $P'(R) = 1/v$, and then he will stop. He will never pay for the maximum provision level, except in the extreme case where $P'(R) > 1/v$ for the full range of the production function.

A homogeneous group

Collective action is about groups of actors, of course, not large individuals purchasing private goods. Therefore, we next consider a slightly more complex case, a completely homogeneous group of 500 affected employees. Unlike our executive, no one of them has extensive financial resources. Each has only $150 available in ready cash. Although it is often possible to borrow money to make a profit, it is rarely possible for a financially strapped individual to borrow money to avoid a loss, so we assume that this budget constraint is real.

We might plausibly imagine either that our group of many individuals is just as interested as the one executive, but poorer, or that they also have a much lower interest in the collective good. Thus, we will analyze two cases, one where these 500 individuals each expect to experience the same unstandardized loss as the executive ($20,000), and the other where their v_i is substantially lower ($2,000). We will assume they are considering contributions to a strategy that costs $cM = \$15,000$ to achieve the maximum. Note that only 100 of the 500 group members need to contribute to achieve this maximum, so the group has the capacity to provide the collective good. Note also that the total value of the good to all 500 employees far exceeds its cost. If they each have a $20,000 interest, the total interest is $10 million. Even if they each have a modest $2,000 interest, the total interest is $1 million. Each group member's standardized available resource level is $t = \$150/\$15,000 = .01$. If the unstandardized value is $20,000, the standardized $v = \$20,000/\$15,000 = 1.3333$, and $1/v = .75$; if the unstandardized value is $2,000, $v = \$2,000/\$15,000 = .1333$, and $1/v = 7.5$.

The optimization problem is the same as stated previously. Instead of one individual deciding whether to make another unit of contribution, we have many individuals deciding sequentially whether to add another contribution to the total. In either case, the maximum profit (if any) occurs when $P'(r) > 1/v$. For small contributors deciding sequentially, the criterion of profitability is

$$g_i(r) = vP(r + R) - vP(R) - r, \qquad (3)$$

which implies that a profit will be made as long as $P(r + R) - P(R) > r/v$, that is, that the change in the provision level exceeds the ratio of the standardized contribution size to the standardized value v. This difference equation expresses the same relation as does the derivative. If our 500 employees each have a \$20,000 interest, they will each contribute their \$150 as long as the slope of the standardized production function $P'(r) > .75$. If their interest level is \$2,000, they will contribute as long as the slope $P'(r) > 7.5$, that is, where the change in P is 7.5 times the change in r.

In keeping with our sequential model, each group member is brought up to the decision point in turn and makes a decision based on what previously approached individuals have indicated they will do, but without coordinating his actions with others or attempting to influence others' actions with his own. Later in this chapter we will relax these assumptions.

Linear functions and other dichotomous situations. If the production function is linear and the group is homogeneous, either all 500 will be willing to contribute or none of them will. Recall that the standardized slope of a linear production function is always 1, so contributions are profitable if the standardized value exceeds 1. If all the employees stand to lose \$20,000, $v = 1.333$, everyone will be willing to contribute, and the collective action will occur at its maximum provision level. In fact, there will be 350 extra potential contributors. By contrast, if all the employees have an interest level of \$2,000, $v = .13333$, and no one will contribute, even though everyone would be better off if everyone paid their \$150. This is the classic generalized prisoner's dilemma that arises because each individual's own impact on the collective good is less than the cost of making her contribution. Acting independently, even though sequentially, each behaves as if she is being asked to pay \$150 to receive \$20 (.01 × \$2000) and, of course, refuses. It is obvious why communication so often leads to a cooperative solution in situations like these, but that is not the concern of this chapter.

The situation is effectively the same if the production function is not linear, but the range of its slopes is always greater than $1/v$ or always less than $1/v$. In the former case, every group member will be willing to contribute everything she can, and in the latter case, no one will be willing to contribute anything.

Decelerating functions. When the production function is decelerating, a homogeneous group of small contributors produces the same analytic result as does one large actor. Individuals should agree to contribute sequentially until a point is reached where $P'(R) = 1/v$, then no individual should agree to contribute to a contract that is larger.

Where a difference arises between the executive purchasing a private good and the homogeneous group of 500 workers is in the assumption one is willing to make about their interest levels. If each of the 500 workers has the same $20,000 interest in the collective good, their willingness to contribute is identical to that of the executive. Assuming the same production function, each is willing to contribute up to the point where $R = $6,000 ($R = .4$); if each has $150, this point is achieved by 40 contributors. In fact, if the 500 workers also had the same resources as the executive, all 500 of them would be willing to pay $6,000 toward the collective good (assuming it has jointness of supply so the maximum cost is constant); this is the point of Chapter 3. However, none of them will be willing to contribute anything after the optimum has been reached.

But if we suppose that the 500 workers have an interest of only $2,000, our model of independent decisions says that each one will be willing to contribute only when the slope of the standardized production function equals 7.5. Our workers would be willing to contribute up to $r = .1$, for example, if $P(.1) > 7.5$. This requires that the initial contributions have very large effects on the provision level.

Again, it is not the number of group members that affects the willingness to make independent contributions, it is the size of the members' interest. And again, the enormous collective profit to be made when the group is large, even if individual interests are small, suggests that there are strong incentives to cooperation and coordination of action. And again, we will not deal with these issues at this point.

When the production function is decelerating, people are not willing to contribute once the optimum is achieved, even if they would have been willing to make the initial contributions. If everyone cares equally about a picnic, we will probably find that once one person spends an hour arranging for a place and another spends two hours arranging for food, it is unlikely that anyone else will volunteer to spend comparable amounts of time on things that are less central to the success of the picnic. Once a core of citizens initiates an anticrime Neighborhood Watch program, it will be difficult to persuade others to do a large share. Once someone has called about a pothole in a middle-class neighborhood, no one else is likely to call. Once 40 employees have each contributed $150 for a total of $6,000 and have reached the point where the production function falls below $1/v$, no more individuals will contribute. Given our assumptions about independent sequential decisions, we would predict that if the production function is decelerative (and the costs and values do not put us in the extremes of the all-or-nothing situations), *some* collective action will occur, but provision of the good with certainty (the meaningful maximum that *could* occur) is quite unlikely.

Accelerative functions. The analytic equivalence between the homogeneous group and the single executive does not hold true for the accelerative case. In fact, quite opposite results hold, even when every individual has an interest greater than the total cost of the collective good, in this case even when all 500 group members have a $20,000 interest. This is because at the initial levels of contributions, $P'(R)$ is less than $1/v$, so no individual should contribute his $150. In our example, where $P(.2) = .005$, the slope is flat enough that the initial contributors (whose interest in the maximum provision level is $20,000) would realize about $5 worth of improvement in the collective good from their $150 contributions. Acting independently, no one would make such an unprofitable initial contribution. If no one makes the initial contributions, the point where $P'(R)$ is greater than $1/v$ will never be reached. If, somehow, contributions happen to be made so that R is at the point where $P'(R)$ equals $1/v$, each additional contributor would obtain a positive net payoff from his contribution. But under the assumption of a homogeneous group making small contributions, this will never happen. This is a generalization of the pattern we saw with the executive: The person with low resources is less likely to contribute than the person with high resources. If the accelerative production function impedes action for homogeneous groups with very high interests compared to their resources, it is even more unfavorable when the interests also are low.

If, somehow, the initial contributions get made, later contributions can become profitable, and collective action will tend to snowball, drawing in more and more people until the maximum is reached. It is accelerating production functions that tend to produce widespread mass action once something starts. In homogeneous groups, though, this should not happen. Instead, what we expect to see in most relatively homogeneous groups of not very resourceful individuals facing accelerating production functions is a lot of nothing going on. Residents of poor areas do not call about local problems, community centers do not get built, lawsuits are not brought, and protests are not organized.

General third-order curves. The general third-order curve had two solutions to equation (2): the first is the minimum net payoff, a net loss, reached at the end of the initial period of low returns; the second is the desired maximum payoff, which occurs at the end of the period of high returns. The key question in this situation therefore concerns the length of the initial, accelerating segment, relative to the resources of the group members. Most commonly, a homogeneous group facing a general third-order production function will exhibit the dynamics of the accelerative curve.

The dynamics of deceleration can occur only if the initial period of low returns can be surpassed. This can happen only if the individual resource level t is high enough, or the initial region of negative returns small enough, to make $g(t) > 0$, that is, to put the initial contributor into the profitable portion of the accelerative region of the production function. If this condition is met, a homogeneous group will exhibit the optimization pattern of the decelerating curve.

More commonly, the initial period of negative returns is longer than t, and no one individual can surpass it. In this more common case, homogeneous groups facing a third-order production function exhibit the dynamics of the accelerative case. That is, no contributions are made, and no collective action occurs. If, somehow, the start-up costs are taken care of and the initial contributions are made, contributors will be pulled in and collective action will proceed to the decelerating portion of the curve where optimization becomes an issue. But normally, the initial problems are not solved and nothing happens.

If we look at the universe of actual contributions to collective action, we find that the vast majority are made when start-up costs are low and the production function approximates the decelerating curve. By contrast, the vast majority of *opportunities* for collective action have significant start-up costs that give rise to the fundamental dynamic of the accelerating case – nothing happens. This fundamental contrast holds, but the dynamics become more complex when we add heterogeneous interests and resources to the analysis in the next section.

Results II: interactions among group heterogeneity, interdependence, and production functions

In this section we explore the interactions among the form of the production function, group heterogeneity, and strategic interdependence. In the process of developing our theory for this chapter, we analyzed the numerical results from a Monte Carlo simulation. These results permitted us to generate general theoretical conclusions that transcend the particular numerical results. The numerical cases provide concrete examples of the effects we found and, in a few instances, allow us to get a feel for the rough size of these effects.

The numerical examples and results presented in this chapter are based on the production functions sketched in Figure 4.2 and summarized in Table 4.1. (More details on the simulation are given in Section 4 of the appendix to this chapter.) We used ten production functions, five decelerating and five accelerating. These were paired, so that each accelerating function had the same series of slopes as one of the decelerating functions, but in reverse order. Since we are not interested in the minute peculiarities of particular functions, we made our numerical analysis more tractable by using spline fits of ten line segments each. Spline fits have "edges" where the slopes change discontinuously; this affects the particular results obtained, but we are aware of this, and never attach substantive importance to these point solutions. Smoother curves would show the same basic patterns, but would have more scattered results.

Detailed rationales for the terms in Table 4.1 are developed in the Appendix, but it will be helpful to give a nontechnical summary here. All of the production functions we used were standardized so that their average slope was 1. The maximum contribution level of one produced the same payoff in all cases. The steepest curves were in Pair 1, and the flattest in Pair 5. The decelerating production functions were everywhere above the linear production function with slope 1; they started with high marginal returns to contributions and then flattened out. The accelerating curves were everywhere below the line; they started with low marginal returns,

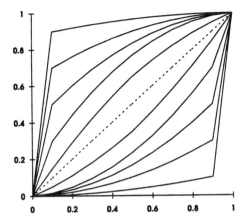

Figure 4.2. Plots of standardized production functions from Table 4.1. The diagonal is the linear production function. Decelerating curves are above the diagonal, accelerating curves below the diagonal. The steepest curves 1 are outside, the flattest curves 5 are inside, and the others are in order between these.

which became progressively steeper. The "critical v^*" is the interest level that must be exceeded if a person is to find it profitable to contribute at that particular point in the production function. As the Appendix explains, this v^* is the reciprocal of the slope at that point. Where the production function is steeper, contributions have a bigger impact and lower interest levels are necessary.

Decelerating production functions

Our discussion so far allows us to say two important things about de-celerative production functions. First, compared with accelerative func-tions, the prospects for *initiating* collective action are quite favorable, since comparatively low levels of individual interest in the collective good are all that is required to motivate initial contributions. This comparison is developed technically in Section 1.3 of the appendix to this chapter and can be seen by inspecting the v^*'s in Table 4.1. Another way of saying this is that a person with a given level of interest in the collective good will obtain a much higher profit from an initial contribution to a decelerating production function than to an accelerating production function. Second,

Table 4.1. *Spline fits for decelerating and accelerating curves*

	Standardized contribution levels									
	0.1	0.2	0.3	0.4	0.5	0.6	0.7	0.8	0.9	1
Curve 1										
Decelerating										
Change in P	0.9000	0.0200	0.0178	0.0156	0.0133	0.0111	0.0089	0.0067	0.0044	0.0022
Slope	9.0000	0.2000	0.1780	0.1560	0.1330	0.1110	0.0890	0.0670	0.0440	0.0220
Critical v^*	0.1111	5.0000	5.5180	5.4103	7.5188	9.0090	11.2360	14.9254	22.7273	45.4545
Accelerating										
Change in P	0.0022	0.0044	0.0067	0.0089	0.0111	0.0133	0.0156	0.0178	0.0200	0.9000
Slope	0.0220	0.0440	0.0670	0.0890	0.1110	0.1330	0.1560	0.1780	0.2000	9.0000
Critical v^*	45.4545	22.7273	14.9254	11.2360	9.0090	7.5188	6.4103	5.6180	5.0000	0.1111
Curve 2										
Decelerating										
Change in P	0.7000	0.0600	0.0533	0.0467	0.0400	0.0333	0.0267	0.0200	0.0133	0.0067
Slope	7.0000	0.6000	0.5330	0.4670	0.4000	0.3330	0.2670	0.2000	0.1330	0.0670
Critical v^*	0.1429	1.6667	1.8762	2.1413	2.5000	3.0030	3.7453	5.0000	7.5188	14.9254
Accelerating										
Change in P	0.0067	0.0133	0.0200	0.0267	0.0333	0.0400	0.0467	0.0533	0.0600	0.7000
Slope	0.0670	0.1330	0.2000	0.2670	0.3330	0.4000	0.4670	0.5330	0.6000	7.0000
Critical v^*	14.9254	7.5188	5.0000	3.7453	3.0030	2.5000	2.1413	1.8762	1.6667	0.1429

Curve 3

Decelerating										
Change in P	0.5000	0.1000	0.0889	0.0778	0.0667	0.0556	0.0444	0.0333	0.0222	0.0111
Slope	5.0000	1.0000	0.8890	0.7780	0.6670	0.5560	0.4440	0.3330	0.2220	0.1110
Critical v^*	0.2000	1.0000	1.1249	1.2853	1.4993	1.7986	2.2523	3.0030	4.5045	9.0090
Accelerating										
Change in P	0.0111	0.0222	0.0333	0.0444	0.0556	0.0667	0.0778	0.0889	0.1000	0.5000
Slope	0.1110	0.2220	0.3330	0.4440	0.5560	0.6670	0.7780	0.8890	1.0000	5.0000
Critical v^*	9.0090	4.5045	3.0030	2.2523	1.7986	1.4993	1.2853	1.1249	1.0000	0.2000

Curve 4

Decelerating										
Change in P	0.3000	0.1400	0.1244	0.1089	0.0933	0.0778	0.0622	0.0467	0.0311	0.0156
Slope	3.0000	1.4000	1.2440	1.0890	0.9330	0.7780	0.6220	0.4670	0.3110	0.1560
Critical v^*	0.3333	0.7143	0.8039	0.9183	1.0718	1.2853	1.6077	2.1413	3.2154	6.4103
Accelerating										
Change in P	0.0156	0.0311	0.0467	0.0622	0.0778	0.0933	0.1089	0.1244	0.1400	0.3000
Slope	0.1560	0.3110	0.4670	0.6220	0.7780	0.9330	1.0890	1.2440	1.4000	3.0000
Critical v^*	6.4103	3.2154	2.1413	1.6077	1.2853	1.0718	0.9183	0.8039	0.7143	0.3333

Curve 5

Decelerating										
Change in P	0.1500	0.1400	0.1300	0.1200	0.1100	0.0900	0.0800	0.0700	0.0600	0.0500
Slope	1.5000	1.4000	1.3000	1.2000	1.1000	0.9000	0.8000	0.7000	0.6000	0.5000
Critical v^*	0.6667	0.7143	0.7692	0.8333	0.9091	1.1111	1.2500	1.4286	1.6667	2.0000
Accelerating										
Change in P	0.0500	0.0600	0.0700	0.0800	0.0900	0.1100	0.1200	0.1300	0.1400	0.1500
Slope	0.5000	0.6000	0.7000	0.8000	0.9000	1.1000	1.2000	1.3000	1.4000	1.5000
Critical v^*	2.0000	1.6667	1.4286	1.2500	1.1111	0.9091	0.8333	0.7692	0.7143	0.6667

the general dynamic of collective action is negative interdependence, since each contribution to a decelerating production function reduces the marginal return of subsequent contributions. This creates the dynamics of optimization and also introduces the possibility of strategic gaming, which we will consider later.

In this section we go beyond our initial discussion and show that decelerative collective goods also exhibit either of two less obvious phenomena: either there will be an "order effect" in which maximum contributions to the good are obtained when the *least* interested group members contribute first, or there will be a surplus of contributors for some region of the curve. Either situation opens the door to problems of strategic gaming that may disrupt the otherwise favorable environment that decelerating production functions create for collective action. To demonstrate these results, we must develop some new ways of talking about production functions.

Willing subsets. The dynamics of decelerative collective goods arise from the fact that individuals' payoffs are higher from initial contributions than from later ones, so more individuals are willing to contribute initially than later. As described in more detail in Section 2.1 of the Appendix, we may speak formally about this fact by defining the *willing subset* for a region of the production function as the set of individuals whose interest in the collective good is high enough relative to the slope of the production function that they are willing to contribute in that region. It should be obvious that, for a decelerating production function, the largest willing subset occurs initially, when no contributions have yet been made ($R = 0$), and that willing subsets get smaller as more and more resources are contributed (R gets larger).[1]

Order effects. In Section 2.2 of the Appendix we describe technically a way of considering both interests and resources to define what we term the *likely subset* for a region, with each individual assigned to the one region in which he should contribute. The likely total group contribution is the maximum contribution level for which there is a non-null likely subset. Because progressively higher interest levels are required for in-

---

[1] The extreme cases in which no group member is willing to contribute anywhere on the curve or in which all group members are willing to contribute everywhere on the curve will not be considered in this analysis, as they are not subject to the processes described in this section.

dividuals to be willing to contribute once others have, total contributions by the group are maximized if people contribute in order, from least to most interested.[2] That is, individuals whose interest level is such that they will contribute initially but not later are assumed to make the initial contributions, while those with higher interest are "saved" for the later regions where a higher interest is required to be part of the willing subset.

There is obviously a problem here. Although total contributions toward a decelerative good are maximized if the more interested contribute after the less interested, it is unlikely that this would actually happen. We would generally expect the *opposite,* that the most interested would contribute first, followed by the next most interested, and so forth. Sometimes contributions might be in random order with respect to interest. But we certainly would never expect people with the least to gain to be the first to contribute.

This implies that interest groups facing a decelerating production function would *not* generally be expected to make contributions in an order that would maximize their aggregate contribution. When the amount of resources available is roughly equal to the amount required, the order of contributions can have a big effect. In our simulations, having individuals make contributions in the order from most interested to least interested reduces the aggregate contribution of the group by as much as 20% to 30% from the optimal least-to-most order. Random orders fall between these extremes.

Consider our employees who stand to lose various amounts of money from the requirement that they live in the city. Suppose they are pursuing a collective strategy with a decelerating production function. Lobbying might have this character, with the initial contributions having the biggest effects, as city council members first confront the employees' feelings of inequity, while later contributions will have progressively smaller effects. Or, perhaps, the employees hire a lawyer, where the simple act of paying a retaining fee and indicating seriousness of purpose has the largest impact,

---

[2] In contrast to the decelerating case, we may quickly dismiss the order of contributions as a factor for accelerating production functions. If a less interested person contributes on an earlier, flatter part of the curve before a more interested person, the more interested person will be even happier to contribute on a subsequent portion of the curve because it is steeper. The only exception is the unrealistic special case in which each person has exactly one chance to decide whether to contribute. In this case, it is desirable to have the most interested persons decide first so that the chances of the less interested person encountering a steep enough portion of the curve to be willing to contribute are maximized.

and additional dollars paid into the legal fund, while having positive effect, have progressively smaller effects. If those with the smallest interests contribute first, those with the larger interests will still be willing to contribute later, and their chances of obtaining a grandfather clause or otherwise achieving relief will be maximized. The question is whether this would ever be a plausible scenario.

We can give some other everyday examples of order effects. Consider a university computer center supported by research grants. All researchers need basic software such as word processing and a major statistical package, while only those with more intensive computer needs would be willing to contribute to more exotic items such as SIMSCRIPT. It would therefore be most rational for the least interested members to buy the basics, freeing resources for the more interested to purchase the other items, which might even prove useful to the less interested, if someone else paid for them. In reality, though, the heavy computer users are likely to make the first purchases of common software items, and the researchers with less interest in the computer are likely to spend their grant money on something else, such as secretarial services, rather than contribute to additional software.

Local voluntary action often exhibits these same dynamics. Many people want the neighborhood association, the Girl Scout troop, or the computer user's group to exist, but few care about planting flowers in the median strip, teaching the girls astronomy, or communicating with a national computer network. The people who would be interested enough to do the additional jobs usually are the same people who took on the basic tasks of calling meetings, taking minutes, and keeping books; they have used up the time and effort they can devote to these groups. Because the others are not interested enough to do anything except basic maintenance for the organization, nothing else gets done.

In short, unless the most interested people can engage in some kind of strategic gaming, restrain their enthusiasm, and withhold their contributions until the less interested make theirs, contributions under decelerating production functions can be expected to be suboptimal. Such strategic interaction is often difficult, since one's greater interest in the collective good is usually obvious. One response to this problem can be seen in fundraising, when a highly interested donor promises to match smaller contributions, thus "forcing" the less interested to contribute "first."

The order effect is a supplementary explanation for the "exploitation of the great by the small" described by Olson (1965, p. 29). The less

interested members free-ride on the initial contributions of the most interested, and total group contributions are suboptimal. The significance of
our analysis is to show that this phenomenon is most acute when the
production function is decelerating and there is not a great surplus of
potential contributions.

Surplus. Decelerating production functions may produce surpluses instead
of order effects. (See Section 2.3 of the Appendix for a technical definition
of *surplus.*) Surplus arises when there are more people willing and able
to make contributions than are needed to provide a given level of the
collective good. There may be a surplus for the maximum provision level,
which means simply that there is a surfeit of resources. But there may also
be a surplus for some lower provision level, with the seemingly paradoxical
result that there are too many people willing to contribute initially, but
none of these are willing to contribute later. Surplus arises at lower provision levels when the difference in slopes across regions of the production
function is large enough to wash out variation in group members' interest
levels, so that all group members are willing to contribute when the slope
is steep, but none are willing to contribute when it is flatter.

We can develop an example of surplus using the steeply decelerating
Curve 1 in Table 4.1. To make the computations easy, let's assume that
$10,000 paid to a lobbyist would certainly ensure passage of the grandfather
clause to protect our suburban-dwelling employees. This is the cost of the
maximum provision level M. According to Curve 1, a total contribution
of $1,000 (standardized $r = .1$) would make the probability of the amend-
ment being passed .9, whereas paying an additional $1,000 would raise
the probability only .02 more, to .92. Recall that the willing subset com-
prises those group members whose interest level is high enough to make
them willing to contribute at a particular point on the production function.
The interest level necessary to be in the willing subset for the first region
is $1,111, whereas an interest level of $50,000 is necessary for the second
region.

Suppose interest (potential loss averted) in having the amendment passed
is normally distributed, with a mean of $2,000 and a standard deviation
of $2,700. Then, about 315 of the 500 affected employees would be
expected to have an interest level greater than $1,111, but no one would
have an interest level greater than $50,000. If the average affected em-
ployee has $200 in resources, the expected pool of potential contributions

from these 315 people for the first $1,000 is $63,000 ($200 × 315), yielding a surplus of $62,000. But none of this is available for subsequent contributions. Even if each of these employees has only $10 that she could contribute, there is a potential of $3,150 that might be tapped by the fund, and a surplus of $2,150.

Obviously, very steep production functions tend to yield very large surpluses. Under the assumptions we have been using to this point, homogeneous groups facing a steep decelerating production function always generate a surplus, for they have enough resources to provide the good with certainty, but are willing to contribute only up to some intermediate level.

Examples of surplus potential contributions to a collective good abound, especially since the phenomenon applies also to the decelerating segments of general third-order production functions. Upper-middle-class neighborhoods usually respond quickly and effectively to proposed threats to or lapses in municipal services. Even though many residents free-ride, the few who do not have sufficient interest and resources to protect the entire neighborhood. Surpluses are often associated with collective goods that are inexpensive relative to their worth, such as office coffeepots, shoveling snow off a privately maintained street, or telephone calls about problems such as potholes.

It is important to stress that the problem of surplus is different from the general dilemma of collective action, although economists often intertwine their discussions of the two. The general dilemma (as formulated by Olson) arises when the payoff to an individual from a contribution to a collective good is lower than the cost of the contribution, even though every individual would be better off making the contribution and having the good than making no contribution and lacking it. In these circumstances, predictions about others' behavior are irrelevant, for contributions are irrational no matter what other people do. In contrast, surplus arises when many individuals find that their own individual payoffs from a contribution *do* exceed the cost of those contributions, and the production function is such that there is no positive payoff from contributions after a certain provision level is achieved.

It is only under conditions of surplus that individuals may rationally consider the possibility that the good will be provided by others. When there is a surplus, an individual who is convinced that everyone else will refuse to contribute should rationally make a contribution, for his own individual benefit from this action will exceed its cost, and he should be unconcerned that others will also benefit. Oliver (1984) reports that active members of neighborhood organizations are *less* likely than token members to believe that their neighbors would engage in collective action in response to a neighborhood problem. Individuals in this situation have a strategic interest in persuading others that they will refuse to contribute.

Idiosyncratic factors or random events may decide who contributes when there is a surplus. Our simple sequential model implies that the first ones who happen to be faced with the decision are "stuck." They will contribute because they find it profitable to do so while those whose turn to decide comes later will free-ride. Although this is extreme, it is probably not far from the reality of many situations.

Surplus creates the conditions for strategic gaming, since individuals might reasonably expect to be provided the optimum level of the good through the efforts of others. There is the ironic possibility that the very surfeit of resources could stymie collective action. One's empirical predictions in this situation depend on the assumptions one brings to bear. Economists generally predict that no one will contribute anything because there is no equilibrium solution; that is, everyone can hope to get the good without paying for it. Social psychologists aware of the diffusion of responsibility literature (Latane and Nida 1981; Piliavin et al. 1981, pp. 120–32) may generalize from small-group experiments and predict that the higher the surplus, the lower the provision level.

Our own predictions are less pessimistic. The question is whether surplus lowers individual probabilities of contributing so much so as to counter the positive effect of having so many more contributors. We think not. The fact that there is a huge aggregate profit to be made opens the door for some sort of resolution. If the value of the good is high enough, relative to the cost of an individual's contribution, the individual may not be deeply concerned about the risk of making a redundant contribution. This is why many people call when the lights go out or a pothole develops. Obviously, the most interested group members are most likely to decide that it is worth it to pay for the good alone, and it is likely that the others expect them to. This will resolve the question of who will pay the cost, again through the "exploitation of the great by the small." Surplus may also create a potential profit for political entrepreneurs (Frohlich, Oppenheimer, and Young 1971), who provide the good for a price, although they must have some sort of incentive available (Oliver 1980) as part of the enterprise.

Heterogeneity of resources. The total contribution from a group is determined by the amount of resources controlled by those interested enough to contribute. Our discussion so far has focused on interest heterogeneity while treating resources as homogeneous. This is reasonable because, in most decelerative situations, the total or mean level of available resources matters much more than their dispersion. Our simulations indicate that heterogeneity of resources around a given mean does not alter the average total contribution. However, if resource levels are randomly distributed with respect to interest levels, resource heterogeneity can increase the variance of the total contribution (depending on sequencing, i.e., the order of contributions) by as much as 100%. That is, if both interests and resources vary randomly across a population, the average total contribution stays the same, but there is a greater between-group variation around this average total that increases with the dispersion of resources. Random heterogeneity increases the uncertainty of outcomes, but not their central tendency.

The situation is different if interests and resources are not only heterogeneous, but positively correlated with each other. This positive correlation may raise the expected (mean) contribution level dramatically: in our simulations, a perfect correlation produced total contributions two to three times larger than those produced under the same conditions with a homogeneous resource distribution. If the most interested group members also have the greatest resource levels, contributions to the collective good are likely to be very high, much higher than one would predict from knowing only the group averages on these factors.

Accelerating production functions

Accelerating production functions yield entirely different dynamics in heterogeneous groups than do decelerating functions. Mathematically, this is because their increasing marginal returns make optimization and instantaneous slopes inappropriate analytic tools. Instead, we have to compare average rates of change, that is, the relation between a contribution of a given size and the total difference it makes in the probability of obtaining the collective good. The concepts we have developed for decelerating curves can be defined for accelerating curves, but they are not very useful for understanding them. Similarly, the ideas we develop in this section may be defined for decelerating curves but are of little value in understanding their dynamics.

We have previously noted the two key features of accelerating production functions. On the negative side, *feasibility* is a central problem because collective action must start at the flattest part of the curve. On the positive side, each contribution moves subsequent decisions to a more favorable part of the curve. Thus, if somehow contributions begin, collective action tends to snowball, involving more and more contributors until the maximum provision level is reached. We believe that accelerating production functions underlie the mass actions popularly associated with the term "collective action," such as political demonstrations or revolutions. They are rare events relative to the grievances that might give rise to them, but they tend to accelerate once they start.

In the absence of contracts or considerations of indirect production, the resolution of the accelerative collective dilemma is highly problematic, depending on the rare circumstance of there being a critical mass of persons whose combination of interests and resources is high enough to overcome the feasibility problem. Groups fortunate enough to have a critical mass can enjoy the collective good; less fortunate groups cannot. Resource and interest heterogeneity are essential to the resolution of accelerative collective dilemmas, for a homogeneous group cannot contain a critical mass. A positive correlation between interest and resources obviously improves the chances of there being a critical mass. The more usual situation of zero or even negative correlation obviously makes the existence of a critical mass much less likely.

In contrast to the decelerating case, resource heterogeneity as well as interest heterogeneity may have significant effects on the prospect for a critical mass when the production function is accelerating. As may be recalled from our earlier discussion, an individual with a given standardized interest v in an accelerative good finds that, after the minimum point where $P'(R) = 1/v$ is passed, his net payoff increases with each unit contributed until the good is provided with certainty. Thus, *individuals whose potential contributions are larger, that is, who have more resources, are more likely to find it profitable to contribute.* This is shown more formally in Section 3.1 of the Appendix. This result has surprising consequences. It leads to the prediction that if two people have the same interest in an accelerative collective good, but one is much richer in resources than the other, the richer person is more likely to find contributing rational. This is not because his opportunity costs are lower (we assume this is not true), but because his larger possible contribution can buy a greater proportionate return. In fact, our computer simulations reveal that often a rich individual with a much *lower* interest will find contribution rational while a poor person with a higher interest will not. Interested wealthy benefactors who provide the good single-handedly represent one resolution to accelerative collective dilemmas. This has been known to happen, but such a resolution is not of great theoretical interest, and its practical importance is limited.

However, a related characteristic of accelerating functions is more interesting and important: as we show formally in Section 3.2 of the Appendix, initial contributions lower the necessary interest for subsequent contributions. A pool of highly interested and resourceful individuals willing to contribute in the initial region of low returns may therefore become a "critical mass" creating the conditions for more widespread contributions. If even one such person exists, she may begin a process in which continuously increasing numbers of group members find that the contributions of others have changed the situation to one in which they, too, wish to contribute. The bandwagon may roll, started by a single person. For the process to start, however, this initiator must have an extraordinarily high interest in the collective good, perhaps several hundred times greater than that necessary to initiate action for a decelerative good (see Table 4.1).

Anticipating indirect production. The prospects for starting collective action for accelerative goods are bleak, but not quite as bleak as our discussion so far implies. If actors have full information about the form of the production function and about everyone else's interests and resources, they know what we know – that they can affect others' contributions by making a contribution of their own – and adjust their own payoff calculations accordingly. We may think of this as "indirect production" of the collective good, in contrast to the "direct production" we have been considering so far. For example, Jones may stand to lose $3,000 if the amendment is not passed and has $1,000 he could invest in the fight. If the production function is like Curve 4 in Table 4.1, the $1,000 "buys" a .0156 probability increase for an expected payoff of $47, yielding a net loss of $953. But suppose Jones knows that if he contributes $1,000 toward the legal fund, he will set in motion a chain of events resulting in others contributing the additional $9,000 necessary to guarantee passage of the bill. If Jones considers this "indirect" production, he calculates a $2,000 profit from his $1,000 investment. This process is similar to the macroeconomic concept of anticipating the multiplier effect of specific investments.

A complete accounting of indirect production can have many complicated steps, since part of the individual's calculation may be that the next person in line will also calculate the indirect effects of a contribution, and so on. These projections need not require any probabilistic inference about others' decisions; they are determinate calculations based on knowledge of the interests and resources of each individual in the group. Even under these conditions, the calculations can be so complex that we cannot model them, and even our ideal rational actors probably would not really compute them.

Indirect production may resolve the collective dilemma when circumstances permit simplifying assumptions that eliminate the problem of computational complexity. Because each contribution makes subsequent ones more profitable, it is reasonable for individuals to believe that "starting the ball rolling" with a good example will produce widespread enough participation to justify the investment, even though they cannot predict the exact chain of events. This is, of course, exactly what happens in all sorts of real-life circumstances. Mass fund-raising drives begin with a core of organizers who assume that if they coordinate the candy sale or door-to-door solicitation, many people will contribute small amounts of money. Campaigns for political office have this character when the candidate starts as an unknown and gradually adds supporters to the bandwagon.

What we term *indirect production* is a common occurrence, but it is not universal, as many budding activists have learned the hard way. It is a structurally rational way to provide collective goods only if the production function is accelerating so initial contributions increase the value of subsequent contributions. Under deceleration, initial contributions move subsequent decisions to *less* productive portions of the curve where the slope is smaller and contributions require higher interest levels. Agreeing to be president of the neighborhood association, for example, rarely starts anything rolling because most residents are sufficiently satisfied if it simply exists. Many voluntary associations have third-order production functions with start-up costs that can be borne by one person. Once someone agrees to be president or chair or leader, the rest of the curve is decelerating; a few more may agree to be secretary and treasurer or coleaders, but the optimum is rapidly reached, and the initial joiners are certainly not followed by a bandwagon full of active members.

Contracts or conventions. Individuals rarely have the kind of full information required to calculate the indirect production from a contribution. However, the same effects can be obtained from explicit or implicit all-or-none contracts. Consider a very simple contract: a group of affected employees agree that they will all contribute specified amounts to the lobbying fund, and that if anyone fails to contribute by a specified deadline the fund will be dissolved and all the contributors will get their money back. This all-or-none agreement provides the same calculation of return as the more complex process of anticipating indirect production. Jones will receive not only the increase in probability directly produced by his own contribution, but also the increase produced indirectly through the contributions of the other parties to the contract. Since the others will not contribute unless an agreement is reached and everyone contributes, we may base each employee's calculation of payoff on the total change in probability produced by the contracted contributions. One way to think of this is that failing to live up to the contract will make the payoff zero instead of what it would have been under the contract. This is formalized in Section 3.3 of the Appendix. An event such as a wildcat strike often involves an implicit all-or-none contract, since individuals can turn around and go back to work if too few others are walking out with them.

When contracts may be reached, we need a different equation for the individual's contribution decision. We will let $gC_i(r)$ stand for the gain to the individual of contributing r to the contract and R be the total contributions from the contract. Then we may write

$$gC_i(r) = vP(R) - r. \tag{4}$$

Contributing to the contract will be profitable whenever $gC_i(r) > 0$, that is, whenever $vP(R) > r$. This may also be expressed as $P(R) > r/v$, which means that the total provision level from the contract must exceed the ratio of the individual's share of the cost to the value he would experience from the maximum provision level.

Obviously, this is a much more favorable ratio than we have encountered before. Continuing the example from the section on indirect production, Jones would need an interest level of $64,103 to be willing to invest his

$1,000 without a contract. But if there are $10,000 in resources committed to the contract, any interest level greater than $1,000 will make Jones's investment in the contract rational. If only $8,000 were committed, which would raise the probability of the collective good by .56, Jones would need an interest of $1,786 to be willing to participate.

All-or-none rules are clearly one solution to an accelerative collective dilemma for a group whose members have only moderate interests or resources. Substantively, these rules might take the form of revokable contributions, the invocation of third parties to enforce contracts, or simply very high levels of trust among the group members. Hardin (1982, pp. 155–230) stresses the importance of what he calls "conventions," norms or agreements that everyone will act in the same way because it is in everyone's benefit to do so. These are the informal or implicit equivalent of all-or-none contracts. Although conventions or contracts are useful resolutions to any collective dilemma, they are especially crucial when an accelerating production function makes any other resolution almost impossible. They should be less important in decelerative situations where the basic problem is declining returns to later contributions. This analysis raises issues that are related to those discussed by Marxist scholars of collective action such as Offe and Weisenthal (1980), who stress that workers face acute collective dilemmas in the conflict between individual and collective rationality and require ideological solidarity (conventions) and union organization (contracts) to overcome these dilemmas.

Since many real-life production functions involve the high start-up costs that characterize accelerating curves, we suspect Hardin is right to stress the importance of conventions in collective action. To the extent that this is true, an understanding of collective action in the face of accelerative collective dilemmas requires attention to the problems and costs of organizing and enforcing contracts, or to the cultural forces that shape cooperative norms.

Summary and conclusions

In general, the problem of collective action is one of getting some relatively small subset of a group interested in the provision of a public good to make contributions of time, money, or other resources toward the production of that good. This subset is the critical mass needed to begin any collective action. Whether it emerges and what role it plays if it does depend on a variety of factors. In this chapter we have attended to one fundamental condition – the shape of the production function – and to the way that production function interacts with the distribution of interest and resources across the group of potential contributors.

Our analysis has stressed the contrast between production functions dominated by increasing or decreasing marginal returns, including third-order S-shaped curves that approximate one or the other extreme. But the contrast is also relevant to the more general S-shaped production function considered over time. In such cases, collective action begins with the feasibility problem of the initial, flat periods of the production function, when it is ruled by the dynamics of acceleration. Most potential collective actions never get off the ground because of this problem, but if any action is forthcoming, it is the most interested group members who will contribute. By the time the group has gathered sufficient contributions to be on the steep portion of the curve, it is mostly the less interested who remain. During this period of high returns, these less interested actors jump on the bandwagon. However, once the later, flatter portion of the curve is reached, it is ruled by the dynamics of deceleration, and the less interested cease contributing. Because the more interested individuals have already contributed on the first part of the curve, the collective action will tend to "top out" at some level well below the maximum.

There is always a collective dilemma, but it is not always the same dilemma. Although many authors *define* all public goods as entailing the free-rider problem, free riding as such is not the crucial dynamic for the accelerating regions of production functions. When the production function is accelerating, others' contributions *increase* one's willingness to contribute and reduce the propensity to free-ride. The accelerative collective dilemma is one of *feasibility,* the problem of inadequate interests and inadequate resources to overcome start-up costs. The usual outcome of the accelerative collective dilemma is that nobody rides free because nobody contributes and there is no ride. However, an "irrational" contributor may well find that, rather than being a "patsy," she is a role model or organizer whose action sets off others' actions and, in the end, vindicates the original contribution.

It is in accelerative cases that the critical mass is likely to fill the role associated with the nuclear metaphor. A small core of interested and resourceful people can begin contributions toward an action that will tend to "explode," to involve more and more of the other, less interested or less resourceful members of the population and to carry the event toward its maximum potential.

Clearly, contractual solutions to the collective dilemma are most important in accelerating cases. Often the resolution of this dilemma depends on the possibilities for organizing, communicating, and coordinating an all-or-none contract. Organization and communication costs then become central issues. It is in this case that the idealistic organizer who sees her role as "bringing people together" and "showing people their true interests" is most likely to fulfill her goal of fostering mass action. In Chapters 5 and 6, we develop a more explicit theory for organizers and their choices.

If, by some mechanism, the group manages to get to the decelerating part of the general third-order curve, or if the initial region of low returns is small (relative to group members' resources), a different set of issues appear to determine the dynamics of collective action. In the decelerating case, the critical mass is likely to be a relatively small subset of a larger pool of interested group members who provide some of the good for the benefit of all. If we may expand Olson's metaphor, free riding is likely in the decelerative case, but the ride is short. That is, there will likely be a ride, and some will ride free (not have to contribute), but the ride will be cut short at the optimum, and no one will pay to finish the trip. It is hard to imagine any resolution, social or otherwise, that would lead to maximum contributions in the decelerative case, although when interests are small relative to costs, social resolutions may be necessary for obtaining the optimum.

We may speculate about which group members are likely to pay for the ride when there is a surplus of available resources. Again, it seems most plausible that those with the highest interest in the collective good would pay, and that they would be faster to act than those with lower interests. It is also likely that other actors would assume that the most interested persons would pay. Thus, considerations of inherent motivation to act and of projections of others' behavior converge on the prediction that the most interested will be most likely to provide the good, even though others might also be willing to do so. For this reason, decelerating production functions seem especially likely to lead to the "exploitation of the great by the small" that Olson describes.

Interestingly, our analysis of order effects indicates that, if there is not a surplus, having the most interested contribute first can lead to a suboptimal outcome. Our analysis is very different from Olson's, but it leads to the same conclusion, that exploitation of the great by the small tends to produce suboptimal results. However, we go beyond Olson and argue that suboptimality occurs when the production function is decelerating and there is no surplus.

If there is a surplus, lots of people may ride free, but it is not entirely clear who will pay for the ride. It seems most likely that the most interested will pay, even though less interested people would also be willing to pay. In this context, of course, people are motivated to appear less interested than they really are, and strategic gaming and misleading statements about one's interests may result. Economists have long been fascinated by the potential complexities that such gaming can introduce, although strategic behavior does not seem to us to be very common in collective action in the social or political sphere. A common resolution to surplus that we have observed is normative reciprocity. People expect that particular actions will have a few contributors and many free riders, but that the contributors should rotate across actions. In neighborhood organizations, it is common for people to feel that they should "take a turn" at serving on the board. Academicians often feel obliged to take a turn as department chair. In sum, an understanding of the differences among production functions, particularly when groups are heterogeneous, is the first step toward recognizing the processes underlying the ebb and flow of interdependent collective actions and toward identifying important differences among them.

Appendix

This appendix provides a more formal treatment of several topics.

1. Basic concepts

1.1. Metric. As described in the text, we choose a metric so that the standardized cost–value ratio is $1/v$. Obviously, the more an individual values the collective good, the *smaller* $1/v$ will be.

1.2. Relating slope and value. We may tie regions of the production function to individuals with particular levels of interest in the collective good. For each point or region of the production function with a unique slope, there is a level of value for the collective good that we will denote v^* such that $P'(R) = 1/v^*$. Among a group of individuals, those whose standardized values v for the collective good are greater than v^* will find it profitable to contribute at point R on the production function, while those whose values v are less than v^* will not find it profitable to contribute at this point. Thus, we may identify which members of a group would be willing to contribute at each point on a production function. Given a portion of the curve, we can identify the group members who would be willing to contribute, or given a set of individuals we may identify the portions of the curve that would attract their contributions. We use this relation extensively in subsequent developments.

1.3. Favorability. To see the relation among linear, decelerating and accelerating production functions, we compare standardized production functions. All have the same lower limit (0, 0) and the same upper limit (1, 1). There is only one standardized linear production function; its slope is 1. The average slope (i.e., the average rate of change) of all standardized production functions must also be 1; some regions will have a slope less than 1, and others will have a slope greater than 1. The slopes of a uniformly decelerating production function continuously decline, so its initial slope must be greater than 1, and its final slope must be less than 1. Conversely, the initial slope of a uniformly accelerating production function must be less than 1, and its final slope greater than 1. An S-shaped production function must have slopes less than 1, greater than 1, and less than 1 in that order. As the differences among the slopes in a nonlinear production function become small and approach zero, all production functions approach the linear production function as a limit, as the differences among their slopes approach zero.

Since $v^* = 1/P'(R)$, the v^* for the initial segments of uniformly decelerating production functions must be less than 1, whereas, for accelerating production functions, v^* for the initial segments must be greater than 1. This means that it is always "harder," in the sense of requiring a higher standardized interest level v, to start collective action in an accelerative case than in a decelerative case. The steeper the curves, the greater the disparity. "Destandardizing" this result, we may say that whenever production functions have the same cost of the maximum provision level cM, so that they can be compared, it is always "easier" to start an action with a decelerating production function than with an accelerating production function, in the sense that a lower value for the collective good is required for the decelerating production function.

2. Decelerating production functions

2.1. Willing subsets.

The analysis of the decelerative case hinges on optimization and the relation between the slope $P'(R)$ and its associated $v^*(R)$. As already indicated, for each point on the production function there is a $v^*(R)$, the level of interest in the collective good an individual must have to be willing to contribute at that point. At each point R, we may sort the members of a heterogeneous interest group into two nonoverlapping subsets: (1) the *willing* $W(R)$, those who would be willing to contribute at that point on the production function, that is, those group members for whom v is greater than $v^*(R)$; and (2) the *unwilling subset,* $U(R)$, those group members who would not be willing to contribute, that is, for whom v is less than or equal to $v^*(R)$. In the decelerating case, the smallest v^* for a particular production function must be $v^*(0)$; furthermore, for any $i < j$, $v^*(i) < v^*(j)$, and therefore, $W(j)$ is a subset of $W(i)$.

Obviously, if the largest v in the population is less than $v^*(0)$, no one will contribute anything, and the willing subset is null for the entire curve. Similarly, if the smallest v in the population is greater than the maximum $v^*(1)$, all group members are willing to contribute across the whole production function, and the willing subset is the total population for all segments of the curve. The rest of the discussion will assume that neither of these extremes holds.

In general, regions of the production function may be described according to the size of the willing subset associated with them. It should be obvious that $W(0)$ is the largest willing subset, and that willing subsets get smaller as R gets larger.

2.2. Allocating resources.

The problem is to determine how many resource units might be contributed by an interest group. We know that, for each region of the curve, there is a willing subset of actors, but we need a way of determining whether they have sufficient resources to do what they are willing to do. The procedure for making this assessment needs to be general enough to allow for unusual shapes of production functions or distributions of interest. We may divide the production function into J regions, each with a different willing subset. Within each region, the same individuals are willing to contribute. Obviously, the number of regions (J) depends on the variability of the slope of the production function (and, therefore, $v*$) as compared with the variability of v in the interest group, but the logic of the analysis is the same whether J is 2 or 2,000. We index the regions by j, which runs from 1 to J, letting R(j) denote the contribution level dividing region j from region j + 1, and B(j) stand for the region of the curve between R(j − 1) and R(j). Each of these B(j) has a willing subset that we now denote by W(j), where W(j) = W[R(j)]. Of course, for m < n, W(n) is a subset of W(m). We then define nonoverlapping sets of individuals L(j) = W(j) − W(j − 1) so that each individual is assigned to the rightmost region to which he is willing to contribute.

Now we are ready to take account of available resources. Let A(j) be the amount of resources available for B(j), where A(j) is the sum of resources across individuals who are members of L(j). We need to compare these available resources to needed resources. Let D(j) = R(j) − R(j − 1); this is the amount of resources used in this region of the production function. If, for every region A(j) is greater than or equal to D(j), there are enough resources so that individuals can contribute what they are willing to contribute. But if this is not true, we need an adjustment process to determine how many resources can be contributed.

We make this adjustment in an iterative procedure, working with each region from 1 to J in turn. If A(j) is greater than or equal to D(j), move on to the next region. Otherwise, move individuals L(j + 1) to L(j), then from L(j + 2) to L(j) and so forth until A(j), the sum of resources across individuals in the revised set L(j), is equal to D(j). (If we are moving an individual who has more resources than are needed for the lower region, we will notationally split the individual into two, placing each in the appropriate subset L(j) and allocating resources to the two regions appropriately.) We then repeat this procedure for the next region, moving individuals from right to left until we run out of individuals and resources. We may refer to the revised subset L(j) as the "likely subset" for that region, that is, the individuals who would be expected to make their contributions at that point on the production function.

This procedure finds the amount of resources the interest group can feasibly contribute given a distribution of interest and resources; it is the point on the curve at which we "run out" of resources.

2.3. Surplus. The surplus in a region is defined as A(j) − D(j). The total surplus is the sum of these differences.

3. Accelerating production functions

3.1. Minimum necessary interest.

Let us define the *minimum necessary interest* $Z(r|R)$ as the value an individual must have to experience a net payoff of zero from a contribution of r units when R units have previously been contributed. Unless it would be ambiguous, we will usually denote the minimum necessary interest from the origin, $Z(r|0)$, with the simpler $Z(r)$. As elsewhere in this chapter, we will work with standardized units, and the term $Z(r|R)$ is the standardized minimum necessary interest.

Solving for the minimum necessary interest requires a different mathematical strategy from the more usual problem of optimizing. The net payoff from a contribution of r units from the origin is $vP(r) - r$. To find $Z(r)$, we substitute it for v in this equation and set the payoff equal to zero to obtain

$$0 = Z(r)P(r) - r. \tag{A1}$$

Solving for $Z(r)$, we obtain

$$Z(r) = r/P(r), \quad \text{for } P(r) > 0. \tag{A2}$$

$Z(r)$ is undefined at $P(r) = 0$; the substantive meaning of this is that if the contribution does not change the provision level of the collective good, there is no interest level that will make the net payoff zero.

In the general case of a contribution of r units beginning with R, we would obtain

$$Z(r|R) = r/[P(R + r) - P(R)], \quad P(R + r) > P(R). \tag{A3}$$

The denominator in equation (A3) is simply the *difference* the contribution makes in the provision level of the collective good. So, in general, the minimum necessary interest is the ratio of the contribution size to the change in the provision level produced by that contribution.

Under the assumptions that define the uniformly accelerating production function, $Z(r)$ decreases (or, more strictly, is nonincreasing) as r increases. That is, the amount of interest in the collective good necessary to make a given contribution rational decreases as the size of that contribution increases. (In contrast, the assumptions of uniform deceleration imply that $Z(r)$ increases with r.)

3.2. Interest and previous contributions. This means that the interest level necessary to make a contribution declines with the amount already contributed by others. We may see this by calculating the derivative of $Z(r|R)$ with respect to R:

$$\frac{\partial Z(r|R)}{\partial R} = \frac{-r[P'(R+r) - P'(R)]}{[P(R+r) - P(R)]^2}. \tag{A4}$$

Since $P''(R) > 0$ in the accelerative case, $P'(R + r) > P''(R)$, making the difference $[P'(R + r) - P'(R)]$ positive. Therefore, $Z'(r|R)$ is always negative in the accelerative case, meaning that $Z(r|R)$ decreases as R increases. Obviously, $Z(r|R)$ increases in the decelerative case with $P''(R) < 0$ (i.e., decreasing slopes); in that case, the interest necessary to make a contribution *increases* as others' contributions increase.

3.3. All-or-none contracts. Let R_c represent the total resources to be contributed by a group of actors acting according to an all-or-none rule, and let $P(R_c)$ represent the provision level associated with R_c. Then an individual's payoff decision equation may be written as

$$g(r) = vP(R_c) - r. \tag{A5}$$

To find the minimum necessary interest for a contribution of size r, we substitute $Z(r)$ for v in equation (A5), set $g = 0$, and solve for $Z(r)$:

$$Z(r) = r/P(R_c). \tag{A6}$$

4. Simulations

The program we used was written in FORTRAN and consisted of several steps. First, each member of a population of 1,000 individuals was randomly assigned an interest and resource level. These distributions were constant, normal, or skewed with a given mean and variance. The skewed distribution was a squared normal distribution, which was chosen for its computational ease.

Second, if necessary, subroutines processed the interest and resource arrays to give them a particular order, such as sequenced from highest to lowest value or to make the interest and resource arrays correlate with one another. Third, a subroutine selected the particular production function desired for the simulation. The functions used were the spline fits described in Table 4.1.

The next set of subroutines had each individual decide how much (if anything) to contribute to the collective good. The decision rules were those described in the text: a comparison of interest and instantaneous slopes for decelerating production functions and a comparison of total contribution and total payoff for the accelerating production functions.

This decision process was repeated ten times, each time feeding back through the program a resource array adjusted for the resources previously contributed. This allowed individuals the opportunity to respond to others' previous contributions. We found that ten iterations were plenty to allow everyone who would ever contribute to do so.

Each "case" (combination of parameters and options) was repeated at least ten times to allow estimation of the effects of random variation in probabilistically generated distributions. Results were written to an output file for examination.

5. Social networks: density, centralization, and cliques

Our discussions so far have ignored the problem of how collective action might be coordinated. We have mostly assumed that individuals contribute independently without coordination, although with knowledge of others' actions. In a few cases, we have shown how simultaneous coordinated actions would affect individuals' decisions, but without inquiring into the ways in which such coordination might be achieved. In this chapter, we introduce an explicit model for this coordination and then examine the effects of different features of social networks on the prospects for coordinated action.

The core of our model of simultaneous coordinated action is the assumption that there is a single organizer who contacts all possible actors and absorbs all the costs of organizing the action. The simultaneous coordinated action is modeled as an all-or-none contract. The organizer is conceived as asking others to participate in a risk-free agreement to make contributions if enough others also agree. As described briefly in Chapter 4, group members will agree to contribute if the total benefit they would experience from the "contract" exceeds their own share of the cost. Our single organizer is usually thought of as one person, but the model would also apply to any small group whose members have decided to pool their resources and act in concert, as if they were one complex person. We have repeatedly stressed that there is no single general process of collective action, but rather kinds of actions. We make no claim that all collective actions are organizer-centered or can be approximated by the organizer-centered model. But we do believe that organizer-centered mobilizations are an extremely common form of collective action and probably the most common source of simultaneous coordinated actions.

We investigate the ways in which the structure of social networks in a group promotes or hinders the prospects for organizer-centered mobilizations in that group. Our analysis is focused on the group level, on the group characteristics that give rise to organizers, not on the individual characteristics of organizers. In our analysis, we give every group member an analytic "chance" to be the organizer, and the dependent variables are whether any such organizer emerges and the highest level of action that could be achieved in that particular group.

The social structure of an interest group of moderate or large size is usually marked by a complex network of social ties that differentiate the relationships among the individual members. Any given organizer is usually in easy and ready communication with some group members but would find it difficult to deal with others. She might not even know that particular individuals actually have an interest in the good. Among our workers, for example, all the affected firemen might know one another quite well, but none of them might easily communicate with, say, three equally affected managers from the mayor's budget office.

That social ties are important for collective action is a commonplace observation in the literature. For example, it is widely agreed that participants in social movement organizations are usually recruited through preexisting social ties (e.g., Snow, Zurcher, and Ekland-Olson 1980), and that mobilization is more likely when the members of the beneficiary population are linked by social ties than when they are not (e.g., Oberschall 1973; Tilly 1978). But exactly how and why social ties are important is less well established. What kinds of ties are most important for collective action? What features of social ties are especially relevant? Are social ties important because they make mobilization less costly or because they connect more people? And how can we distinguish these explanations?

In this chapter we restrict organizers to mobilizing only those individuals to whom they have previous social ties. We then compare groups with different patterns of social ties (social structures) to see how these patterns affect collective action. The first and most important analysis we report considers differences among groups in their overall frequency or density of social ties and the extent to which the ties are centralized in a small number of group members. In addition, the cost of using a tie for communication or coordination is varied. The second analysis we report compares groups with different levels of cliquing, where *cliques* are defined as subgroups within which organizers may mobilize but across which mobilizing is forbidden.

It is important to remember that all of the variables for this analysis are ultimately conceptualized at the level of the group. However, we do add an important new factor to the model at the individual level; each group member is now allocated her own social network of other group members whom she can organize. This ego network (Burt 1980, p. 91), or "organizer network," is defined by direct, asymmetric "send" links: A is linked to B if it is physically and socially possible for A to ask B to participate in a given collective action. We treat the cost of communicating across a tie as a separate variable from the existence of the tie itself.

We assume asymmetry of ties because we believe that stratification and other social realities often prevent a person from approaching someone who could approach him.[1] A police lieutenant might recruit patrolmen who would be wary of initiating discussions with him. We consider only the direct ties between potential organizers and potential participants, ignoring the "second-order" or indirect ties that have often been investigated by social network theorists (Dorean 1974; White, Boorman, and Breiger 1976; Arabie 1977; Burt 1978, 1980; L. C. Freeman 1979; Alba 1981; Marsden 1981, 1983). We also do not distinguish the "strength" of the tie (Granovetter 1973). Although such variables are of great importance in understanding social networks, incorporating them would require factorially more complex models – much too complex for us to manage either through analysis or simulation.

Study 1

Variables

At the group level, the model that structures the first analysis in this chapter concerns six key variables. The dependent variable, as usual, is the amount of resources contributed toward the collective action. The major independent variables, which require further discussion, are density, centralization, organization costs, and group heterogeneity in interests and resources.

---

[1] These asymmetric ties may be mutual. A's link to B does *not* preclude B's link to A; it just does not entail it. In the simulation, the two links (A to B and B to A) would have independent probabilities of occurrence. Our analysis assumes that the mutuality of ties has no effect, which is true in our simulation.

Density

The assumptions noted above greatly simplify our treatment of networks. Let t_i be the number of ties (i.e., the "out-degree") for individual i, and T the total number of ties in the group. If the total size of the interest group is N, the maximum number of possible ties (send links) within the group is simply $N(N - 1)$, and the overall interest group *density* D is the proportion of possible ties that are actually realized, or $T/N(N - 1)$. Similarly, the density d_i of each individual's ego network is $t_i/(N - 1)$. In general, therefore, the mean of the individual network densities equals the overall group density.[2]

In terms of our example, density is best imagined as varying between cities. Since the affected employees in each city need to have a clause passed by their own council, they constitute separate, isolated, and comparable interest groups. Consider the cities Alpha and Beta. Alpha is fairly isolated, and most of its affected employees live in a single suburb, Centauri. They attend Centauri's churches, send their children to Centauri's public schools, and belong to Centauri chapters of social and service clubs; and all are served by the same local telephone exchange. In contrast, Beta is part of an ethnically diverse two-state megalopolis, and its affected employees are scattered across a dozen different suburbs in two states and four counties. They rarely see one another after work. They go to different churches, send their children to different schools, read four or five different newspapers, and pay toll charges for telephone calls between many of the suburbs.

We would find virtual unanimity among social scientists in predicting that the employees in Alpha are more likely than those in Beta to organize collective action. Other things being equal, the large number of social interconnections in Alpha provides a solid basis for interdependence, while their virtual absence in Beta is surely a hindrance. We have noted that it is practically a truism among social movement theorists that social networks

---

[2] For network specialists, the term *density* often refers to the extent to which the people known by one person tend to know each other. We are using the term in the nonspecialist's sense of number of actual social ties in a group divided by the number possible. This seems the only reasonable term for such a concept at the group level. When group size is fixed, as it is in our example and simulations, there is an equivalence between the total number of ties in a group, the density (total ties divided by number of ties possible), and the average number of ties per member (total ties divided by number of members). Thus, we often use these three terms somewhat interchangeably, although, of course, when group size is not held constant, they are not equivalent.

are important for recruiting participants (see, e.g., Oberschall 1973; Tilly 1978; Fireman and Gamson 1979), and these theorists are supported by a fair amount of empirical evidence. (See Snow, Zurcher, and Ekland-Olson 1980 and Walsh and Warland 1983 concerning participation in movement organizations, or Cohn 1985 on participation in a clerical workers' strike.) The basic argument was even important to Marx, who reasoned that employees who are in regular contact with one another will develop a "habit of cooperation," and be more likely to act collectively than will employees who work in isolation.

Centralization

But there is more to know about an interest group's social ties than simply how many there are. We also need to know how they are structured. In the present analysis, the aspect of structure on which we shall focus is the extent to which the ties are *centralized* or concentrated in a few individuals rather than being spread more evenly across the whole group. In contrast to density, whose effects on collective action are both important and obvious, the effects of network centralization have been little explored in the literature and appear to be quite complex.[3]

To illustrate, consider the cities Delta and Epsilon. The affected employees of Delta have the same total number or density of social ties as the employees of Epsilon. However, these ties are distributed quite differently. Delta has annexed all its potential suburbs. Its affected employees are therefore not suburbanites, but residents of Delta's "exurbs," lightly sprinkled around a sparsely settled rural fringe. They shop in the city's many shopping centers and attend city churches. In fact, they share only one important local institution – the county primary and secondary schools, which serve the entire rural area. The one affected city employee, who is on the county school board, therefore accounts for a very high proportion (let us say 50%) of all the ties among affected employees.

Social ties among affected employees in Epsilon are much less centralized. Epsilon is the central city of a small metropolis, and affected

---

[3] Again, because we consider only direct asymmetric ties, our use of the term *centralization* is different from the more complex usage of network theorists, e.g., Freeman (1979). We are referring simply to the tendency for a few people to account for most of the ties, while the network concept of centrality refers to the extent to which any particular person is an important link in the indirect network relations of others.

employees live in a number of contiguous suburbs with diffuse and indistinct social and economic boundaries. There are a few dozen churches that serve larger or smaller catchments depending on the denomination. Service clubs have loose geographical bases and draw in residents of adjacent suburbs. There are eight municipalities, four school districts, and three suburban newspapers with distinct, but partially overlapping territories. Different employees see each other in different contexts.

To make a prediction about the prospects for Delta and Epsilon, we have to assess the effect of the different levels of centralization of network ties. We have to decide whether collective actions are more likely to thrive where a small number of people know many others (while most know almost no one) or where many people each know some others (but no one knows a large number). The centralization around the school board in Delta suggests the possibility of efficient coordination of action by the affected employee who knows everyone else. But it also means that if the school board member is incompetent, or is just not interested in spearheading the collective action, no alternative affected employee has much of a chance to get things going. On the other hand, the crisscrossing social ties and overlapping memberships in Epsilon evoke images of more diffuse potential loci for action. If one person doesn't show initiative, perhaps another one will. The problem in Epsilon is that no one person is in a social network position to efficiently gather together some major proportion of all the affected workers. There are advantages and disadvantages in either situation, and in the absence of good theory, it is not obvious how these will balance out.

Given a specific group density, the centralization of an interest group's social network may be defined as the standard deviation σ_t of the number of ties across the ego networks of all group members. When all of the group's ties are concentrated on one individual (and everyone else has none), the group's network is fully centralized and σ_t is very large. When all group members have the same number of ties, the network is completely decentralized, and σ_t equals zero. The standard deviation of the ego-network densities $\sigma_d = \sigma_t/(N - 1)$, and may be interpreted similarly. When N is treated as fixed (as it is in the following simulation, where N = 400 for all groups), there is a direct equivalence between the standard deviation of ego-network densities and the standard deviation of numbers of ties, since the former is just the latter divided by N − 1.

Organizing cost

Our third independent variable is organizing *cost,* that is, the cost of using one of the social ties for some purpose, such as asking the person to participate in a collective action. This variable is often confounded with network density in work on social ties. To some extent we committed this confounding in our comparison of Alpha and Beta. Factors that make it cheaper to communicate across social ties, such as free local versus costly message-unit telephone rates, may also help determine whether such ties exist at all. Empirically, the two are often correlated. However, a *theoretical* distinction between the presence or absence of ties and the cost of using them is needed, because each factor may have a different effect on the prospects for collective action.

To illustrate this issue, we need a three-way comparison, such as among cities Mu, Sigma, and Rho. Suppose Mu's affected employees average ten ties to other affected employees and generally have to pay message-unit charges for calls to one another. Sigma's employees also average ten ties, but all the suburban areas are in the same extended calling area. Finally, Rho's employees average fifteen ties but have the same message unit charges as Mu's. Clearly, we would expect the prospects for collective action to be worse in Mu than in either Sigma or Rho. But what prediction do we have about the prospects for success in Sigma compared with those in Rho? Another way of asking this is, if one were in Mu, would there be a bigger effect of increasing the number of employees who know each other or of devising a cheaper mode of communication among those who already have social ties? A real group of employees might have to decide if its efforts to generate collective action would be helped more by social gatherings and other efforts to increase the group's density of social ties or by finding ways to reduce the cost of communication among people who already know each other, perhaps by printing a directory of home addresses and telephone numbers. This is really a question about comparative rates of change, and it does not have an obvious answer.

The effects of different *kinds* of organizing costs are complex and will not be treated here. In the present model, we continue to make the very simple assumption that organizing costs are exactly proportional to the number of parties to the all-or-none agreement, and that this constant cost per participant is a characteristic of the interest group that does not vary with the organizer or the particular individuals involved. Thus, average costs may be higher in one city than another because of telephone cost differences, but employees of the same city are assumed to face identical costs per network member recruited.

Interest and resource heterogeneity

In the current analysis, we expect the effects of the network variables to interact with the degree of resource and interest heterogeneity in the interest group. Remember that although all present employees who live outside the city share an interest in an exemption, they differ in the magnitude of that interest, depending on such factors as how easy it would be for them to get another job, whether they own or rent their home, and whether their spouse is employed. They may also vary in the amount of time and money (i.e., resources) objectively available to them.

The simulation

The following analysis again builds from the simple to the complex. We first consider groups that differ only in their organizing costs. Next, we vary the density of network ties, and then their centralization. The results to that point are essentially analytic, although we create a data set to compare the relations among these variables to those from the simulation. The last step in this analysis involves varying the dispersion of interest and resources around their means. The resulting interactions do not permit analytic solutions, and we again investigate with data produced by a rather complex simulation of the process. Unlike previous chapters, where the simulations we used to generate our theory faded into the background in explaining it, the results of this analysis remain complicated enough that we will present them explicitly and describe our interpretations.

Fixed parameters and algorithms

Although the underlying model of collective action used in this chapter is the same as for previous chapters, the parameters of the numerical simulation are somewhat different. As before, the standardized provision level P of the collective good ranges between 0 and 1, standardized individual contributions r and total contributions R are expressed as proportions of the amount needed to achieve the maximum provision level, and an individual's interest v in the collective good is expressed as the value that would be experienced from the maximum provision level. We may think of this either as the probability that a dichotomous good such as a grandfather clause is achieved or as a proportion of some maximum possible provision level.

As before, this standardization means that, if the production function is linear, the total amount of resources contributed equals the provision level, that is, $P(R) = R$. However, we argued in Chapter 4 that simultaneous coordinated action is especially important when the production function is accelerating and start-up costs need to be surpassed. When the production function is accelerating, each contribution increases the value of subsequent contributions, and contracts for simultaneous coordinated action are less likely to raise issues of strategic gaming. For these reasons, we conducted this analysis with an accelerating production function, $P(R) = R^{1.2}$, $0 < R < 1$. The particular choice of function is essentially arbitrary.

All groups have an arbitrary 400 members. All members have resources that may be spent either for organizing or for making a contribution to a contract organized by another. Organizing costs are paid wholly by the organizer, are proportional to the number of group members who agree to contribute to a contract (regardless of the sizes of their contributions), and do not vary among individuals in a group, although they vary between groups. As a further simplification, we do not permit organizers to make direct contributions to the collective good, even if they have resources left over after organizing.

As we have seen, the total resource and interest levels of the group as a whole have an enormous influence on the prospects for collective action. Since we are interested in other independent variables, we must constrain these factors to ranges that neither guarantee nor prohibit contributions. We set the *mean* of the distribution at .06 for resources and .15 for interest. The interest mean is substantially higher than the resource mean so that many group members will meet the criterion $P(R) > r/v$, which permits contracts that produce provision levels between 0 and 1.

Operationalizing the variables

The group outcome (the dependent variable) is operationalized as the best possible outcome across all possible organizers in the group. Each group member is a possible organizer, and we calculate the total contribution from his best possible contract given the specific others to whom he has social ties. We then select the one organizer in the group whose contract commands the highest total contribution. His contract becomes the *group's* contract, and the group payoff becomes this total contribution raised to the 1.2 power. Since payoff and contribution are perfectly correlated, we use the latter in our regression analyses. In other analyses, we transform this continuous contribution/payoff variable in three ways: into the dichotomy between achieving the maximum possible (contribution total 1.0 or more) and not; into the dichotomy between failing totally (contributions total 0) and not; and into the trichotomy among total failure, partial success, and maximum success.

For each independent variable, we define a range of values of interest. The actual values assigned to each case on each variable are systematically generated or randomly selected from the uniform distribution defined by that range. These uniform distributions do not mean anything substantive; they are continuous analogues of the equal-cell Ns in a standard fixed-effects analysis of variance design.

Individuals' personal network sizes (or out-degrees), resources, and interest are distributed lognormally within each group. As we have previously argued, it is most plausible to assume these distributions are skewed, both because they are constrained to be nonnegative and because one would generally expect to find a large number of group members low and only a few high on each variable. In most groups there are many more people who are very poor than are very rich. The choice of the lognormal, rather than some other skewed distribution, is largely practical.

Interest and resource *heterogeneity* are operationalized as the *standard deviations* of lognormal distributions. Among groups, these range from .01 to .06 around the resource mean of .06 and range from .025 to .15 around the interest mean of .15.

Organizing cost (C) is defined as the cost to the organizer per each contributor to a contract and is standardized to the same metric as *r*. It varies among groups from .001 to .010 in increments of .001. Organizing is never free, but its cost ranges from insignificant to prohibitive, given organizers' resource levels. Each of a group's 400 members faces the same organizing cost.

The density and centralization of group networks are operationalized in a nonstandard way because these numbers must be integers. We operationalize a group network's density as the *mode* of a lognormal distribution of individuals' personal network sizes within the group, and the group's centralization or dispersion as the difference between the mode and the "largest possible" personal network size, meaning the size above which falls less than .0005 of a lognormal distribution with the given mode. In these data, the correlation between the mean and the mode of the distribution of personal network sizes is .99, while the correlation between the standard deviation and our operationalization of dispersion is .96. The range among groups for modal personal network size was set as low as possible, ranging from 1 to 10. Dispersion was chosen to ránge from 2 to 20, a range that seemed on its face to provide extensive variation among groups in the degree of centralization of network ties. The largest possible group size is the sum of mode and dispersion, and therefore ranges from 3 to 30 with a flat bell shape. The range of modes is extremely unfavorable for successful contracts, but the range of largest possible sizes includes a good proportion that can achieve certainty.

Actual assignment of network sizes to individuals within the groups used a computer algorithm to produce the frequency distribution of integers that is the best approximation to the lognormal distribution defined by the mode and the largest possible group size. Because the largest possible group size is the level at which 1 in 2,000 networks would obtain, while the groups have only 400 networks, the actual size of the largest group in these frequency distributions is a little lower, especially when the dispersion is high (but the correlation between the two is .98).

Network ties are randomly assigned to group members in accordance with this frequency distribution. For example, an individual might be randomly determined to be able to organize (i.e., "send to") 8 others. The particular 8 would be randomly chosen from the 399 other group members entirely independently of the presence or absence of other ties. That is, the fact that A can organize B has no effect on the probability that B can organize A and the fact that A and B can both organize or be organized by C has no effect on the probability of a link between A and B.

Results

Although we are ultimately interested in the interactions among all five of the independent variables at once, we introduce them in three stages so that the results for the simpler cases may be used as baselines for interpreting the more complex.

Case 1: homogeneous groups

We begin our analysis by considering interest groups that have no *within-group* variance on any important characteristic. Each member therefore has .06 in resources, an interest of .15, and some constant number of other group members she could organize. Under these circumstances, all group members, and the networks of those they could organize, are completely equivalent. The total group's contribution is simply proportional to the number organized. In turn, the number organized is determined by the least favorable of two constraints: the number of others each group member has a tie to that permits organizing (i.e., organizer network size) and the number she can afford to contact (i.e., the available resources per person divided by the per capita organizing cost, or r/C). The outcomes for the ranges of variables used in our simulation are easy to calculate, as summarized in Table 5.1. These results are not intrinsically interesting, since they are a direct product of the ranges selected for organizing costs and network sizes. They provide the baseline information that the simulation has been parameterized so that homogeneous groups cannot provide the good with certainty and have only a 1 in 5 chance of being able to provide an intermediate level of the good. As it should, the model indicates that groups with more social ties among their members and lower organizing costs should support more collective action.

Case 2: heterogeneity in social ties

The next step in our analysis is to permit heterogeneity in organizers' network sizes, that is, variation among groups in network centralization. As long as interests and resources remain invariant within the group, the group's total contribution is still solely a function of the *number* of individuals organized. The organizing cost constraint remains the same, so that every group member can afford to contact exactly r/C others. The only difference from Case 1 is that individuals differ in the sizes of their personal networks. The key to analyzing Case 2, therefore, is to recognize that the best *group* outcome is simply the outcome for the group member

Table 5.1. *Summary of the homogeneous case*

Description	Symbol	Outcome		
		Certainty	Partial success	Failure
Resources per person (assumed constant)	r	.06	.06	.06
Minimum necessary total contribution to achieve specified outcome	M	1.0	.47	0
Minimum network size for minimum total contribution, $n' = M/r$	n'	17	8	0
Maximum organizing cost permitting contact of n' others, $C' = r/n'$	C'	.0035	.0075	Any
Proportions having $n \geq n'$ for groups in simulation with (modal) network sizes drawn from uniform distribution between 1 and 10		0	.3	.7
Proportions having $C \leq C'$ for groups in simulation with organizing cost drawn from uniform distribution between .001 and .010		.3	.4	.3
Proportions constrained to each outcome by the least favorable of n and C for the distributions used in the simulation		0	.21	.79

Note: A total contribution of 1 achieves certainty because of the standardization. A contract for total contributions less than 1 is viable if $r/v < P(R)$. For $r = .06$ and $v = .15$, $r/v = .4$. For the production function $P = R^{1.2}$, the minimum R necessary to meet the constraint is $M > .47$.

who would make the best organizer, and that the best organizer is always the one with the largest organizer network.

Thus, when resources and interests are homogeneous in a group, analysis of the effects of degree of centralization is simply a matter of determining the *largest* organizer network. The density and centralization of a group's network ties jointly determine the largest network size in that group. The higher the average number of ties (density) in the group, the larger will be the largest network. For a given density, greater centralization leads to even larger networks, since available linkages become concentrated on a few sociometric stars, such as the Beta school board member. Of course, as centralization increases, the sizes of most group members' personal networks decrease. One's intuition might suggest that this decrease in the ''typical'' personal network size would have some harmful consequences,

Table 5.2. *Summary of the case of heterogeneity in network sizes and homogeneity in interests and resources*

Description	Outcome		
	Certainty	Partial success	Failure
Proportions having $C \leq C'$ for groups in simulation with organizing cost drawn from uniform distribution between .001 and .010	.3	.4	.3
Proportions with $n_{largest} \geq n'$ for groups in simulation with largest network sizes determined by modal network size uniformly distributed between 1 and 10 and distance between mode and largest possible network size uniformly distributed between 2 and 20	.34	.56	.10
Proportions constrained to each outcome by the least favorable of n and C for the distributions used in the simulation	.11	.52	.37

Note: Computations of minimum necessary network size and maximum possible organizing cost are the same as for Table 5.1 and are not shown.

but for organizer-centered actions in homogeneous groups, this intuition is false.

Table 5.2 shows the outcome distributions for the ranges of variables used in our simulations. The proportions constrained to each outcome by the organizing cost distribution is unchanged. The difference in outcomes is due entirely to replacing the distribution of the *modal* organizer network size in Table 5.1 with the distribution of the actual *largest* organizer network size in Table 5.2.

Just as for the homogeneous case, the particular proportions shown in Table 5.2 are not intrinsically interesting, as they are directly determined by the parameter ranges chosen. It is clear, however, that network centralization (heterogeneity of network sizes) permits much greater rates of success. The explanation for this is straightforward. A successful outcome depends only on the size of the *largest* organizer network, and heterogeneity around a mean increases the proportion falling above some value greater than the mean. This constraint interacts with the organizing cost constraint just as in the homogeneous case, with the outcome determined by the least favorable of these two constraints.

This substantive finding – that, for a given density, centralization in a group's network promotes collective action – has *not* been recognized in the literature. Although the importance of well-connected organizers is understood, there has been little recognition in theoretical discussions that properties known to make for good organizers imply group-level characteristics that give rise to them, network centralization, in this case.

Case 3: resource and interest heterogeneity

Understanding the effects of the group's network variables on collective action becomes much more difficult when groups are allowed to be heterogeneous in interests and resources as well as personal network sizes. Under these circumstances, outcomes are due to the conjunction of several probabilistic events. For collective action to occur, the group must contain at least one organizer network with enough resourceful people that the sum of their contributions forms a viable contract. That same network must also have an organizer who can afford to contact enough people to form the contract. In our symbolic language, if M is the amount needed for a viable contract, C is the cost per contributor, and k is the number of contributors, then the maximum provision level is achieved if $\Sigma r_k \geq M$ and $r_{org} \geq kC$. These factors alone mean that there are three probabilistic elements: the organizer's resources, the size of the organizer's network, and the resources of that network's members.

Additionally, the members and organizer are constrained by their interests, since those who could make especially large contributions, or organize a large network, will not do so if their interests are too low. In symbolic terms, the constraint for each individual is $P(\Sigma r_k) = (\Sigma r_k)^{1.2} > r/v$. These simultaneous inequations are difficult to solve because Σr_k is recursively determined. Individuals' willingness to contribute depends on how much others are contributing.

When resources and interests vary within the group, it is not necessarily true that the organizer network with the largest number of members will make the largest contribution of resources. There are sampling fluctuations within the group in the composition of each organizer network, and when network sizes are small (e.g., 3 to 27 in our simulations) and the independent variables are lognormally distributed, these fluctuations can be very large. Within most of the ranges of our simulation, the outcome from a particular set of parameters varies widely, depending on the "luck" of the joint distributions of the variables.

The complexity of the case is reflected in the complexity of the computer program that we use for its Monte Carlo simulation. The indirect way in which interest constrains resources requires an iterative algorithm to search for the best contract for a particular organizer with a particular network, and this algorithm must be repeated across all the organizers in a group. In brief, for each organizer, the algorithm searches for the best set of contributors from his network given the organizer's resource constraint. When the resource and interest conditions neither assure certainty nor force failure, numerous iterations can be required to find the best partial success contract or to determine that such a contract is impossible. The program implementing this process takes a long time to run. For this analysis we have generated 2,794 groups, with each group constituting a single case.

Effects of resource and interest heterogeneity. Our central interest is in the effects of a group's network characteristics, but we begin with a brief summary of the effects of resource and interest heterogeneity to provide a proper context for those results. As Table 5.3 shows, resource and interest heterogeneity increase the *dispersion* among groups in rates of collective action. A comparison of the first line (taken from Table 5.3) with the second shows that resource and interest heterogeneity increases *both* the proportion of all groups achieving certainty and the proportion failing completely.

The rest of the table breaks groups into the outcome that would be expected from the group's "network" variables (i.e., those in Table 5.2) alone and, within these groups, separately shows the effects of raising the heterogeneity of resources and interest. Inspection of these subtables reveals that resource heterogeneity has clear positive effects if the group network variables would predict failure for homogeneous groups, clear negative effects if the network variables would predict achieving certainty, and stronger negative than positive effects if the network variables would predict a partial success. The effect of interest heterogeneity is more irregular: it is clearly negative if the group network variables would predict achieving certainty, somewhat negative if they would predict partial success, and small and irregular if the network variables would predict failure.

Overall, these data show the importance of what we call the "mean level" effect of heterogeneity. If a distribution's mean is sufficiently high, more heterogeneity hinders collective action; if the mean is too low, heterogeneity helps. This effect is more clear-cut for resources because we

Table 5.3. *Effect of resource and interest heterogeneity of outcomes, by outcome network that variables would produce in a homogeneous group*

| Cases | Proportions | | | | | |
	Certainty	Partial success	Failure	N	Mean	S.D.
Homogeneous (analytic results)	.11	.52	.37	1,900	.46	.38
All heterogeneous (simulation)	.19	.31	.50	2,794	.38	.42
Failure if homogeneous Resource deviation	.08	.23	.69	1,007	.19	.33
Low 1	—	.29	.71	252	.16	.26
2	.02	.31	.67	268	.19	.32
3	.12	.21	.67	243	.20	.35
High 4	.19	.09	.72	244	.21	.38
Partial success if homogeneous Resource deviation	.17	.39	.45	1,537	.41	.41
Low 1	.11	.53	.37	395	.48	.40
2	.17	.41	.42	398	.45	.40
3	.20	.35	.45	366	.37	.41
High 4	.20	.25	.56	378	.34	.42
Certainty if homogeneous Resource deviation	.83	.16	.01	250	.95	.17
Low 1	.89	.11	—	61	.99	.03
2	.90	.10	—	63	.97	.13
3	.75	.20	.05	65	.91	.22
High 4	.77	.23	—	61	.92	.21
Failure if homogeneous Interest deviation	.08	.23	.69	1,007	.19	.33
Low 1	.11	.18	.71	267	.22	.37
2	.09	.18	.74	224	.18	.34
3	.10	.22	.68	249	.19	.33
High 4	.03	.33	.64	267	.17	.27
Partial success if homogeneous Interest deviation	.17	.39	.45	1,537	.41	.41
Low 1	.26	.34	.40	378	.50	.44
2	.16	.34	.50	364	.40	.42
3	.15	.40	.45	392	.40	.40
High 4	.10	.47	.43	403	.36	.36
Certainty if homogeneous Interest deviation	.83	.16	.01	250	.95	.17
Low 1	.97	.03	—	58	.99	.06
2	.81	.19	—	66	.96	.15
3	.86	.12	.02	65	.94	.19
High 4	.64	.33	.03	61	.90	.22

have set the mean resource level relatively low and the mean interest level relatively high.[4]

Effects of the group's network variables. Treating groups as the units of analysis, we want to assess the effects of organizing costs and the density and centralization of network ties, as well as to determine how these effects interact with the level of resource and interest heterogeneity. As Table 5.3 indicates, however, the distribution of the outcome variable is quite unusual. Half of the cases fall at the low extreme of 0, that is, complete failure; nearly 20% fall at the other extreme of 1, achieving certainty. The distribution of the 30% that fall between these extremes has a rough bell shape around a mean of .61; it is a bit flat (kurtosis = − .417) and has a small negative skew (− .382).[5] To be sure that the mode of analysis does not distort the results, we analyzed three dependent variables (total contribution level, whether the maximum was achieved, avoiding complete failure) in two ways (ordinary least squares [OLS] regression and probit analysis). All yield the same basic patterns of results. We report only the standard OLS regression using the total contribution level.

In Table 5.4, we show the linear regression of our outcome variable, the total contribution of the most successful organizer network in the group, on the group's three network variables (organizing cost, density, centralization of networks) separately for groups with different levels of interest and resource heterogeneity. In the first row of the table a comparable regression is reported for data from Case 2 (resources and interest homogeneous), to provide a baseline for comparison.[6] For Case 2, the total

---

[4] Recall that the mean interest level is set at 2.5 times greater than the mean resource level. Increases in interest heterogeneity increase the proportion of group members whose interest level is below their resource level, i.e., too low to contribute. Only when resource heterogeneity is very high, meaning that there are a few group members with very high resource levels, is interest heterogeneity potentially beneficial. Obviously, for a variable on which high values deter collective action, heterogeneity is beneficial when the mean is high and harmful when the mean is low.

[5] If interest were always exactly 2.5 times the resource level, there would be no outcomes falling between 0 and .47, but because both vary, interest is sometimes greater than 2.5 times the resource level, and there can be partial successes below the .47 level.

[6] To provide an appropriate baseline for comparison, we created a data set consisting of 1,900 cases, one for each possible combination of 10 modal network sizes, 19 largest network sizes, and 10 levels of organizing costs. The outcome for each of these cases when each individual has resource level .06 and interest level .15 was determined analytically and added to the data set. (The outcome is entirely determined by the three manipulated variables, so there is nothing probabilistic in these data.) The same regressions were performed on these data as on those generated for the heterogeneous case.

Table 5.4. *Linear regression of total contribution level on contacting cost and the density and centralization of network ties, separately for different levels of resource and interest heterogeneity*

	Unstandardized			Standardized			
	Cost	Density	Centralization	Cost	Density	Centralization	R^2
Homogeneous	−.10	.03	.02	−.78	.22	.27	.72
All heterogeneous	−.05	.08	.03	−.29	.56	.45	.60
Resource dispersion							
Low 1	−.06	.08	.03	−.36	.54	.47	.64
2	−.05	.08	.03	−.33	.58	.46	.64
3	−.05	.08	.03	−.28	.54	.45	.59
High 4	−.03	.08	.03	−.18	.56	.42	.56
Significance of difference[a]	<.0001	N.S.	N.S.	—	—	—	—
Interest dispersion							
Low 1	−.05	.04	.08	−.29	.51	.51	.60
2	−.05	.08	.04	−.28	.55	.47	.62
3	−.05	.09	.03	−.28	.59	.42	.62
High 4	−.05	.08	.03	−.31	.60	.39	.59
Significance of difference[a]	N.S.	.29	<.0001				

[a]This is the *p* for an *F*-test on the difference of slopes across the four heterogeneity levels for each independent variable taken one at a time. See footnotes in text for model specification.

group contribution is exactly determined by the three independent variables, but in a way that is only approximated by a linear regression, as indicated by R^2 less than 1. We do not know what the best equation relating the three group network variables to the outcome is for Case 3, but it is helpful to compare the linear approximation to that for Case 2.

The variances of cost, density, and centralization differ, so we require standardized coefficients for comparisons of the effects of different variables within equations, along with the unstandardized coefficients for comparisons of the effects of the same variable between equations. For each independent variable, we report the result of a significance test for the difference in the unstandardized coefficient depending on the level of interest and resource heterogeneity.[7]

[7] Table 5.4 shows the *p* values for six *F*-tests that tested each of the three independent variables separately for interaction with resource and interest heterogeneity. The restricted model in each case was $Y = b_0 + b_1M + b_2S + b_3C + \Sigma_{bk}h_k$, where b_0 is the intercept,

In examining Table 5.4, three important patterns emerge quite clearly.[8] First, and perhaps foremost among these, is the fact that all three independent variables are strong predictors of the group's level of contribution. Only for organizing cost under conditions of high resource heterogeneity is there a standardized coefficient (beta) less than .2. As we have noted, we expected that the overall density of ties and organizing cost would be strong predictors of collective action. However, the consistently positive effect of centralization is a new result not anticipated in the literature.

The second significant pattern in Table 5.4 is that the importance of organizing cost as a constraint on collective action declines with resource heterogeneity. In the "homogeneous" data, the coefficient for organizing cost is much larger than the coefficients for either the mode (density) or the spread (centralization) of group network ties. This relationship *reverses* for the "heterogeneous" data, where the coefficients for both mode and spread are much higher than for organizing cost, and the coefficient for organizing cost declines significantly as resource heterogeneity increases. The third important pattern in Table 5.4 is that the coefficient for centralization declines significantly as interest heterogeneity increases.

Discussion

No theory or simulation that hopes to reflect the most commonly held understandings of the empirical social world could fail to find that the sheer density of an interest group's network and its organizing costs are important predictors of collective action. Our "news" is the strong positive impact of the group network's centralization on collective action, and the interaction of all three independent variables with interest and resource heterogeneity.

M is the modal network size, S is the spread of network sizes, C is the organizing cost, and the h_k are three dummy variables to represent the four levels of heterogeneity of either resources or interest. The full model in each case is $Y = b_0 + b_1M + b_2S + b_3C + \Sigma_{bj}h_j + \Sigma_{bk}h_kX$, where X is either M, S, or C. That is, the full model allows the independent variable in question to have a different slope for each heterogeneity level. To aid interpretation, Table 5.4 shows the coefficients for the independent variables for separate regressions for each heterogeneity level.

   [8] In general, results from analyses using the dependent variables "avoiding failure" and "achieving certainty" closely replicate those using the group's total contribution. The effect of organizing cost on avoiding failure declines but not significantly with increasing resource heterogeneity. The effect of density (mode) on achieving certainty increases with resource heterogeneity but decreases with interest heterogeneity. Otherwise, all three dependent variables show the same results.

For a given level of group network density, the centralization of ties means that group members are more heterogeneous in the number of ties each has. Some of our results can be explained by the general principles determining whether heterogeneity promotes or impedes collective action. The overall positive effect of centralization is due in part to the mean-level effect. The modal personal network size in the simulation is always too small to achieve certainty and usually too small to support even partial success, so heterogeneity around the mode is necessary for there to be any organizer networks large enough to support collective action. This effect obviously obtains only when the average organizer network is too small. If the average personal network size is large enough to support collective action, we would not expect centralization to be beneficial on this basis.

The declining effect of centralization as interest heterogeneity increases may be explained as a "conjunction of probabilities." The joint probability of two or more independent events must be lower than the marginal probability of either one of them. Thus, increasing the heterogeneity of two or more variables at the same time tends to have a negative effect on the outcome. In the present case, as centralization and interest heterogeneity jointly increase, the risk grows that the organizer of the single largest network (in a group with mostly very small personal networks) will not be interested enough to organize her network. Although the effect of centralization is always significantly positive in our simulation, even for the highest levels of interest heterogeneity, the decline in the size of the effect might seem to suggest that there are situations in which centralization would not be beneficial. However, we believe that this suggestion is false, because of selectivity.

Selectivity

We believe that the most important theoretical insight to emerge from our analysis is the formulation of the concept we call "selectivity" and the recognition of its role in the processes we have described in this chapter and the previous two chapters. We consider selectivity so central to the development of the theory of the critical mass that we shall put off discussing some of these results until the next chapter, which is devoted to a full explication of the concept.

Briefly defined, *selectivity* refers to the fact that organizers often must select among the members of their networks which individuals to recruit into the collective action. We had to decide on some procedure by which organizers would make these decisions. Brief consideration suggested that they would want to choose those individuals likely to contribute the most resources. Thus, we wrote a computer program that rank ordered all the members of an organizer's network on their probable contributions if asked by the organizer and had the organizer select the top $k = r_o/C$ of them, where k is the number chosen (truncated to the nearest integer), r_o is the organizer's resource level, and C is the cost per contact. Thus, we implicitly built selectivity into our model without recognizing its enormous potential for affecting collective action.

Obviously (in hindsight), allowing the organizer to select the best subset of his network maximizes collective action in a very important way. It turns out that larger organizer networks promote collective action, but not in the way we had expected. Our original idea, which still seems to us to be what the literature implies, was that larger networks promote collective action because they permit *more people* to be organized. But as group heterogeneity increases, it turns out that the most important predictor of successful organizing is happening to have the few large contributors together in the same organizer network, so they can assure a successful contract. That is, knowing more people turns out to be important for being able to reach the few *right* people. This is why organizing cost (which constrains the number of people the organizer can mobilize) has a declining effect as group heterogeneity increases. Although it is arguable that we should have anticipated the effects of this process, the fact is that we did not. Our reconsideration of this process constitutes Chapter 6.

Centralization and "weak" ties

We may draw out some of the implications of our analysis even at this point, however, by considering its relation to Granovetter's (1973) important and frequently cited analysis of the effects of strong and weak ties. Granovetter argues that strong ties tend to form cliques, while weak ties tend to bridge cliques and bring everyone into the same network, so that weak ties are a better basis for collective action. The imagery of this argument suggests that decentralized nets and centralized wheels of weak ties would be equally effective network structures for collective action. Our results would imply that it is not weak ties per se that are useful, but their tendency to be centralized. Residents who are all bridged by *the same* weak tie, to a parish priest, for example, are more likely to be mobilized than those linked by the same number of weak ties distributed more widely through crosscutting associational memberships. Our claim in this regard is, of course, quite consistent with a huge social psychological literature on communication networks (for a summary, see Michener, DeLamater, and Schwartz 1986, pp. 418–421), and Granovetter would doubtless agree that the same number of ties will be more effectively employed if they are centralized than if they are decentralized.

Where we might part company with Granovetter is that our results would suggest that the "bridging" function of weak ties is relatively unimportant for collective action. Again, our position is that collective action tends to happen when a critical mass of interested and resourceful individuals can coordinate their efforts. There is generally no need for *all* of the aggrieved population to be mobilized and no need for all the members of a population to be mutually reachable. Thus, we are suggesting that it is possible to be increasingly specific in our claims about just how and why social networks are important for collective action.

The fact that association membership promotes collective action has been said to demonstrate the importance of weak ties for providing bridges among friendship cliques. Our analysis indicates that the important structural fact about associations is that they are centralized. Since both theoretical approaches predict that organizations are important, it would be difficult to construct critical tests at an aggregate level. Case studies might indicate whether collective actions tend to be coordinated through the leaders of organizations (favoring the centralization analysis) or through nonleaders who use the organization as a recruiting ground for events outside the aegis of the organization (favoring the weak-ties analysis).

At least in principle, empirical tests could also be constructed for our predictions that organizing costs are less important constraints as group heterogeneity increases, and that successful organizing is more a matter of *whom* you can mobilize, than of *how many* you can mobilize. Centralization, and its effect on creating some very large organizer network, should remain important even when only a few members are mobilized, since an organizer with a larger personal network is more likely to know the right few people.

Study 2: cliques

A fundamental part of Granovetter's argument is his proposition that strong ties of friendship and kinship could not provide an organizational basis for collective action because they tend to *clique,* and that cliques hinder action. Over the past several decades, cliquing has probably been the most commonly studied aspect of social structure in groups. By *cliquing* we refer broadly to a structural condition in which groups become internally differentiated into two or more subgroups within which social ties are common, but between which ties are rare or nonexistent. From Moreno (1934) to White et al. (1976), from studies of juvenile delinquency (e.g., Akers, Krohn, Lanza-Kaduce, and Radosevich 1979) to studies of the interlocking directorates of corporations (e.g., Mizruchi 1987), theorists and researchers have argued that such substructuring is an important determinant of all kinds of social processes.

At first glance, it seems obvious that cliquing should have serious consequences for the emergence of collective action from the group as a whole. A second glance, however, suggests contradictory possibilities for the nature of that effect. On the one hand, dense within-subgroup social networks created by cliquing might allow organizers to quickly and effectively gather the resources needed to launch collective action. On the other hand, as in Granovetter's discussion, barriers between cliques may prevent organizers from reaching beyond the confines of their small subgroup to bring together those individuals whose combined resources and interest would make collective action viable. Our analysis was designed to throw some light on these issues and test these predictions within the context of our model.

Cliques

We define the presence of cliques in a group in terms of barriers to social ties between specified individuals. To simplify our analysis (and distinct from Granovetter's approach) these barriers are assumed to be totally transitive, so that they define subgroups that are isolated from one another. If A can have a tie with B but not with C, then C cannot have a tie with B. Thus, organizers may have ties only within their own clique and are prohibited from recruiting individuals not in their clique. This definition of cliques does not imply that all members of a given clique have social ties with one another. In fact, an individual may be a member of a clique but be an isolate and have no social ties at all. His clique membership is defined by the fact that he is structurally *able* to have such ties, even if he does not develop them. The imagery is something like the Capulets and

Montagues, in which no member of either clan could befriend anyone from the other, but any individual could remain an isolate, even within his own group.

In our simulation, cliques within groups are always equal in size. If there are four cliques, each will have 100 members; if there are five, each will have 80. Individuals within each group may differ in the number of other group members with whom they have a social tie, but all of the groups we create have the identical total number of social ties (i.e., density). Again, these ties, along with resources and interest, are distributed lognormally within the group, with the distributions defined by the *mode* and the *practical maximum* of network sizes. In the present analysis, the mode is held constant at 4 and the practical maximum at 20. This means that the largest possible personal network for any individual within any of our groups is 20 others. As before, assignment of a number of social ties, and the specific others to whom the individual is tied, are done by a random process within the constraints defined by cliques.

The independent variable of primary interest is the number of cliques in the group. For this analysis we have selected four levels. Level 1 is actually a control, where there is only one clique, which is the same as saying there are none. Level 2 groups each have two 200-member subgroups. Similarly, Level 5 groups each have five 80-member cliques, and Level 20 groups each have twenty 20-member subgroups. Two cliques is obviously the least substruction of the group that is possible. Five was selected as a convenient intermediate number of cliques.

Twenty cliques is the largest number possible for a distribution of personal network sizes with mode set at 4 and practical maximum at 20. With 20 cliques in a group of 400, each clique is of size 20. Clique sizes smaller than 20 would force the largest network size to be smaller than 20, thus forcing a change in the network size distribution. Thus, clique sizes cannot be any smaller than 20 and still hold the effect of network size constant. We know from Study 1 that personal network size has a large effect on the prospects for collective action, so comparisons of the effect of cliquing in this experiment would be artificially biased against collective action for numbers of cliques greater than 20. It is interesting to see from this reasoning why a group divided into a very large number of cliques simply cannot generate collective action. However, for the present analysis, we prefer to keep the comparisons within a range that does not force a clique effect through structural fiat.

It is important to note that, in this analysis, membership in cliques is assigned randomly, in the same manner as membership in organizer networks. In real life, cliquing usually follows some pattern defined by a social variable of interest, in which similar individuals choose one another. Our analysis seeks the ''pure'' effect of cliques on collective action, independent of patterns of association.

Simulation

Except as noted, the simulation is the same as for Study 1. For all groups, the mean resource level is .06 with standard deviation .03, while the mean interest level is .15 with standard deviation .075. Because it adds another level of process to the simulation reported in Study 1, the computer algorithm for each simulated 400-person group is even more complex and time-consuming to run, so the sample size is small. One hundred 400-person groups are generated. Each group has a particular randomly determined distribution of interest and resources across its members. Each group is then randomly divided into cliques four times, one at each level. This within-group strategy of comparison reduces random error and increases the efficiency of our assessment of the effect of cliquing on the outcomes. Network ties are determined and assigned as in Study 1, except for the constraint that ties can occur only within cliques. The rest of the collective action model proceeds as in Study 1. For each of these 400 cases (100 groups × 4 cliquing levels), the total contribution from the best contract is determined.

Results and conclusions

Our results do not present clear answers to our principal research questions. The means and standard deviations for the total contribution level over the 100 groups in each of the four levels of cliquing are presented in Table 5.5.

A mean total contribution of approximately .63 is common to all four levels of cliquing in Table 5.5. However, this result is not in itself interesting, as it merely reflects the parameterization of our model. The distribution around this mean is similar to what we found in Study 1. The shape is essentially bimodal, with modes at the minimum (0) and maximum (1) provision levels, a rough threshold at the .4 provision level arising

Table 5.5. *Number of cliques and maximum contributions to collective action*

No. of cliques per group	Number of groups (N)	Mean contribution (mean CMAX)	S.D. of CMAX
Level 1[a]	100	.651[b]	.309
Level 2	100	.664	.322
Level 5	100	.625	.350
Level 20	100	.619	.374

[a]Level 1 indicates group has a single clique, i.e., is not segmented at all; Level 2 indicates there are 2 cliques; etc.
[b]Reported as the amount contributed by the most successful network in the group divided by the total amount of contribution needed to provide the collective good with certainty. Scores for each group may range from 0 to 1.

from the ratio of the mean resource level to the mean interest level, and a fairly even distribution between this threshold and the maximum.

Complete failure (total contributions of 0) was the result for approximately 18% of the groups (ranging from 14% to 23% for different levels of cliquing). The maximum provision level (1) was achieved by 22.5% of the groups. This fraction ranged from 18% to 26% over the four levels or cliquing.

The number of cliques seems to make very little difference in the outcomes. Significance tests for differences among the four levels of cliquing taken at once, or for any planned comparison between the baseline of no cliquing (Level 1) and some higher number of cliques, do not allow rejection of the null hypothesis of no difference. However, the standard deviation of the contribution level appears to increase with the number of cliques. Most of these comparisons are also not significant when appropriate tests (F-tests, $p = .05$, in this case) are applied. However, when we compare the variance among groups with 20 cliques with the variance among groups with no cliques, the former is significantly larger.[9]

It seems plausible that increasing the number of cliques would increase the variability of the outcomes. Depending on how interests and resources happen to be (randomly) distributed across the cliques, large potential donors may be in the same clique or different cliques. If they fall in the

[9] Some caution must be applied to this finding as the underlying distribution of the dependent variable is not normal, contrary to a major assumption of the F-test for comparing variances.

same clique, the probability of being in the same organizer network goes up; if they fall in different cliques, the probability of being in the same organizer network is zero. Highly cliqued groups have two steps of random processes operating, rather than one, and will therefore have a larger stochastic component – and hence variance – in the process of network formation.

However, this is a secondary finding when compared to the main result that number of cliques had no effect on mean levels of contribution by groups. Do these findings lead us to dismiss the likelihood of any such effect? Two considerations prevent us from confidently reaching that conclusion. The first is that nonrejection of the null is not the same thing as acceptance of the null. This is particularly the case for the simulated data we have produced. Although differences among levels of cliquing were not statistically significant, they were relatively clear and in a direction that makes sense. More cliques meant less collective action. Perhaps more clearly, more cliques meant greater variance between groups in the amount of collective action.

The second consideration is that the logic for negative effects of cliquing on collective action is quite strong when the level of cliquing is taken to an extreme. We have already noted that because our selected levels of mode and spread allowed the largest organizer networks to reach 20 members, the smallest cliques we allowed for this analysis also numbered 20. Consider, however, the effect of removing this constraint. In that case we might have as many as 200 cliques of 2 persons each. Under these conditions we might not be able to maintain the density of social ties that existed with a mode of 4, and results would not really be comparable. However, we might further assume that all members of all cliques are, in fact, tied to each other, creating the greatest possible density. Under these extreme conditions it is hard to see how any collective action would ever emerge from any of the groups. There would have to be two enormously resourceful and interested individuals sorted into one of the 2-person cliques through a random process for a clique to produce collective action, and this is an event of extremely low probability.

More generally, if there are enough cliques that no clique is larger than the minimum critical mass, no collective action can ensue. This may interact with the heterogeneity of resources; for example, when heterogeneity is high enough for one person to provide the good, cliquing cannot have an effect. Pursuing these interactions is difficult within the simulation model we have used, and we leave this question to further research.

Taking these two considerations together, we believe that our conclusions should be temperate. All in all, it seems that within moderate, and therefore realistic, levels of cliquing, the effects of cliquing on expected levels of collective action are at most very small and possibly nil. The lack of effect probably stems from the fact that randomly assigned social networks within cliques are as likely to be as large as are those within uncliqued groups – with the largest networks reaching the identical high numbers. Since the placement of individuals within cliques is also random, there is probably little mean difference between the networks generated with and without cliques. This means that the basis for cliquing is crucial. As we have mentioned, cliques are almost never based on random sorting in the real social world. Instead, similar individuals tend to group together. There is every reason to suppose that these cliques frequently correlate with interest and/or resources. The rich know mostly other rich. Those committed to a cause are friends with similarly committed individuals. When such correlation exists, it becomes more likely that some social network within, for example, a rich clique, will contain several individuals with substantial resources. If those in the clique also share interests, as they generally do, cliquing may increase collective action rather than decrease it.

It appears that cliques can substantially affect collective action only because they can influence the composition of organizer social networks or because they can limit the sizes of those networks. Without these secondary processes, the "pure" effect of cliquing is either small or nonexistent.

6. Selectivity in social networks

As we have developed our understanding of how organizers would use their social networks in mobilizing collective action, we have come to understand the importance of the process we have called "selectivity." Selectivity is the ability to focus mobilizing efforts on the members of a population who are most likely to contribute or who are likely to contribute the most. Once we assume that collective action usually involves selected members of a population rather than a whole population, we need to develop some systematic theory regarding how processes of selection interact with group characteristics and mobilization strategies. In this chapter, we develop two alternate approaches to modeling the selection process and provide detailed quantitative analysis of the complex interactions they imply. Both models require many simplifying assumptions, so neither is particularly realistic. Nevertheless, each illuminates the dynamics of situations approximated by the model.

Consider the decisions being made by an organizer in the field. If she can afford to contact everyone in her network, she does, and there is no selection involved. But suppose that organizing costs are high and her resources are low. Then she can only contact some fraction of the people she knows and could potentially organize. Whom will she contact? Most often, past theorizing has implicitly assumed that organizers randomly pick targets. This assumption is implicit in the use of the group mean as the estimate for the amount of contribution the organizer can expect to get from each contacted participant – as if she randomly chooses from her network. But random choice would be silly and wasteful. Instead, an organizer operating under resource constraints should approach those individuals whose contributions are most certain or seem likely to be largest. That would maximize outputs of contributions for inputs of resources spent on organizing. Posed this way, the process of selection is obvious: the organizer should rank order all the members of her social network according to their expected contributions and choose as many as she can afford to contact, beginning at the top and proceeding down the list until she runs out of resources to put into organizing.

Selectivity as information

Note that the organizer's preferred behavior is completely dependent on having the information she needs to rank the members of her network. In all of the analyses to this point we have assumed that organizers have such knowledge, not only about the individuals in their own networks, but about all other group members. Here we move beyond this simplification and begin to develop an understanding of the role of information in collective action.[1]

In this chapter, the larger interest group recedes and attention is focused on the organizer's network. Of course, the characteristics of the total interest group always constrain the characteristics of networks, but we simplify our analysis by ignoring these. We assume that the interest group is large enough to impose no size constraint on the network, and that its distribution of potential contributions is always identical to the network's. It should also be noted that when we understand the factors that differentiate networks, we also understand much of the differences between groups, since the level of collective action in each group is determined by the level of collective action of its most successful network.

As before, we assume that every individual has an expected contribution of size r_i; we make no assumptions about the individual process that creates r_i, but we do assume that it is determinate for each person (or that the organizer is an expected value maximizer who is not worried about risk). An organizer is assumed to have a total amount of fixed resources r_o, and the total cost of organizing is linear with k, the number mobilized.[2] If c is the cost per person mobilized, then the total cost of mobilizing is kc. Thus, an organizer can afford to mobilize $k = r_o/c$ people. We assume

---

[1] In Chapter 7, the notion of imperfect accuracy is modeled as choosing among distributions with different means, but not knowing about the specific people within those distributions.

[2] We are very much aware that this is actually a highly restrictive and unrealistic assumption, although it may sound plausible to many readers. We use it to gain purchase on the general problem. When our analysis is understood, it will be readily apparent that it could be elaborated and extended by analyzing a variety of functional forms for organizing costs. See Chapter 8 for more on this issue.

that the production function is linear or accelerating, so that the organizer's payoff is maximized by maximizing the number mobilized, subject to the organizer's resource constraint. We also assume that k is large enough to make mobilizing profitable rather than unprofitable. Thus, we focus only on the number mobilized and the size of their contributions, without worrying about the organizer's total payoff. Obviously, if the production function is not accelerating, or there are concerns about whether the organizer can mobilize enough people to pass the profit threshold in the production function, the results in this chapter would have to be merged with a production function analysis to generate predictions.

Some numerical examples

To understand the actual effects predicted by the theoretical models developed in this chapter, we need to work with plausible numerical examples. Because the probability distribution for potential contributions is always different for every mobilization, every network, and every organizer, it and the effects of selectivity will vary greatly across empirical cases. However, we can get a feel for how and when selectivity can play an important role in mobilization by examining a variety of numerical examples with varying degrees of heterogeneity. Although our exact numerical results depend on our choice of examples, we can identify systematic relationships that transcend them.

Our examples are a family of standardized two-parameter lognormal distributions.[3] We use this family because it is nonnegative, has varying skew, and is mathematically tractable. Contributions of time or money cannot be negative and are usually quite skewed, with many people giving little or nothing and a few giving a great deal. A two-parameter lognormal cannot take on the value zero, but it can have a mode that is a very close approximation to zero. To focus attention on the shape of the distribution,

---

[3] Lognormals are distributions of variates whose natural logs have a normal distribution. They have a lower limit of zero. Their skewness and kurtosis (peakedness) both increase as the standard deviation increases. A lognormal with mean equal to its standard deviation is a close approximation to an exponential distribution. Using our standardized curves with mean 1 and standard deviation expressed as a proportion of the mean, when the standard deviation is less than .3 of the mean, the normal and lognormal are rough approximations of each other. For larger standard deviations, normal curves would necessarily have part of their range below zero, which is inappropriate for a contribution distribution. A lognormal of the same standard deviation essentially piles the lower part of a normal distribution into a large mode just above zero and has a longer positive tail.

Table 6.1. *Lognormal distributions with mean 1*

		Standard deviation					
Cumulative probability	Top fraction	0.3	0.8	1	3	10	20
0.01	0.99	0.48	0.15	0.10	0.009	0.001	0.000
0.05	0.95	0.59	0.25	0.18	0.026	0.003	0.001
0.1	0.9	0.66	0.32	0.24	0.046	0.006	0.002
0.2	0.8	0.75	0.43	0.35	0.089	0.016	0.006
0.3	0.7	0.82	0.54	0.46	0.144	0.033	0.014
0.4	0.6	0.89	0.66	0.58	0.217	0.058	0.027
0.5	0.5	0.96	0.78	0.71	0.32	0.10	0.051
0.6	0.4	1.03	0.94	0.88	0.47	0.17	0.094
0.7	0.3	1.12	1.13	1.10	0.71	0.31	0.18
0.8	0.2	1.23	1.42	1.43	1.14	0.61	0.40
0.9	0.1	1.40	1.93	2.06	2.23	1.58	1.17
0.95	0.05	1.55	2.49	2.79	3.87	3.44	2.84
0.99	0.01	1.90	4.02	4.93	10.87	14.89	15.04
0.995	0.005	2.04	4.80	6.06	15.88	25.45	27.70
0.999	0.001	2.38	6.89	9.30	34.64	76.81	97.55
0.9995	0.0005	2.52	7.93	10.99	46.93	118.04	159.18
0.9997	0.0003	2.63	8.75	12.35	58.036	159.46	224.25
0.9998	0.0002	2.72	9.48	13.59	69.101	204.15	297.18
Mode		0.879	0.476	0.354	0.032	0.001	0.0001

Note: Entries in the body of the table are the values associated with a given cumulative probability. The top fraction is 1 minus the cumulative probability.

we standardize all examples to mean 1, so that the standard deviation is expressed as a proportion of the mean.

Table 6.1 and Figure 6.1 show the distributions that we will use in our examples. All have mean 1 and standard deviations varying from a very low .3 through .8, 1, 3, a very high 10, and an extremely high 20. In Figure 6.1, note that the skew and kurtosis for σ of 10 and 20 are so extreme that their modes near zero cannot be plotted on a scale that includes their right tails, but their shapes are comparable to that for $\sigma = 3$, only more extreme. Reading Table 6.1, if the standard deviation is 1, the median (cumulative probability equals .5) is about 71% of the mean, and the mode is about 35% of the mean. About 5% (top fraction equals .05) would be expected to contribute 280% or more of the mean level, and 1 in 5,000 (top fraction equals .0002) would contribute more than 1,350% of the mean. This standardized table can be used for any mean simply by multiplying all values by the mean. For example, continuing to use a standard

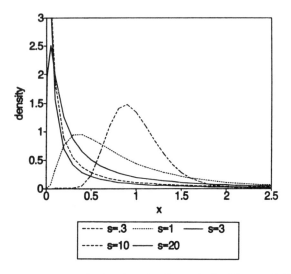

Figure 6.1. Density functions for six standardized lognormal distributions used in examples. Mean $\mu = 1$ for all; standard deviation s for each is indicated in legend.

deviation of 1, if the mean contribution were expected to be $10, the median would be $7.10, the modal contribution would be $3.54, and so forth.

Inspection of this table and figure shows the effects of heterogeneity on the contribution distribution, when the mean is constant. It is especially instructive to compare the modes, medians, and the upper tails of the distributions. When the standard deviation is low, most contributions cluster around the mean, and even the largest contributions are only two or three times the size of the smallest. As the heterogeneity goes up in these skewed distributions, the typical contribution gets closer to zero, while the largest contributions can be hundreds of times greater than the mean level.

The range of variation in these examples is entirely plausible. In the United States, income (individual or household) has a roughly lognormal distribution with a standard deviation about .8 of the mean,[4] so this distribution might approximate monetary contributions from the general pop-

---

[4] Income is only approximately lognormally distributed, so this equation cannot be used to give exact estimates of mean or median incomes, but the degree of heterogeneity used in this example will give a good idea of what can be expected when contributions of money are drawn from national samples.

ulation, if expected contribution is some constant proportion of income. The least heterogeneous distribution ($\sigma = .3$) might approximate fundraising in a middle-class school district, where nearly all parents contribute some money, but no one's contributions are extremely large. By contrast, in the most skewed distribution ($\sigma = 20$), most people contribute essentially nothing and a few contribute a great deal. If the units are dollars, this would say that the vast majority give almost nothing, 10% give a dollar or more, 1% give $15 or more, one in 1,000 gives $100 or more, and one in 5,000 gives $300 or more. If the units are hours per year spent volunteering, the highest contribution level (297) works out to about 6 hours a week, which is a quite plausible upper value in a distribution where the mean is an hour a year. As extreme as these distributions may seem, even more extreme distributions are entirely plausible.

Model 1: targeting the big by eliminating the small contributors

We will explore the effects of selectivity using two different models that make different assumptions. For our first model, we imagine an organizer who can afford to contact only a relatively small proportion of a larger group. (Recall that we assume that there is a per capita organizing cost.) In this model, selectivity is information that permits the organizer to eliminate some of the group as known low contributors and thus pick only from among those known to have larger contribution levels. But even after some are eliminated, the remaining pool of "high" contributors is heterogeneous and too large for the organizer to be able to contact all of them.

We may now formalize this conception. The organizer has a network of n people, each of whom has a potential contribution size r he will make if asked; these potential contribution sizes have density function $f(r)$ with mean μ and standard deviation σ. The organizer is resource constrained, and she can afford to mobilize $k = r_o/c$ members of her network. For this model, we must assume that k is substantially smaller than n throughout the range of possible choices. If the organizer has no information about network members' expected contributions, she chooses contributors randomly. In this case, her expectation for the contribution of any one individual is μ and the expected contribution of k individuals is $k\mu$. What she would like is information that would permit her to focus her efforts on those who will make the largest contributions. In this first conception, however, she cannot provide an exact rank ordering of all potential contributors. Instead, she has *partial* information that permits her to sort the network into larger and smaller potential contributors. In our example, an organizer might know that the affected managers in the city's department of administration, for which she works, all have more to lose and more resources than the affected clerks, but she cannot differentiate among persons within these groups. Or she may be able to sort the list of all city employees into those who do and do not live in the suburbs (thus separating those who are likely to make substantial contributions from those who are not) but cannot further distinguish among those who live in the suburbs.

Reflecting this idea, our mathematical model assumes that the organizer can accurately divide the n people in her network into two nonoverlapping subsets: the subset "High," which contains the m individuals whose r_i are largest, and the subset "Low," whose $n - m$ individuals all have smaller r_i than those in High. The organizer knows who is in High and who is in Low, but cannot rank order the individuals within the subsets. This information is quite imprecise, but it does have the advantage of narrowing the focus of the organizer's efforts. Even if m is significantly larger than k, the ability to eliminate the subset Low of small contributors will increase the total contribution she can obtain with her resources. As long as $k < m$, making subset High smaller and smaller (and m smaller and smaller) will always increase the total contribution the organizer can mobilize, as mobilizing can be restricted ever more narrowly to the largest potential contributors. Thus, organizers may choose to expend resources in gathering more precise information about their network members. The analysis we develop in this section requires that the information is always partial and k is always substantially smaller than m. If the information gets good enough for attention to be focused on exactly the best k contributors, the model in this section will not apply, but our second model will.

Selection ratio

Our measure of the degree of selectivity is the fraction $w = (n - m)/n$, which we term the *selection ratio*. The ratio indicates what portion of the organizer's network is in subset Low and has been withdrawn from his target group. If w is .5, the lowest half of the distribution has been withdrawn, and mobilization focuses on the top half. If w is .95, the lowest

95% of the distribution has been withdrawn, and mobilization focuses on the top 5%. The minimum of w is zero, which means that there is no selection and the whole network is the target of mobilization. The maximum w is $(n - k)/n$. At this maximum point, the organizer has identified the k largest contributors and R_k is maximized. As n increases to very large numbers and m is very small relative to n, the selection ratio w approaches 1 as a limit.

Selectivity inflation function

$R_{k|w}$ is the expected total contribution from k individuals selected from a network with selectivity w, that is, from which the lowest w have been eliminated. A total can always be expressed as the product of the number of elements and their mean, so we can write

$$R_{k|w} = k\mu_w, \tag{1}$$

where k is the number of contributors and where μ_w stands for the mean of the selected subset when selectivity is w. We may define the *selectivity inflation function* for a given organizer, $S_f(w)$, as the ratio of μ_w to μ. The selectivity inflation function shows how much the average contribution level is improved by restricting mobilization to the selected subset. It is important to remember that each different density function $f(r)$ will have a different $S_f(w)$ function, and that the density function f is always specific to a particular organizer's network. If $f(r)$ is continuous and differentiable, $S_f(w)$ will be a continuous and differentiable function of w. The derivative of $S_f(w)$ with respect to w is always positive, so that increasing the selectivity always increases the inflation function.

When selectivity w is 0, the selectivity inflation function $S_f(w)$ is 1: that is, when there is 0 selection, the organizer chooses targets from the whole group, and the selected mean equals the total network mean. When the selectivity w is small, $S_f(w)$ is only slightly greater than 1. As the selectivity increases and the target of mobilization narrows, $S_f(w)$ gets larger; its maximum varies with $f(r)$, m, and n. We will be exploring the interrelation among these factors in this chapter.

We may use the selectivity inflation function to obtain a new expression for the mean of the selected fraction of a distribution:

$$\mu_w = \mu S_f(w), \tag{2}$$

that is, the mean of the selected fraction equals the overall mean (μ) times the selectivity multiplier. It is then a straightforward matter to write a new expression for the expected total contribution of the selected fraction:

$$R_{k|w} = k\mu_w = k\mu S_f(w). \tag{3}$$

This equation says that the expected total contribution from the selected fraction of an organizer's network equals the number of contributors times the overall mean potential contribution level of the network as a whole times the selectivity inflation function for that selection level (which is of course specific to the particular network's distribution of potential contributions).

In this chapter, all distributions are assumed to be lognormal with $\mu = 1$, and $S_\sigma(w)$ is the selectivity inflation function for the lognormal with the given standard deviation. For example, $S_{.8}(w)$ refers to the S function for the standardized lognormal distribution with mean 1 and standard deviation .8. Table 6.2 and Figure 6.2 show $S_\sigma(w)$ for our example distributions.[5] In understanding the logic of S, it may be helpful to examine Figure 6.3, which is a different way of plotting the distributions shown in Figure 6.1. Instead of the density functions shown in Figure 6.1, Figure 6.3 represents the same distributions as reflected ogives (cumulative probability distributions), with the cumulative probability on the horizontal axis and the variate (x) on the y-axis. Expressed this way, it can be seen that the S function for a distribution is the same general shape as its reflected ogive, except that the S function is always greater, as the S associated with each x is the weighted mean of all the values greater than x.

We may use Table 6.2 to give an example of the effect of selectivity on the total contribution level. If the standard deviation σ is .8 and the selectivity level is .5, we look up $S_{.8}(.5)$ in the table and find 1.52. This says that if we withdraw the bottom half of the network, the mean potential contribution of the selected top half of this organizer's network is 1.52 times the overall network mean, or 50% larger. For this same distribution, $S_{.8}(.8)$ equals 2.23, indicating that when the selectivity level is .8 and 80% of the distribution is withdrawn from the target, the mean of the selected 20% of the distribution is over twice the size of the overall network mean. We may translate these numbers into total contributions by assuming that the mean contribution is $10 (and, thus, the standard deviation is $8), and

---

[5] The values in Table 6.2 are numerical approximations. It will be clear that the arguments we develop do not depend on the accuracy of these computations.

Table 6.2. *Selection inflation functions for lognormal distributions with mean 1 (numerical approximations)*

Selection level	Standard deviation					
	0.3	0.8	1	3	10	20
0	1.00	1.00	1.00	1.00	1.00	1.00
0.1000	1.05	1.09	1.09	1.11	1.11	1.11
0.2000	1.09	1.18	1.19	1.24	1.25	1.24
0.3000	1.14	1.28	1.31	1.41	1.43	1.42
0.4000	1.18	1.39	1.44	1.61	1.66	1.66
0.5000	1.23	1.52	1.60	1.88	1.98	1.98
0.6000	1.29	1.69	1.80	2.25	2.44	2.45
0.7000	1.36	1.91	2.08	2.81	3.17	3.21
0.8000	1.46	2.23	2.49	3.78	4.56	4.70
0.9000	1.62	2.83	3.28	5.98	8.14	8.71
0.9500	1.77	3.48	4.19	9.09	14.02	15.69
0.9900	2.11	5.27	6.83	21.26	43.74	54.77
0.9950	2.26	6.17	8.21	29.45	68.13	89.63
0.9990	2.59	8.53	12.04	58.20	173.67	255.63
0.9995	2.73	9.71	14.03	76.62	254.08	389.97
0.9997	2.84	10.62	15.59	92.54	330.26	526.48
0.9998	2.92	11.41	16.97	107.81	408.61	663.44

Note: The "selection level" is equivalent to the "top fraction" in Table 6.1. Entries in the table are the values of the selection inflation function, which is the mean for the portion of the distribution between that point and positive infinity.

that $k = 100$ people can be contacted. If there is no selection, the expected total contribution is $k\mu = 100(\$10) = \$1,000$. If there is enough information to restrict mobilization to the top half of the distribution ($w = .5$), the expected contribution is $k\mu S_{.8}(.5) = 100(\$10)(1.52) = \$1,520$, an increase of $520. If mobilization can be restricted to the top fifth of the distribution ($w = .8$), the expected contribution is $k\mu S_{.8}(.8) = 100(\$10)(2.23) = \$2,230$, an increase of $1,230. Thus, even when the heterogeneity is moderate and the information is only partial, expected contributions can be substantially increased.

It should be noted that the selection inflation function we have defined approaches infinity and becomes meaningless as the population size n approaches infinity or w approaches 1. At this mathematical extreme, the selected subset is distorted by the discrepancy between infinite theoretical distributions and finite actual populations of people. However, we conduct our analysis within the range of plausible population sizes and selection

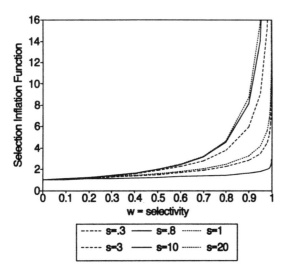

Figure 6.2. Selection inflation function (S) for six standardized lognormal distributions with mean $\mu = 1$ and standard deviation s indicated in legend.

ratios, and within this range, the selectivity inflation function stays within reasonable and interpretable limits.

Basic relationships

Table 6.2 can be used to see the general effect of the selectivity inflation function and how it is affected by the selection ratio and the dispersion and skew of the population of a network. We have seen in previous chapters how important these factors are at the level of the group and thus know that our analysis of selectivity must explicitly examine its association and interaction with network heterogeneity.

Inspection of Table 6.2 reveals several patterns. The most obvious pattern is that most of the action is in the right-hand tails: when selection is high (greater than .8), all inflation functions shoot up, and they go higher the greater the heterogeneity. More specifically, both w and σ are positively related to S, and additionally w and σ have a strong positive interaction effect so that w has a much stronger effect when σ is high, and conversely. Substantively, this says that the effects of selection are most pronounced when selection is very high, that is, when mobilizing efforts can be targeted

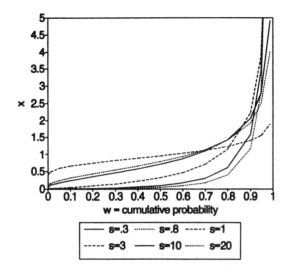

Figure 6.3. Six standardized lognormal distributions plotted as reflected cumulative probability distributions; each has mean $\mu = 1$ and standard deviation s as shown in legend.

on a very small fraction of the distribution. Furthermore, the effects are greater the greater the group's heterogeneity.

It is important to remember that this analysis holds the *mean* contribution constant and thus the overall group (and network) total contribution also constant. For a given mean, more heterogeneous groups have more of both larger contributors and very small contributors. As heterogeneity increases, the mean for the withdrawn Low subset is lower, and the mean for the selected High subset is higher.

The partial derivative of the payoff R with respect to the selection w is

$$\partial_w(R) = \mu k d S_f(w). \tag{4}$$

This derivative is always positive; selection always helps. For the more heterogeneous groups, the inflation function is also accelerating (positive second derivative) through most of its range, so that a change in selection has a greater effect the more selection there already is. When σ is relatively low and the curve is bell shaped, as it is for normal distributions and lognormals with small standard deviations, there is a relatively flat portion of the curve near zero, and selection across this portion of the curve improves the payoff but at a declining rate, until the edge of the bell is reached. The second derivative of S is negative for normal curves for $w < .295$. For lognormals, the second derivative is negative for $w < .17$ for $\sigma = .3$, for $w < .03$ for $\sigma = 1$, and for $w < .0005$ for $\sigma = 3$; for $\sigma = 10$ and 20, the second derivative of S is always positive within the range of our numerical calculations. Once the initial low flat portion of the curve (if any) has been surpassed, selection has an accelerating effect on the total payoff.

At this point, we may make a few interesting static comparisons, always remembering that these require the assumptions we laid out at the beginning of this section. When the organizer's resources are limited and constraining, the information to exercise greater selectivity always improves the total contribution. The more narrowly organizers are able to identify a small circle of large contributors, the greater total contribution they can obtain for their efforts. For any given level of information permitting selectivity greater than zero, the total contribution will be greater the *more* heterogeneous the group. And, finally, the increment in total contributions from more information is always greater the greater the group's heterogeneity.

It is important to review the assumptions and logic that lead to these results. The mean for all these curves is the same. If there is zero selection and k individuals are chosen randomly, their expected total contribution is the same regardless of the degree of heterogeneity. But if there is any selection, the expected total contribution is greater the greater the heterogeneity. The reason for this is quite straightforward and not dependent on our examples. If the mean is constant, increased heterogeneity means both that the largest potential contributions are bigger and that the smallest potential contributions are smaller. Thus, for any $w,$ the contribution level of those withdrawn is lower the greater the heterogeneity, and by necessity the average contribution level of those selected is higher. The heterogeneity effect is zero if there is no selection and quite small if the selection level is low. But if the selection level is .5 or more, the effect of heterogeneity on the expected contribution level becomes substantial. If the selection level is greater than .9, the heterogeneity effect becomes enormous.

Increasing k versus increasing w. Our discussion so far has ignored information costs and simply noted that greater selectivity increases the total contribution of a given number of contributors. But, of course, information may not be costless.   If we are to model the strategic choices of organizers, we have to assume that they weigh the cost of obtaining more information against the increment in contributions that the information would produce.

In considering this problem, it is most reasonable to assume that resource-constrained organizers face a trade-off between k and w, that is, between how *many* people they can contact and how much information they can use to be selective in their mobilization. They can contact more people less selectively or fewer people more selectively. Thus, the "cost" of information may be understood as a reduction in k, the total number the mobilizer can afford to contact.[6]

Whether information is worth a decrement in the number mobilized depends on the relative costs of mobilizing individuals and obtaining information. This would obviously vary greatly from situation to situation, but the selectivity inflation function permits us to analyze the problem. Recall that $R = \mu k S_f(w)$. If information is traded for number mobilized, w and S will go up, while k will go down. Using primes to denote the changed values, the total contribution will be improved in the trade as long as k'/k is greater than $S(w)/S(w')$. If we begin with zero selectivity, $w = 0$ and $S = 1$, and by substitution, $R = \mu k$. In this initial case, the total R is increased as long as k'/k is greater than $1/S(w')$.

Working with Table 6.2, it is readily seen that a given change in w produces a bigger change in S for more heterogeneous groups. Thus, in more heterogeneous groups, information can cost more – in terms of reducing the number contacted – and still be worthwhile because of the greater increase in S. Another way of saying this is that information with a given fixed cost is more likely to be worthwhile in a more heterogeneous group. At the other extreme, if the group is homogeneous, increasing the selectivity does *not* increase S, and information is not worth any reduction in k.

Thus, the question is whether the information is worth its cost in a particular instance. We may analyze this problem systematically by defining a cost function Q as the fraction k'/k, where k' is the smaller number contacted selectively, and Q expresses this smaller number as a proportion of k, the number the organizer can afford to contact unselectively. We let

---

[6] Notice that this question is meaningful only if we assume, as we have, that k is enough smaller than m that either k or w can change without imposing a constraint on the other.

Q be any *inverse* function of w and write $Q(w)$. If Q declines proportionately with w, $Q(w) = 1 - w$. Figure 6.4 shows this cost function and two others plotted against distributions of $1/S$. When the cost function is always below $1/S$, as it is for all distributions in subplot (a) for $Q = 1 - w$, no level of information is worth the price, and an unselective mobilization strategy is preferred. There is a minimum at $w = 1$ in this case; the greater the selectivity, the worse the total payoff. At the opposite extreme, if the cost function is always above $1/S$, as it is for all but the least skewed distribution in subplot (b) for $Q = 1 - .5w$, the payoff steadily increases with selectivity, just as it does when the information is costless. Finally, when the cost function crosses the $1/S$ curve, as it does in subplot (c) where $Q = 1 - w^2$, information is profitable for the regions for which $1/S$ is below the cost function, and not profitable for those above.

To find the optimum selectivity level that maximizes the total contribution within the profit range, we now interpret k as a constant and write a revised equation for R:

$$R = \mu k Q(w) S_f(w). \tag{5}$$

The derivative of R with respect to w is

$$dR/dw = \mu k[S_f(w)dQ(w) + dS_f(w)Q(w)]. \tag{6}$$

This derivative equals zero when

$$S_f(w)/dS_f(w) = - Q(w)/dQ(w), \tag{7}$$

that is, when the ratio of the selectivity function to its derivative equals the negative of the ratio of the cost function to its derivative. (Recall that the derivative of the cost function must be negative, so its negation is positive.) When the cost function is always above or below $1/S$, minima and maxima occur at the extremes of $w = 0$ and $w = 1$. When the cost function is intermediate relative to $1/S$, the maximum occurs at the point at which the expected value of another contributor, $S_f(w)$, is large enough relative to dS, the marginal improvement in S, to make another contributor worth more than an increase in the average level of contributions.

The overriding determinant of our results in this section is the cost of information relative to the cost of mobilizing. When information is cheap relative to the cost per individual contacted, more information is

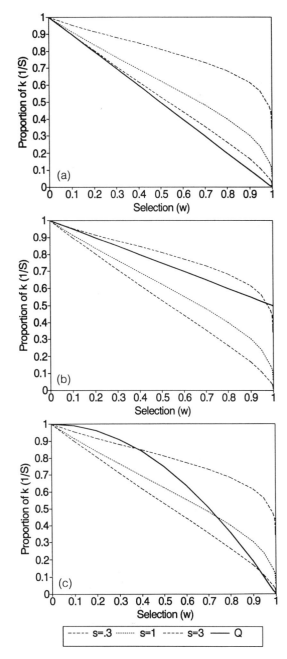

Figure 6.4. Trade-off between cost of information (Q) and value of information expressed as $1/S$ for three standardized distributions with mean $\mu = 1$ and standard deviations s as shown in legend. The value of information exceeds its cost when the $1/S$ curve is below the Q curve. (a) $Q = 1 - w$; (b) $Q = 1 - 0.5w$; (c) $Q = 1 - w^2$.

always better, up to the limits of our model.[7] Readily available inexpensive information is always worthwhile if the target population is heterogeneous and is more worthwhile the more heterogeneous the population. Conversely, when the per capita cost of information is expensive relative to the per capita cost of mobilizing, zero information and unselective mobilization are always preferable.

When the cost of information is moderate in terms of the reduction in how many people can be mobilized, there is an optimum amount of information to obtain. Information is worth more when little has already been obtained. As the amount of information increases, a point is reached where its cost in further loss of contributors is not offset by the benefit it produces in the average contribution level.

Our results also show a strong interaction between information costs and a group's heterogeneity. The more heterogeneous the population, the more costly information can be and still be worth obtaining. In an extremely heterogeneous population, it can even be worthwhile to pay for information that requires a proportionate or greater decrease in the number of people mobilized.

Model 2: the trade-off between number mobilized and network size

To this point, we have assumed both that organizers' resources are small relative to the target population, so that only a small fraction of the network can be contacted, and that information was incomplete, permitting only the distinction between the upper and lower fractions of a distribution. In this section, we change assumptions and thus change the kinds of situations we are modeling. Instead of partial incomplete information about a network, we assume full information about the initial network. That is, we assume that the organizer can perfectly rank everyone in her network by their expected contribution size. What was problematic in the previous section is unproblematic here. If the organizer has a network of size n and she can afford to contact k of them, she will certainly contact the top k/n

---

[7] Recall that, in this section, we assume that the network is large enough relative to k and w that they can be treated as independent, i.e., that w is not so high that everyone in the selected subset can be contacted.

fraction of the distribution. Thus, the contacted population equals the selected population and $k = m$.

In this second model, we take a quite different approach to selectivity. We still work with the effects of selectivity as captured by w. However, w is not an independent factor, but rather itself depends on k and n, with $w = 1 - k/n$. The selectivity inflation functions given in Table 6.2 can be used to show how the fraction k/n (i.e., $1 - w$) and the distribution of r mutually determine the total contribution and can be used to make predictions of differences between groups.

In this model we return to the image of the organizer's network as part of a larger interest group. We assume that she has full information about people *within* her network, but zero information about group members outside her network. For example, a firefighter may know all about each of her fellow affected firefighters, but nothing specific about affected police officers. In this conception, the organizer may bring someone into her network by obtaining information about that person that permits her to unambiguously insert that person in her ranking of network members. Our organizer therefore considers whether to spend all her resources contacting the top k members of the existing network or instead to expend some resources on expanding n, the network size, by getting information about new people. As before, we assume that the organizer's resources are limited and interchangeable, so that expending resources on expanding the network entails costs in reducing k, the number contacted.

To simplify the problem, we assume that the statistical distribution of the larger interest group is the same as that of current network, that is, the same mean, the same standard deviation, and the same form. This assumption is unrealistic, but it provides a useful baseline.

The expression for the total contribution generated by this selection process is similar to that of the previous section, but its interpretation is more complex because now $w = 1 - m/n = 1 - k/n$. The total contributed by k individuals whose mean is μ_w still equals $k\mu_w = k\mu S_f(w)$. Obviously, increasing k has a simple positive effect on the total: more contributors contribute more. However, there are also indirect effects operating through the selection inflation function, which consist of a positive effect for n and a negative effect for k.

The indirect effect of increasing n is always positive because it reduces the selection ratio and thus increases μ_w. If n increases, w increases, and so do S_f and μ_w. That is, getting information about one more person and adding him to an organizer's network increases the total expected contribution. This effect is not because more people contribute; that is explicitly ruled out in the definitions of terms. Rather, it arises because there is a chance that this new person will contribute more than the worst contributor among those previously selected.

In addition to its direct positive effect, increasing k also has an indirect *negative* effect on μ_w. This arises because our assumptions now mean that *by definition* selectivity declines as the number contacted increases. This indirect negative effect is always smaller than the positive direct effect, of course, since the net effect of increasing k and adding a contributor must always be positive. However, as the size of the indirect negative effect varies, the marginal value of an increase in k varies. We will show that, under some conditions, the marginal value of k can even be less than that of n, and gaining information and adding a network member (who may or may not turn out to be a good contributor) can be worth more than contacting someone already in the network. If it is recognized that the *expected* contribution of an unknown person from the larger group must be the group mean μ, it can be seen intuitively that this situation arises when the worst two contributors of the selected k from the existing network would together contribute less than μ. This condition arises when k is large relative to n so that very small contributors are selected. When the distribution is skewed, there are many potential contributions that fall far below the mean.

To address this issue formally, it will be helpful to consider the partial derivatives of R with respect to k and n. We begin by rewriting equation (3) in terms of k/n, where $k/n = 1 - w$:

$$R(k/n) = k\mu_w = k\mu S_f(k/n). \tag{8}$$

The partial derivatives are

$$\partial_k(R) = \mu[S_f(k/n) + (k/n)dS_f(k/n)] \tag{9}$$

and

$$\partial_n(R) = -\mu[dS_f(k/n)k^2/n^2]. \tag{10}$$

Comparing ∂k and ∂n

Since n and k are in comparable units of whole people, it is meaningful to compare their partial derivatives to determine the relative value of changes in each for increasing the total contribution. Both partials are always positive, but they vary with σ and k/n (or w). The separate plots in Figure 6.5 compare the partials (divided by the mean) with respect to k (number contacted) and n (size of pool) for each of our example distributions.

These plots show that the partials for k and n cross, so that the ∂n is greater than ∂k for low selectivity (low w, high k/n), while ∂k is greater than ∂n for high selectivity (high w, low k/n). This is a very interesting result. Organizers normally want to expend their own resources so that they can mobilize more people. When the selection level is high and only a small portion of the existing network can be contacted (and there is full information about the network), this is the proper strategy. It is worth more to add another contributor than to gain information about a new person whose potential contribution level is unknown.

But the organizer's normal approach does not apply when he can afford to contact a large proportion of his existing network. When the selection level is low, obtaining full information about a new person and adding her to the network is worth more than contacting an additional person already in the network. As the series of plots shows, the curves for ∂n and ∂k cross at higher and higher selection levels as the heterogeneity σ increases. For our example distributions, the crossing point is close to zero for σ = .3, but increases as σ increases and is above $w = .8$ (i.e., $k/n = .2$) for our two most heterogeneous distributions. When heterogeneity is low, contacting more people is almost always worth more than gaining information about new people. But when heterogeneity is very high, the picture changes. After the top 20% or so of contributors have been contacted, it is worth more to gain information about new people than to keep contacting the remaining group members. This occurs, of course, because most people in these very skewed distributions are very small contributors.

Discussion of Model 2

It is perhaps worth stressing that the partial derivative for n is always positive, even when it is smaller than the partial for k. Having a larger available pool to choose from always improves the total contribution level. This is a pure "group-size" (although this time, of course, specifically a *network*-size) effect, which is completely independent of considerations of organizing cost or resource levels. It is always better to have a larger

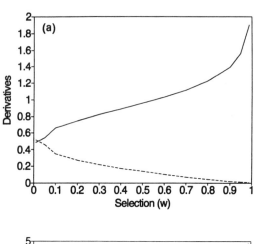

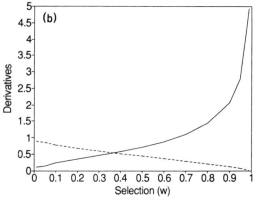

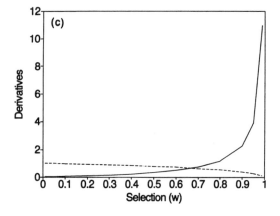

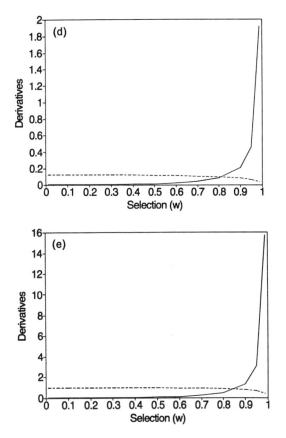

Figure 6.5. Relation between partial derivatives for N (number in network) and k (number mobilized) for standard lognormal distributions with mean $\mu = 1$ and various standard deviations. k, Solid curve; N, dashed curve. Standard deviations: (a) 0.3; (b) 1; (c) 3; (d) 10; (e) 20.

pool of potential contributors. As the figure shows, this effect is largest when selection is low and heterogeneity is high. Its upper limit is 1 (i.e., μ), which is approached for very heterogeneous distributions when the selection level is very low.

In our first model, the relative costs of information and mobilizing were the overriding determinant of the outcome. Here, we do not include a direct cost term that tells us whether the cost of a change in n is comparable to the cost of a change in k. Clearly, if one cost term is significantly greater than the other, the outcome will be determined by the relative costs. However, if they are of comparable magnitudes, we may draw the following conclusions from the present analysis.

First, when the organizer is sharply resource constrained and can afford to contact only a small fraction (10% or less) of his existing network, the value of an increment in k greatly exceeds that for n. This situation of a small k/n can also be created by a very high level of existing information that makes the network size n very large. (Recall that, in this model, the definition of a network is the set of people about whom the organizer has full information.) Thus, when only a small proportion of the existing network can be mobilized, all available resources should be spent on mobilizing, not on gathering new information about others, unless information gathering is extremely cheap relative to mobilizing. Cheap here means very cheap, that is, a per capita cost of information that is a tenth or less of the per capita cost of mobilizing.

Second, when k/n is not small (e.g., $>.1$), the values of increments in k and n are of roughly comparable magnitudes, so that even relatively small differences in the relative cost of each will exert a significant effect on the outcome.

Finally, the value of more information (a change in n) is significantly higher than the value of mobilizing another person (change in k) when nearly all of the existing network can be mobilized so that selectivity is low. Although these differences are small enough to be outweighed by differences in costs, we generally expect that information seeking about new people is worthwhile when an organizer can easily afford to contact most of the people he already knows. Furthermore, the more heterogeneous the group, the higher the values of k/n for which the value of learning about new people is greater than that of contacting existing network members.

In practical terms, when a mobilizer can afford to contact virtually everyone in her social network, it will actually be worth more to expend resources on gaining information about new people to add to the available network (even one at a time) than to contact every last person already known.

Since this can be a substantively significant result, it is useful to review the assumptions on which it rests. Most importantly, we assume in Model 2 that both the members of the existing network and everyone who is added to it are drawn randomly from the same underlying population (the total group). That is, the mean, standard deviation, and distributional form are identical for those about whom the organizer has information as well as for those about whom he knows nothing. In this case, the issue is whether a person chosen essentially randomly from the total group is likely to prove willing and able to contribute enough to compensate for losing the smallest contributions from those in the existing network. The answer from partial derivatives is basically that if a very large proportion of the existing network can be contacted, the two smallest contributors in the existing network are probably worth less than one randomly chosen member of the larger interest group. This occurs only when nearly all of the network can be mobilized if heterogeneity is low, but occurs at rather high selection levels ($k/n < .2$) if the heterogeneity is very high.

If the organizer's network is a result of previous efforts at information gathering from an unknown population, the assumption of identical distributions may approximate the truth. The assumption may also be true if the basis for the organizer's network is unrelated to the issue in question. However, the assumption that the distributions are the same is generally implausible, as the factors that would cause an organizer to know a lot about people would most likely be correlated with their potential contribution level. But, unrealistic as the assumption is, it gives us a very useful baseline. If it is known that the existing network has a lower mean contribution level than the larger interest group, the relative value of information gathering is very high, unless resources are very limited and k/n is very small.

More commonly, we would expect that the network members have a higher mean potential contribution level than the larger interest group. In this case, the value of mobilizing would generally exceed that of information gathering over most of the range of k/n. But unless they have already been heavily screened, at some point the low end of the distribution of network members will involve small enough contributions that information gathering about new people becomes worthwhile. That is, organizers who have enough resources to contact nearly everyone they know will still probably find it profitable to expend some resources on learning about people in the larger interest group.

Conclusions: selection and information

We have developed two somewhat different models for the selection process in collective action, but both models yield similar patterns of results. In this section, we talk about these general patterns and discuss their likely implications for cases that fall outside the realm of our oversimplified assumptions. We have two rather different sets of results, depending on whether we treat the level of information as given, or as something for which an organizer pays.

Static comparisons

The most important static comparison between groups or networks is always μ, the mean level of potential contributions. We have not discussed the mean much because its effect is obvious and thus theoretically uninteresting. But its practical importance is overriding. Other things being equal – or even close to equal – wealthier, more interested networks are likely to contribute more than poorer, less interested networks.

Against the baseline created by μ, the heterogeneity of a population and the organizer's level of information can have enormous effects on the prospects for collective action. If we consider two organizers who are resource constrained and can only afford to contact a small proportion of their networks, it will often be the case that more total contributions can be obtained from a network with a lower mean but high dispersion and skew than from a network with a higher mean but little variability around that mean. Another way of saying this is that it actually does not matter so much what the mean potential contribution level is for the network as a whole, but rather what it is for the *subset* of the population that the mobilizer can afford to mobilize.

Whether this is true depends on the level of information possessed by the organizers. If information is high and the mobilization is highly selective, much greater contributions can be obtained from a very heterogeneous group than from a more homogeneous group. In our first model, "high information" is translated as being able to restrict mobilizing efforts to a small upper fraction of the distribution (high w). In our second model, "high information" is translated as having full information about a very large number of people n, so that the number mobilized can be chosen as the small upper fraction of a distribution (small k/n arising from large n).

Where the "network" is understood as the people about whom the organizer has information, there is always a strong interaction between the level of information and network heterogeneity. Comparing organizers whose resources and mobilizing costs are equal (so k is equal), and whose networks have the same distribution of potential contributions, the organizer with more information will always be able to mobilize a greater total contribution, and the size of this advantage will be directly related to the degree of heterogeneity. The interpretation of this result is slightly different for our two models. In both cases, k is taken as a given. For Model 1, we assume networks of comparable sizes n and treat information as the extent to which mobilizing efforts can be restricted to a top fraction. Within the limits of the model, the greater the information, the greater the total payoff, and the magnitude of this effect interacts positively with the degree of heteroge- neity. When both information and heterogeneity are high, there is an accelerating relation, where information is worth more and more, until the limits of the model are reached.

For Model 2, we treat n as a variable, and ask how large is the network about whom the organizer has full information. The more people the organizer has information about, the larger is n and the smaller is k/n. The larger the n, the greater the information, and the higher the expected total contribution from k individuals; this effect is larger when σ is larger. The expected total accelerates as the fraction k/n declines, although each in- dividual increment to n makes a smaller and smaller difference as n in- creases, so each unit of information in the form of a new person has a declining marginal value.

Organizer's decisions

Our static comparisons treat the information level as exogenously deter- mined and show that more information is always better. We get a rather different view if we treat the organizer's level of information as under his own control and assume that the organizer makes trade-offs between mo- bilizing more people less selectively and mobilizing fewer people more selectively. Here, the cost of information can be understood as a reduction in k, the number mobilized. Although differing in their details and inter- pretations, both of our models show the same basic results.

First, the relative per capita costs of information and mobilizing always have very large effects that can dwarf other relations. When information is cheap relative to mobilizing, it is always worth having more of it; when it is expensive relative to mobilizing, it is never worth its price. Costs can never be ignored.

When the costs of information and mobilizing are of comparable orders of magnitude, we see significant optimization results that interact with the degree of group heterogeneity. In all cases, information is worth the most when there is little of it, and is always worth more the more heterogeneous the network is. In Model 1, we found that additional information is worth the price in terms of a reduction in k, up to the point where the expected contribution is high enough that the loss of a contributor is not worth the increase in the average contribution level. This point occurs at higher information levels when the heterogeneity is higher. In Model 2, we found that adding a person to the network is worth more than mobilizing a person when a high proportion of a heterogeneous network is to be mobilized (so that selection is low). The crossover point for the effects of n and k occurs at higher levels for more heterogeneous distributions.

In both interpretations, it is important to keep in mind the central role organizers' resource constraints are playing. Information matters because organizers are resource constrained and thus have the problem of maximizing total contributions for a fixed input. It is also important to recognize that, in the big picture, the degree of heterogeneity in potential contributions is subject to strategic choice. Different kinds of contributions have differing levels of heterogeneity, and different specific goals elicit differing levels of heterogeneity in interest levels. Thus, our analyses can be used to investigate the expected value of alternate action strategies.

7. Reach and selectivity as strategies of recruitment

With Ralph Prahl

Organizers typically care a great deal about the collective good and are willing to spend substantial portions of their personal resources to help get it. However, they have limited resources and time and cannot do everything at once. Thus, they have to think strategically about how they will go about recruiting others to participate. In Chapter 6, we considered two models for the effects of information on the selectivity of the recruitment process. In the present chapter we discuss the general idea of selectivity using a different mathematical strategy and explore the trade-offs organizers make between the quality and quantity of their recruits.

The existing literature focuses on two simple but related distinctions regarding recruitment strategies. The first is between strategies that concentrate on the social networks of members of the movement in order to recruit and strategies that use more impersonal methods (Gerlach and Hine 1970; Oberschall 1973; John Wilson 1973; Useem 1975; Tilly 1978; Snow, Zurcher, and Ekland-Olson 1980). The second distinction is between strategies that result in the recruitment of solidary blocs of people, such as church groups, and those that result in the recruitment of isolated individuals (J. Freeman 1973; Oberschall 1973; Fireman and Gamson 1979; Zald and McCarthy 1979; Jenkins 1982).

In this chapter we make the somewhat different, although related, analytic distinction between *reach* and *selectivity*. The reach of a recruitment strategy is the number of people who are contacted; while the selectivity of a strategy is the extent to which it contacts the portion or subgroup of the whole interest group that is most likely to make substantial contributions to the cause.

Thus defined, it is clear that any organizer would prefer both complete reach, in which she can contact all members of the group, and complete selectivity, in which only those likely to contribute the most resources are contacted. In our example, the organizer would like to contact all of the affected employees or just those employees who are the most likely to join the collective action. However, given their resource constraints, organizers often must make strategic trade-offs between the two. In other words, we assume that it is generally impossible to achieve both high reach and high selectivity.

Obviously, the opposite combination of low reach and low selectivity is to be avoided. This leaves the organizer to choose between strategies with high reach and low selectivity, or those with high selectivity but low reach. The former include mass events such as rallies, demonstrations, or meetings; population-blanketing strategies such as canvassing, leafleting, or petitioning; and advertising strategies using media such as television, newspapers, or radio. In our example, mailings and demonstrations that might get on television would fit this model. Strategies with high selectivity and low reach include personalized modes such as recruitment from social networks and grapevines. Meetings on the topic called by the relevant trade unions might serve the purpose for our employees.

A formal model of recruitment under conditions of interdependence

The simplicity of the notion of selectivity tends to disguise the fact that there are actually many desirable qualities for which potential recruits can be selected. In keeping with our general approach, however, the most important characteristics are obviously the willingness of contacts to contribute resources to the cause (interest) and their ability to do so (resources). In this chapter we attempt to determine the conditions favoring selecting for high interest levels versus those favoring selecting for high resource levels.

The model of recruitment we use represents the decision process undertaken by an organizer and is somewhat different from the models that have been presented in previous chapters. Some additional simplifications are introduced so that the effects of other complications can be analyzed. The model consists of a set of assumptions the organizer makes about the collective good that he means to provide, the members of the collectivity among whom he attempts to recruit, and the recruitment strategies among which he must choose. The organizer's costs and benefits do not themselves enter the model. However, we do make two fundamental assumptions concerning the organizer's decision process. First, as we have already noted, we assume that he is resource constrained and thus will have to make trade-offs between reach and selectivity in recruitment. We investigate the marginal benefit of each under varying circumstances. Second, we return to the assumption that the organizer has perfect information about the interests and resources of each of the group members and understands the group members' decision rules, so that he can perfectly predict how they will respond to his recruitment efforts. Beyond this, the scope conditions are the same as those in Chapter 5.

Recruitment strategies

We define a recruitment *strategy* as a package of techniques used by an organizer to communicate information about a collective action campaign to a subset of an interest group. If he has good information about the specific individuals in the group, he would prefer to pick precisely the individuals who are likely to make the biggest contributions. We have investigated the consequences of this kind of individual-level selectivity in one of the models in Chapter 6. This kind of recruitment requires that the organizer have a great deal of prior information and almost necessarily follows the lines of friendship and close personal acquaintance.

Organizers are not always able to recruit among people they already know well. Even if they have information about individuals, it may take the form of probabilities of contributing, rather than the actual amount a particular request will obtain. In Chapter 6, we modeled this situation as information that could eliminate a certain proportion of a single group as known low contributors. In this chapter, we instead imagine that organizers choose recruitment strategies that target different subgroups with different mean levels of interests or resources. For example, advertising in a newspaper targets the readers of that newspaper. A direct mail solicitation targets the people on the mailing list. Leaflets tacked to telephone poles target those who walk in the area leafleted.

We describe the subgroup targeted by a particular recruitment in terms of (N) the number of people contacted, (μ_r) the mean and (σ_r) the standard deviation of their levels of mobilizible resources, and (μ_v) the mean and (σ_v) the standard deviation of their levels of interest in the collective good. For example, recruiting through television advertisements reaches a large sample of people, but one with fairly low means and large standard deviations for both resources and interest. Recruiting at a union rally on behalf of the issue in question would probably reach a modest number of people (depending on the size of the union and rally) with relatively homogeneous interest levels and possibly more variable resource levels. Target subgroups that both are very large and have high interest and resource levels would be ideal, but the organizer normally has to make a strategic trade-off between larger target subgroups with lower and more diverse interests and resources, or smaller target subgroups with higher interest and resource levels. These trade-offs are the heart of the present analysis.

The success or failure of the recruitment drive hinges on the decisions of the set of people who are contacted, as they each interdependently decide how much, if anything, to contribute to the cause. However, because the organizer chooses the sample of people who make these decisions, the outcome of the drive depends ultimately on his choice of a recruitment strategy.

The organizer's decision

From the perspective of the organizer, the key outcome is not the decisions of targeted individuals, but the decisions of all members of the targeted subgroup as an aggregate. It is entirely possible that the organizer will be able to use her knowledge about the group and its various subgroups to predict the overall outcome of a recruitment drive without being able to predict the decisions of specific individuals. This principle is well understood in marketing and is widely employed in professional fund-raising. However, in a standard marketing problem each consumer makes an independent decision. In this analysis we consider the more complex problem of ''consumers'' who base their decisions partly on the decisions of others and partly on their expectations of how their own behavior will influence others.

Using our model of interdependent decisions to predict the aggregate contribution from a subgroup requires an iterated solution. We may picture the organizer as deriving her expectations in stages. In the first stage she expects each individual contacted to use all available information to estimate the total level of contributions with and without his own contribution and to make an initial decision about whether or not to contribute on this basis. In the second stage the organizer expects each contacted individual to calculate the decisions of all other members of the target subgroup in the first stage (using the individual's full information about the others) and to use this information to make a revised decision. This continues through subsequent stages, with individuals using the information they have calculated from the previous stage to arrive at a revised decision. Because we assume full information, the estimated *total* contribution is the same for all potential recruits at each stage, although, of course, the *individuals'* contributions will vary. Because everyone has full information, including the organizer, we imagine that the organizer is able to follow through everyone's logic and end up with a good estimate for the total contribution this subgroup can be expected to make. In the remainder of this section we develop a function to represent this process.[1]

We start by assuming that the distributions of both interest and resources across a subgroup are continuous, with probability density functions given by $v(y)$ and $r(x)$, respectively. The number of members of the target subgroup ("contacts") is represented by N. The number of contacts with interest and resource levels between any two points (p_1) and (p_2) are thus given by

$$N \int_{p1}^{p2} r(x)\, dx \qquad \text{for resources,} \tag{1a}$$

$$N \int_{p1}^{p2} v(y)\, dy \qquad \text{for interests.} \tag{1b}$$

The equilibrium total contribution is found iteratively. If only resources are a factor, the total contribution will be given by

---

[1] In some ways, this analysis is quite similar to Granovetter's (1978) threshold models of collective behavior. Because a given level of interest in the good corresponds to a given level on the production function at which an individual will be willing to contribute to it, the assumption of interest heterogeneity is equivalent to Granovetter's assumption of a distribution of threshold levels at which individuals are willing to contribute. Furthermore, the iterative solution to the problem of an equilibrium level in collective action is structurally similar to Granovetter's solution. A primary difference is that, while Granovetter assumes that each successive value of the function $F(A)$ actually occurs, here it is assumed that $F(A)$ is calculated in the minds of recruits.

$$E = N \int_0^\infty xr(x) \, dx, \tag{2}$$

which is the number of contacts times the sum of every possible value for each contact's level of resources, weighted by the probability that the value would occur. This expression simply equals N times the mean resource level, that is, the total resources of all contacts.

However, targets of recruitment are not certain to contribute. A contacted individual will contribute only if the marginal gain from his contribution exceeds the cost of his contribution, that is, if

$$v_i[P(A + r_i) - P(A)] > r_i, \tag{3}$$

where A is the "assumed" total contribution made by all other group members if i does *not* contribute.

Thus, the estimated total contribution must be weighted by the probability that each subgroup member's interest is high enough to motivate a contribution. Adding this consideration to (2) yields

$$E = N \int_{x=0}^{\infty} \int_{y=K}^{\infty} xr(x)i(y) \, dy \, dx, \tag{4}$$

where $K = x/[P(A + x) - P(A)]$.

To find the equilibrium contribution level, an initial assumed value (A) is used to calculate E. The revised value of E is then used as A in the next iteration, and the process continues until A converges to E. At equilibrium, the expected contribution is

$$E = N \int_{x=0}^{\infty} \int_{y=K}^{\infty} xr(x)i(y) \, dy \, dx, \tag{5}$$

where $K = x/[P(E + x) - P(E)]$.

Verbally, the recursive equation (5) may be interpreted in the following way: at equilibrium, the level of assumed contributions will be equal to the number of contacts times the sum of all resource values possible for each contact, weighted both by the probability that each value will occur and by the conditional probability that the contact will have a high enough interest level to want to contribute it to the cause.

Even if the explicit rounds of decisions that underlie this equation do not actually occur, it is meaningful as the equilibrium outcome of a recruitment drive: not necessarily a determinate result, but the level of total contribution at which the pressures resulting from the interdependence of contacts will be in equilibrium. An organizer would reasonably regard the solution to the equation, if there is one, as the most likely result of a particular recruitment strategy. Organizers would plausibly seek to maximize E as they choose among alternate recruitment strategies. In the remainder of this chapter we will examine the implications of this equation.

Results

We are interested in exploring how the equilibrium outcome defined by equation (5) changes as recruitment strategies are employed with higher reach (i.e., N of target subgroup) or greater selectivity (i.e., mean of resources or interest in target subgroup). The outcomes themselves, and the way they change as a function of N, μ_v, and μ_r, depend on the exact nature of the distributions $r(x)$ and $v(y)$. It is impossible to evaluate all plausible functional forms of these distributions and a very complex problem to permit both μ_v and μ_r to vary at once. For this reason, we have analyzed equation (5) in a series of cross sections, in which some things are held constant while others are varied. Our first analysis shows the effects of varying N when both μ_v and μ_r are held constant. This shows the effect of emphasizing reach in a recruitment strategy. Our second and third analyses hold individual resources and interest (and hence μ_v and μ_r) constant across the group in turn, thus permitting us to see the effects of emphasizing selectivity for interest versus selectivity for resources.

As usual, our analysis uses lognormal distributions for interest and resources. Replications with truncated normal distributions yield substantially similar results, and our detailed interpretation of the results permits us to show why the patterns of the findings do not depend on the particular distribution chosen. In this analysis we examine the effects of increasing the *mean* of a distribution and hold the shape of each distribution constant by setting its standard deviation equal to a constant proportion of the mean.

All analyses use the production function $P(R) = R^2$, that is, the payoff level of the collective good equals the square of the total contribution level. Our reasoning and general conclusions will later be shown to apply to any accelerative function. This particular choice is essentially arbitrary. We selected it because it makes the solution to equation (5) tractable and permits us to give very clear numerical examples of how the model is behaving. Substantively, this is a rather sharply accelerating function that accentuates the possibilities for contributions inducing other contributions.

Resources and interest constant: a baseline

We begin with the simplest, and perhaps the least realistic, of all possible cases, in which both interest and resources are constant across the entire group, that is, the group is homogeneous. In this case, the integrals for their cumulative distributions are replaced by constants. The contribution of each contact, should he decide to contribute at all, is simply r. Because all contacts have identical resource and interest levels, all will make the same (dichotomous) decision about whether or not to contribute. Thus, A, the assumed contribution level in equation (3), will be the amount produced if everyone else contributes, that is, $r(N - 1) = (rN - r)$. Making this substitution into (3) and rearranging terms gives

$$v > r/[P(rN) - P(rN - r)], \tag{6a}$$

which simply says that everyone's interest level has to be greater than the ratio of his contribution level to the increment in the collective good produced by the *last* contributor. Rearranging to solve for the resource level, we obtain

$$r > 1/\{v[P(rN) - P(rN - r)]\}. \tag{6b}$$

Since the units for v and r are arbitrary, but are assumed to be in the same metric, it is often more useful to rearrange the terms to obtain an expression for the ratio of resource level to interest level:

$$r/v < P(rN) - P(rN - r). \tag{6c}$$

Equation (6c) says that the ratio of resource contribution level to interest level has to be less than the difference the last contributor would make in the payoff from the collective good. Because P is accelerative, of course, treating one's own contribution as the last contribution is the most favorable assumption possible for evaluating the marginal impact of a contribution.

Our assumed production function, $P(R) = R^2$, can provide a particularly transparent case with which to illustrate how the variables affect collective action. Because this form of the accelerative production function is itself mathematically simple, we have no trouble simplifying (6a) to read

$$v > 1/[r(2N - 1)]. \tag{7a}$$

Rearranging terms to obtain the equivalent of (6c), we obtain

$$r/v < 2N - 1. \tag{7b}$$

It will also be helpful later to isolate r and N in this equation:

$$r > 1/[v(2N - 1)], \tag{7c}$$

$$N > 2(r/v + 1). \tag{7d}$$

Equation (7b) makes it clear that steeply accelerating production functions are highly favorable for simultaneous coordinated collective action. Even if $N = 1$, contribution is desirable if v simply exceeds r. As N gets larger and larger, r can exceed v by larger and larger multiples: it can be up to three times as large for $N = 2$, up to 9 times as large for $N = 5$, 39 times as large for $N = 20$, and 1,999 times as large for $N = 1,000$.

Another angle on the same relationship can be seen by considering the standard equation for the net gain of contributing to an all-or-none contract, where the gain to an individual is a function of the total contribution by all group members:

$$g = vP(R) - r. \tag{8a}$$

If a group is homogeneous, all the r's are equal and the total contribution R of all group members equals Nr. Then we may rewrite the contribution equation as

$$g = vP(Nr) - r. \tag{8b}$$

If we make the substitution $P(R) = R^2$, we obtain

$$g = v(Nr)^2 - r = vN^2r^2 - r. \tag{8c}$$

Differentiating g with respect to N, we obtain

$$dg/dN = 2vr^2N. \tag{9}$$

There is no optimum N; the derivative is zero only when N is zero (since v and r are assumed to be nonzero constants). This means that the effect of contacting one more person is larger and larger as N increases. This effect is bounded only by the finite limits on the population size. The value *to each potential recruit* of contributing to the collective action goes up as the size of the pool of potential recruits (N) goes up. Within the framework of these assumptions, *larger* target subgroups are more likely to give rise to collective action than smaller ones.

To summarize, if resources and interests are constant, there is no value in attempting to be "selective" in recruitment, and only increasing the reach of recruitment has any advantage. This is comparable to the result in Chapter 6 that selectivity has no value in homogeneous groups, and that only the number of contributors matters. If the production function is accelerating, increasing the reach of a recruitment strategy has a strong positive effect on the payoff each individual can receive from the collective good and thus on the prospects for coordinated collective action. Each additional person added above the threshold simply adds r to the expected total contribution.

Selectivity for interest

In this section of the analysis, we hold resources constant and compare the gains from increasing the reach of recruitment to the gains from increasing the selectivity for interest. This case would apply if the collective action is such that each individual who decides to contribute must necessarily make the same size contribution. This would be the case if people are being asked to march in a demonstration, sign a petition, or vote in a referendum. In such cases, the organizer cannot affect the average resource level of the target subgroup, but might employ a selective recruitment strategy focusing on those who are especially likely to be interested in the collective good. In this case, equation (5) simplifies to

$$E = NR \int_{x=K}^{\infty} v(y)\, dy, \quad \text{where } K = r/[P(E + r) - P(E)], \quad (10)$$

which may be read as the number of contacts times the resource level times the proportion whose interest is high enough to make them willing to contribute. All contributions will be of the same amount, so the only question is how many people will contribute.

We investigated the behavior of equation (8) when $v(y)$ is a lognormally distributed random variate with mean μ_v and standard deviation σ_v. A large number of "experiments" were conducted. The first step for each was to select baseline levels of N, r, μ_v and σ_v; these were generally chosen to be as low as possible without making a successful recruitment drive impossible. Then, with everything else held constant, first N and then μ_v was increased incrementally, and a plot was produced showing how its increase affected E.

The results are shown in Figure 7.1. Verbally, they may be described as follows. The plot relating number of contacts (N) to the outcome of the drive traces the x-axis until it reaches a threshold value, $T(N)$. Thereafter it forms a monotonically increasing but decelerating curve, reaching an asymptote with a slope equal to r. The curve decelerates while N increases the probability that others will contribute. As it approaches the asymptote, all N persons are already contributing, and adding a person to N simply adds (his) r to E.

The plot relating mean interest of potential recruits to the outcome of the drive shows both similar and dissimilar effects. This curve also traces the x-axis until it reaches a threshold value, $T(v)$. However, it then jumps discontinuously to a positive value. The discontinuity arises because it never happens that just one person contributes r; instead, the mean interest of the subgroup has to be high enough that a good number of people will all be motivated to contribute in one interdependent swoop. After this jump, further increases in the mean subgroup interest will increase the expected total contribution, but the curve decelerates until it reaches an asymptote with a slope of zero. Once the mean interest level is high enough to ensure that even the least interested members in the subgroup are willing to contribute, increases in μ_v add no more to the expected payoff level.

When v varies, the locations of the thresholds $T(N)$ and $T(v)$ depend on the specific form of the production function being used, as well as on the probabilistic distribution of v. They are therefore difficult to solve for directly. However, the locations of both thresholds follow a similar logic, in which changes in N or μ_v affect the probability (q) that one or more group members will have interests higher than some critical value (v_q). It is these individuals who will actually contribute at the threshold and start

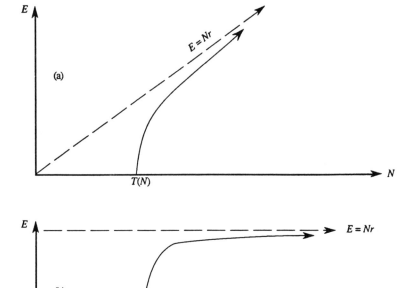

Figure 7.1. Expected outcome with resources (r) constant. (a) Effect of increasing number of recruits (N) when mean interest (μ_v) is constant. (b) Effect of increasing mean interest (μ_v) when number of recruits (N) is constant.

the ball rolling for further contributions by other group members. Increases in either μ_v or N increase the probability q.

We may illustrate these processes by considering again the relatively simple case in which $P(R) = R^2$. For this production function, the threshold value of μ_v occurs when μ_v is high enough that there is some v_q that satisfies

$$v_q > 1/r[2Nq - 1], \tag{11}$$

where the term Nq is the *number* of people in the upper tail of the interest distribution who have interest greater than v_q. When this inequality is satisfied, it means that as defined for this particular production function, there exists a large enough subset of target subgroup members with sufficiently high interest that they will actually contribute.

Similarly, the threshold value of N occurs when N is high enough that the probability function produces a sufficiently large number of target subgroup members in the tail of the interest distribution above the critical value (v_q) to form a subset for which

$$N_q > 2(r/v_q + 1). \tag{12}$$

Selectivity for resource

In this section we consider the case in which resource levels vary while interests are fixed. Although interest levels are never actually constant in real-world groups, we can conceive of a situation in which the variability in resources is high enough relative to the variability in interest levels to make interest levels act almost like a constant. This would be especially true if the group is defined so as to include only people with a known positive interest in the good, and if the collective action requires the kind of resources that are heterogeneous in the group. Collective actions requiring monetary contributions are especially likely to fall in this category, as wealth is generally distributed quite unequally. In this case, organizers attend to the average resources of different subgroups. Examples of campaigns in which selectivity for resource was dominant include the NAACP, which, for most of its formative years, emphasized contributions from whites on the grounds that they had more to offer; the "Live AID" Rock Telethon of July 13, 1985, which, according to one of its organizers (*New York Times,* July 18, 1985), concentrated on musical acts that would appeal to people in the more affluent age brackets; and "large donor" charitable fund-raising, which concentrates on the very wealthy and corporations.

When interest is held constant, equation (5) simplifies to

$$E = N \int_{x=L}^{\infty} xr(x)\, dx, \quad \text{where } L = v[P(E + x) - P(E)] \tag{13}$$

which is the number of contacts times the expected contribution of each.

The contribution expected from each contact is calculated by weighting all resource levels that are high enough to produce a contribution by the probability that those levels will occur. Here, the lower bound of the integral is a recursive but determinant expression representing the minimum amount of resources that a contact must control in order to be able to choose rationally to contribute it to the cause. At levels above the cutoff point established by this expression, a contribution will yield a profit, while at levels below the cutoff point any contribution will yield a loss.

The behavior of equation (11) was investigated through repeated experiments in a manner directly parallel to that of the previous section. Here, the first step is to specify baseline levels of N, v, μ_r, and σ_r. Then N and μ_r are each increased incrementally, and the effects on E are plotted. The main difference between the algorithms is that while the lower bound of the interest distribution can be calculated directly, the lower bound for the resource distribution must be calculated iteratively, making the numerical calculation of the solution more difficult.

The results in this section are rather different from those preceding. Consider first the effects of expanding the reach of recruitment (i.e., increasing N) as shown in Figure 7.2a. Once again there is a threshold; but here the jump is discontinuous. Because interest is constant, when N gets high enough relative to μ_r and v to make contributing rational, everyone in the subgroup contributes. From this point on, each additional unit increase in N simply adds one more contributing person to the total. Although the resource level varies randomly from individual to individual, on the average each additional subgroup member adds μ_r to the total, making the outcome E a linear function of N with slope μ_r. Comparing Figures 7.1a and 7.2a, we see that, in the two cases, the differences in the effects of increasing recruitment reach (N) are concentrated around the threshold. If interests are constant, it is always all the subgroup or none of it who contribute. When interests vary, there is a period above the threshold when only part of the targeted subgroup contributes. Once N is large enough to make it rational for even the least interested subgroup members to contribute, the linear relations between N and E in Figures 7.1a and 7.2a are identical.

The effect of selectivity for resources is very different from that of selectivity for interest. Once again there is a threshold that must be obtained. However, once this threshold is obtained, *all* members of the group

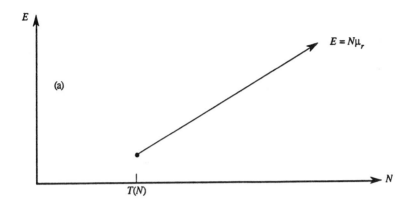

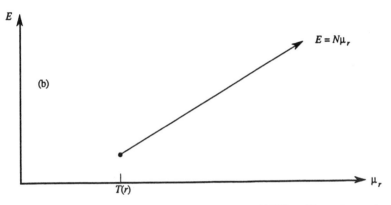

Figure 7.2. Expected outcome with interest (v) constant. (a) Effect of increasing number of recruits (N) when mean resources (μ_r) is constant. (b) Effect of increasing mean resources (μ_r) when number of recruits (N) is constant.

will be willing to contribute (since they have the same interest), and the total contribution will be $N\mu_r$. Each additional increment in μ_r raises E, the expected total contribution, by N times the size of the increment.

Because the effects of variation in resources are so much more straightforward than are those of variation in interest, it is much easier to calculate thresholds for a given production function. Returning to our simple case, in which $P(R) = R^2$, the threshold for reach (N) occurs when $N = 2(\mu_r/v + 1)$. For selectivity on resources, the threshold occurs when $\mu_r = 1/[v(2N - 1)]$.

Summary of results

It will be useful to pull together the results of our analysis in a brief review. It should be recalled that the specific results are for the production function $P(R) = R^2$. However, the general patterns of relationships will hold true for all accelerating production functions. It should also be recalled that the underlying model of interdependence is simultaneous coordinated action, which permits actors to compare their own costs against the combined benefit of the coordinated action.

Expanding reach (N). When both resources (r) and interest (v) are constant in the group as a whole, the expected contribution level (E) is zero until a threshold is reached. This threshold is a function of v, r, and the production function (P). For $P(R) = R^2$, the threshold is $N > 2(r/v + 1)$. After this threshold, each additional person contacted adds r to E. Each additional person contacted adds $2vr^2$ to g, the gain each *individual* obtains from the collective action, so that larger contacted subgroups are much more profitable for their members than are smaller subgroups. If v is constant but r varies around mean μ_r, the results are the same except that μ_r is substituted for r.

If r is constant but v varies around mean μ_v, the threshold value of N has a probabilistic element depending on μ_v, σ_v, and the form of $v(y)$, the probability density function for the interest distribution. The threshold is the point at which some of the subgroup members' interests are high enough to make them willing to contribute. The slope of the relationship between N and E immediately beyond the threshold depends on the nature of $v(y)$ and P, but the curve in this region is decelerating toward the asymptote $E = Nr$, which is reached when N is high enough that even the subgroup members with the lowest interest levels are willing to contribute.

Selecting for interests. For a given resource (r) and targeted subgroup size (N), the threshold for an individual's interest level is $v > r/[P(rN) - P(rN - r)]$. For the production function $P(R) = R^2$, this threshold is $v > 1/[r(2N - 1)]$. If interests are constant within a group, and hence within any subgroup, the interest level (v) acts as an on–off switch for collective action: either no one contributes and $E = 0$, or everyone contributes and $E = Nr$. If interests vary, there is a threshold value of μ_v with a probabilistic element depending on the nature of $v(y)$ and P, which is the point at which some subgroup members' interests are high enough to make them willing to contribute interdependently. There is a region beyond this threshold with a positive but decelerating slope where increases in μ_v make a greater proportion of the subgroup willing to contribute. As μ_v gets high enough that virtually all individuals contacted are willing to contribute, the curve relating E to μ_v approaches the horizontal line $E = Nr$.

Selecting for resources. For a given subgroup size N and interest level v, an individual will contribute if her resource level surpasses the threshold $r > 1/v[P(rN) - P(rN - r)]$. For the production function $P(R) = R^2$, the threshold is $r > 1/[v(2N - 1)]$. If the interest level is constant across individuals contacted, each increment in r above the threshold (if resources are constant) or μ_r (if they vary) raises E by N times the increment.

Discussion

Our analysis points to two key features of recruitment to collective action: the importance of thresholds and the relative ineffectiveness of recruitment strategies focused on interest, rather than on resources or numbers.

Threshold effects in recruitment

Perhaps the most striking feature of our results is the universality of threshold effects. For a given combination of all other variables, each variable has a threshold below which increments in it make no difference in the prospects for collective action. Contacting another person increases the chances of success only if enough other members have already been contacted to reach the threshold. Shifting a recruitment strategy so that it is somewhat more selective, that is, so that there is an increase in the mean level of resources or interest in the targeted subgroups, increases the chances of success only if the subgroup is already resourceful or interested enough to reach the threshold. That is, threshold levels of interest, resource, and raw numbers of contacts must be met in order to avoid a complete organizing failure. This finding has profound implications for organizers.

First, and perhaps most important, it can help to explain the sometimes dramatic fluctuations in the level of activity in various collective action campaigns. Because of threshold effects, relatively small fluctuations in the recruitment efforts of organizers can have a dramatic effect on the total level of contributions to their cause. If people are willing to act if, but only if, enough others also act, a slight increase in the number willing can push a subgroup across the threshold and start a cascade of interdependent action.

Second, an organizer unable to find a recruitment strategy that achieves threshold levels of reach and selectivity (on either resources or interest or both) will be unable to recruit any contributors to his collective action. This suggests that, in some situations, it will be irrational for organizers to attempt to recruit new members to their cause, despite the obvious desirability of doing so, simply because any such attempt will be doomed to failure. Organizers who do not perceive the problem may conscientiously expend a great deal of effort on recruitment and achieve nothing. The failure would lie not with the recruiting ability of the organizer, but either with the lack of a critical mass for action within the group as a whole or with the lack of an effective recruitment strategy for reaching the critical mass.

There are two main reasons why an organizer may be unable to meet the threshold levels necessary to successfully recruit new members to his cause. Each has significant implications. First, an organizer may be unable to succeed simply because she cannot afford to pay the recruitment costs necessary to reach the threshold levels. Both high reach and high selectivity will usually have high associated costs, and poorer organizers may be unable to meet these costs to the extent necessary. This suggests that, quite apart from the fact that well-to-do collectivities have more resources to mobilize on their behalf than do poor ones, poor collectivities may not contain any potential organizer who herself has sufficient resources to be able to organize successfully. This lends credence to the idea, long an article of faith among activists, that poor collectivities frequently need an organizer from outside the group to catalyze them into action.

Second, an organizer may be unable to reach the necessary threshold levels because of the characteristics of the group from which he must select a subgroup to contact. An obvious example of this possibility is the case of a collectivity in which there is a negative correlation between the resource and interest level of members – a situation that may exist for many collective goods that primarily benefit underprivileged groups. When resource and interest levels are negatively correlated in this way, it may be difficult or impossible for organizers to find a target subgroup that meets threshold levels for both variables. Targeting more people will not help because the new contacts will still be unable to act. Selecting a more interested or resourceful subgroup will not work because selection for one entails selection against the other, and both are necessary. Instead, the organizer will have to act directly to increase the interest in the collective good of resourceful members of the group or increase the resources available to those members with high interest.

Both approaches are employed by activists, under the name of "consciousness building" and "empowerment." Consciousness building usually entails training members of a collectivity to have a better understanding of their objective interests or of their class position, so that they will be more inclined to work toward ends that are desirable from the point of view of the organizer. Empowerment usually means training potential participants in collective action to make better use of resources that they already command, thus effectively increasing their resource level. While there is nothing new in saying that consciousness building and empowerment are important elements in collective action, the threshold effects discovered in the previous section suggest that, in some cases, organizers may need to use such strategies in order to successfully mobilize any new participants at all.

A third major implication of threshold effects in the resource level, interest level, and number of contacts for a collective action is that they create a strong pressure for organizers to devote more or less equal attention to all three of these parameters. Even the most mass-oriented of movements must devote some attention to the resourcefulness and interest levels of their potential recruits; even the most conspiratorial or elitist must devote some attention to raw numbers. This suggests that when organizers employ simple recruitment strategies, these will usually include some emphasis on both reach and selectivity.

However, in some cases it may be difficult to meet all the necessary thresholds with a single strategy. Strategies that result in the recruitment of large numbers of people, such as advertising in mass media, tend to be very unselective for levels of interest and resource. Strategies that allow the organizer to be highly selective, such as direct recruitment from social networks or appeals through "movement" publications, tend to result in relatively small numbers of actual recruits. Organizers are therefore pressured to adopt complex combinations of strategies that emphasize one or another of these concerns, thereby assuring between them that all necessary threshold levels are met. Organizers are frequently aware of the need to combine recruitment strategies in this fashion. As John Wilson (1973:175–6) has noted:

Peace groups like CND, civil-rights groups like CORE, new left groups like SDS, Fascist groups like the Mosleyites, adventist movements like the Jehovah's Witnesses have all combined an openness for general support with a shrewd assessment of those who are most likely to contribute to the cause. The result has usually been a two-step sequence of recruitment in which the initial contact is made at rallies, demonstrations, mass meetings, and through the mass media. This diffuse approach is then followed up with personal contact and a more individualized approach in which the scarce resources of members' time and money can be allocated more discriminately in the direction of the probables.

The first step of this two-step process of recruitment may be seen as emphasizing the sheer number of contacts. Rallies, demonstrations, mass meetings, and advertising in mass media are all alike in that, if successful, they guarantee the presence of large numbers of people with at least a moderate interest in the collective good being sought. The second step may be seen as a way of sifting through this large number of potential recruits to find those individuals who have the most interest in the collective good and the most resources available to help provide it. Although this example represents a sequential combination of strategies, organizers may also employ different recruitment strategies simultaneously. For example, an environmental organization may garner large numbers of contributors by canvassing, while simultaneously reaching a few highly resourceful and interested individuals by more selective means.

Limits to the effectiveness of recruiting for interest

Our analysis shows that increasing the number of contacts or increasing the average resource level of those contacted both continue to improve the collective outcome throughout the accelerative range of a production function, while increasing the average interest level of those contacted is beneficial only if the initial level of interest among those contacted is relatively low. Once the interest is high enough that everyone is willing to contribute, increasing the interest adds nothing. As Figure 7.1 shows, most of the variation in the impact of interest selectivity occurs in a very small range around the threshold point.

This suggests that organizers who face no problem exceeding the threshold for all factors will find it much more rewarding to emphasize the raw numbers or the resource level of their potential recruits, rather than their interest level. Organizers should stress selecting for interest or raising interest only if the average interest in the group is so low that no one is willing to act.

This suggests that interest levels are most problematic at the beginnings of recruitment drives. These results seem to imply that as organizers become more successful over time, they will tend to become more concerned about the resources and number of their contacts, and less concerned about the contacts' interest in the collective good. In short, success changes the rules by which organizers must operate. If we assume that the "natural" constituency of a collective action is that subgroup of people who have the most interest in the collective good, this suggests that social movements would tend to move away from their natural constituencies and toward constituents with greater resources as they become more successful.

Implications for specific strategies

Finally, we return briefly to the typology of recruitment strategies presented at the beginning of this chapter. The first thing that must be noted about this scheme in light of the discussion in the previous two sections, is that it must be refined. We now know that the effect of selectivity vis-à-vis reach will depend to a large extent on whether selectivity for resource, interest, or both is the dominant concern for organizers.

Furthermore, the strong pressure on organizers to diversify their repertoire of recruitment strategies to meet various thresholds means that this typology may be too simple to adequately represent the kinds of choices that organizers must make. Rather than choosing a specific type of recruitment strategy, it may be that most organizers choose how to best combine strategies to fit their needs.

These provisos noted, however, there are two specific hypotheses suggested by this analysis. The first is that most strategies, or combinations of strategies, commonly employed by organizers of moderate resources will devote more or less equal attention to reach and selectivity. The second is that the organizers most able to mount large campaigns will tend to devote less emphasis to interest selectivity than to resource selectivity and reach, due to limitations on the efficacy of recruiting for interest.

Few, if any, strategies emphasize either reach or selectivity exclusively. Rallies, demonstrations, and other events staged for mass consumption are primarily reach-oriented strategies; however, they also have the useful feature that they tend to select only those members of the group who have the modicum of interest required to attend the event. Technologically mediated strategies, such as mass mailings and telephone campaigns, would seem to be clear examples of sacrificing selectivity for raw numbers of contacts; however, as McCarthy and Zald (1973, 1977) have pointed out, techniques such as market research and sophisticated mailing lists, which afford recruiters a good deal of information about the potential targets of their actions, are becoming increasingly common. Advertising in mass media would appear to be another reach-oriented strategy. However, what appears to be increasingly popular is recruitment through specialized media: Civil rights organizers advertise in black newspapers; a musicians' co-operative buys time on a progressive radio station; crusaders against gun control buy space in a magazine for hunters. In each case the number of people reached by the advertising is diminished compared to less special-ized media, but the probability that those reached will have a significant interest in the good is increased. The same type of selectivity is frequently the goal of blanketing strategies such as leafleting and canvassing. Leaf-leters choose carefully which streets to work, frequently maximizing the efficiency of their efforts by working the busiest streets available. Can-vassers frequently clamor for the most well-to-do or generous neighbor-hoods. In each case, the apparent primacy of either the reach or selectivity of a strategy is mitigated by techniques that place added emphasis on the other factor.

Large, well-established campaigns for collective goods can take interest levels for granted and focus on numbers or resources. The United Way can mount numbers-focused campaigns attempting to saturate whole work-places and neighborhoods in order to create significant social pressures on individuals to contribute. The United Way and all other major charities devote a great deal of their efforts to large-donor fund-raising, particularly from corporations. Established pressure groups such as the NRA or NOW can emphasize both the numbers and the resource levels of their contacts, simultaneously advertising on network television and seeking a few large contributions through more private means. Well-endowed university foundations usually concentrate more on locating the most resourceful alumni than on locating those with the strongest school spirit. These strategies make sense for organizations that are generally popular and that anticipate no difficulty in meeting threshold levels. For these organizations it is more rewarding to concentrate their efforts on the number and the resourcefulness of their contacts than on their interest. By contrast, organizers of relatively unpopular causes, such as American Communists or those opposed to animal nudity, nearly always target their appeals to an audience that has been highly selected for interest or at least potential interest, because more generalized populations can never exceed the threshold interest level.

In conclusion, we turn to the issue of specific, testable hypotheses that flow from the model presented here:

1. If threshold effects or pronounced gyrations in the outcomes of actual collective action campaigns occur at all, they will occur immediately after some event significantly changes the size, resourcefulness, or mean interest level of the collectivity.

2. Complex recruitment strategies, which combine attention to numbers, interest levels, and resource levels, will tend to promote more successful collective action campaigns.

3. As movements thrive, the mean resource levels of new recruits will increase relative to their mean interest levels.

4. Movements in which there is a negative correlation between interest and resource levels among potential recruits will tend to achieve very little until organizers take action to influence one or the other of these variables; thereafter, threshold effects are likely to occur.

Some of these hypotheses might yield to testing through a carefully designed experiment in which a large number of small groups, each including an organizer and a set of potential recruits with stochastically assigned resource and interest levels, attempt to attain a collective cash incentive offered by the experimenter. However, a more fruitful approach to hypothesis testing might be to focus on historical assessments of the extent to which the hypotheses have held true in major collective action campaigns and social movements.

8. Unfinished business

It is a commonplace to observe that intensive scrutiny of a given social (or physical, for that matter) phenomenon tends to reveal its complexity and open more questions than are answered. So, of course, has it been with our examination of the problem of collective action. In hindsight, we see that each of the specific analyses in this book is relatively narrow, which is to say that each is focused on a particular kind of collective action that arises under a particular set of conditions. Thus, we certainly do not claim to have arrived at some comprehensive account of the dynamics of collective action. Instead, we have introduced or drawn attention to a list of variables, some new tools, and a general orientation toward analyzing distinct collective action problems. These beginnings obviously leave much left to be done. Alternative assumptions and questions may lead to quite different lines of inquiry and theorizing. At least, that is our hope.

In this chapter we first review briefly the analyses we have already undertaken and the answers we have found. We then call attention to some of the "unfinished business" that we think is most worth pursuing by ourselves and others. Obviously, new imaginations may find even more interesting issues to pursue and ways to pursue them. Our intention is simply to offer some places one might start.

Summary and discussion of results

The first substantive issue we addressed (in Chapter 3) was the group-size problem as posed by Olson. We argued that, contrary to Olson's claims, there is no consistent group-size effect on the prospects for collective action. Putting it baldly, you have to put group-size effects *into* your theory, and you will get out exactly what you have put in.

Some past critics have argued that there must be a group-size effect because the total payoff must be divided among the N group members.

That is, they are trying to say that there must be a group-size effect, by definition. These critics fail to realize that such a relationship is certainly not *necessary* for public goods, in part because each increment in the denominator N may well "automatically" increase the total group payoff in the numerator, depending on the level of jointness of supply. The quotient, the individual payoff, may increase, decrease, or be invariant with N. Empirical information or theoretical assumptions about the relation between individual payoffs and group size are required before the effect of group size on the prospects for providing nonexcludible collective goods can be deduced. There simply is no general result.

Because we were trying to make a particular point about social movements and political goods (which are usually jointly supplied), we ended Chapter 3 with some strong language about the value of large groups. But all of those claims flow directly from our interest in jointly supplied goods and group heterogeneity. They certainly do not apply to homogeneous groups or to goods with zero jointness of supply or crowding effects. We see little value in arguing about whether most collective goods are jointly supplied or whether most groups are heterogeneous: sometimes they are, and sometimes they are not. Instead, our analytic conclusion is simply that, when groups are heterogeneous, group size tends to have a positive effect on the provision of jointly supplied collective goods, and a negative effect on the provision of goods whose cost increases proportionately with the number who share in them.

In Chapter 3, we also pointed to a theme that became central as our work progressed – the importance of the critical mass of large contributors to collective action. We showed how collective goods that benefit many can be paid for by a few, and how the number of contributors can paradoxically be smaller when the total group is larger, if the group is heterogeneous and the good has high jointness of supply. Distinguishing the critical mass of contributors from the whole interest group and arguing that collective action depends on the former rather than the latter became the central enterprise of the rest of the book.

Chapter 4 took up the matter of production functions and showed that the dynamics of collective action are illuminated by distinguishing accelerative actions or phases of actions from decelerative actions or phases. In both cases, there is a distinctive role to be played by the critical mass of large contributors, but this role is different in each case.

When production functions are decelerative, there are diminishing marginal returns to contributions and negative interdependence, that is, each contribution lowers the value of the next contribution. In the decelerative case, the critical mass of large contributors tends to provide a free ride for the less interested or less resourceful members of the interest group. We showed that the economists' fascination with issues of strategic gaming and indeterminacy should be confined only to those cases in which the production function is decelerative *and* there is a surplus of contributors. We showed further that when there is no surplus, there are strong order effects, wherein contributions will be maximized only if the improbable happens and the *least* interested contribute before the most interested. It is in the decelerative case that we find the "exploitation of the great by the small" or, more precisely, the exploitation of the most interested by the less interested.

When production functions are accelerative, there are increasing marginal returns to contributions and positive interdependence, so that each contribution increases the value of the next contribution. In the accelerative case, the critical mass of large contributors overcomes the start-up costs and creates the conditions that make smaller or less interested members of the interest group willing to contribute. We argued that free riding is *not* the problem in the accelerative case, unless all public goods dilemmas are said to be free riding by definitional fiat. That is, individuals are not motivated to let others pay for the collective good, because others' contributions make people *more* willing to contribute. Instead, the central problem in the accelerative case is efficacy, that is, the problem of overcoming the start-up costs. We showed that collective action in the accelerative case may be aided by positive interdependence and "indirect production" considerations, in which initial contributors consider not only the direct effect of their contributions on the collective good, but also the effect of their contributions on the likelihood of others' contributions.

We also demonstrated that collective action is "easier" in the decelerative case, in the sense that the critical mass of initial contributors requires a lower interest level to be willing to contribute than when the production function is accelerative. However, collective action in the accelerative case tends to be self-reinforcing and explosive, if it starts at all, while collective action in the decelerative case tends to be self-limiting.

When we put the general third-order curve back together, we argued that the early phases of a collective action are dominated by the accelerative phase and the problem of start-up costs, that the middle phase is the period of positive interdependence and growth, and that the last phase is dominated by optimization and self-limiting processes. Those who care the most have already contributed, and those who have not yet contributed have already been satisfied by the amount of action that has already occurred.

Our analysis in Chapter 4 is a static comparison, carried out as if each collective good's production function is inherent in the nature of the good itself. However, production functions are actually tied to specific strategies for achieving a collective good. People or groups can and do *choose* production functions, albeit within limits set by the nature of the good. For example, they are frequently able to choose between self-help and political strategies. They can often choose between doing things themselves and mobilizing others to do those things. They can redefine a specific collective good in a slightly different way so as to create somewhat different interest groups. They can choose actions that require time or those that require money. All of these choices can be made with an awareness of the interests, resources, and social ties of the population of people from whom they might elicit contributions to the collective action.

In Chapter 5, we explored the problem of how networks affect collective action, focusing on the very narrow situation of an organizer-centered mobilization with an accelerative production function and perfect information. Even within these narrow bounds, we found ample complexity. We distinguished three features of social networks: the overall prevalence of ties in a group (density), the degree to which those ties are centralized around one person rather than spread evenly across a group (centralization), and the cost of communicating across a tie. As we would expect, a higher overall prevalence of ties promotes collective action, and higher communication costs hinder it.

Less obvious, until the details of the model are understood, is the result that network centralization always has a positive effect. In an organizer-centered mobilization, what matters most is the size of the *largest* network among the group members. Thus, the concentration of ties around one person has a very positive effect on collective action. These basic effects hold but are specified when the level of group heterogeneity is considered. The value of centralization increases as *resource* heterogeneity increases. When resources were distributed heterogeneously throughout the group, limitations on the key organizer (the one with the largest network) set by the amount of resources she might devote to mobilizing become much less important. Instead of having to mobilize the whole large network, mobilizers in a group heterogeneous on resources can be successful by mobilizing a *selected* subgroup. Organizers with large networks are more likely to be in contact with the few large contributors in the group, and thus do not have to pay the costs of mobilizing a large number of people. Even though there was some risk that the organizer who knew everybody would not be interested enough to organize (especially when interest heterogeneity was high), within the ranges of our parameters, the negative effect of this risk was much smaller than the positive centralization effect.

Clearly, the centralization result is not general, but depends greatly on the details of our model, particularly organizer-centered mobilization and an accelerative production function. However, this exercise demonstrates that "network effects" should be construed neither simply nor simple-mindedly. The effect of the structure of network ties on collective action *always* depends on the specific organizational structure of the collective action.

Once we recognize how intertwined are the structure of networks and the structure of collective action, a host of analyses present themselves. What happens in decelerative production functions? What are the trade-offs between doing the whole collective action yourself (if you can) and paying to mobilize others? What if two-step mobilizations are permitted, with level-one organizers mobilizing level-two organizers who mobilize participation? What if we permitted organizers to join forces, instead of using the preemptive model? Now that we understand how resource and interest heterogeneity are operating, what if we expand their ranges and more explicitly consider the size of the risk that the person who knows everyone may block mobilization instead of facilitate it? We pose these questions without answering them, at least for now.

In Chapter 6, we expanded our examination of the phenomenon whose importance for the process emerged in our initial consideration of networks – selectivity. Although the point is obvious, once made, little in the literature has recognized that if an organizer has the ability to choose whom to organize, he will devote his efforts to the largest potential contributors. For this analysis we continued to assume heterogeneous groups, organizer-centered mobilizations, and accelerative production functions. In this context, we explored the value of information about contribution sizes. We set the problem up in two different ways, so as to approximate two different kinds of situations. Our static results were that organizers with more information that permits them to target their efforts will accumulate higher contribution levels, and that this effect is greater for more heterogeneous groups. In our more dynamic analysis, we imagined a fixed level of organizer resources and modeled the trade-offs involved in the organizer's decision between spending resources on mobilizing and spending resources on getting information. Our most basic results were that information that increases the level of selectivity is worth the price in reduced numbers mobilized when the initial selectivity is low, and that information is worth more for more heterogeneous target populations.

The issues raised in Chapter 6 are clearly relevant to professional fundraising in the nonprofit sector. More broadly, the analysis speaks to the choice between general population mobilizations and specialized mobilizations and to the conditions under which it pays for organizers to move beyond their current networks and seek out information on new people. The results indicated that, if the interest group is heterogeneous, it may be a big mistake to focus attention on mobilizing as many contributors as possible, instead of on targeting mobilization selectively. Within the framework of our assumptions, this approach provides a way to compare different uses of resources, depending on the heterogeneity of the group.

Chapter 7 also concerned the general idea of selectivity and targeting mobilization, but approached the problem differently. In Chapter 6, we took each individual's contribution size if asked as a given and discussed information regarding specific people and the benefits that can be obtained from using information to target a mobilization. By contrast, we used an equilibrium model to describe a whole group in Chapter 7 and examined the effect on this equilibrium of changing group characteristics. In Chapter 6 the degree of heterogeneity was varied around a given mean, while in Chapter 7 the degree of heterogeneity was constant and the means differed. Additionally, we distinguished between resources and interest as determinants of the overall expected contribution level in Chapter 7, which we did not do in Chapter 6. We continued to assume accelerative production functions and organizer-centered mobilizations.

The analysis in Chapter 7 revealed two main patterns. First, for each of the key independent variables (number of contributors, the average of network members' interests, and their average resources), there is always a threshold level for collective action. If the threshold of any one of the variables is not met, there is zero payoff for mobilizing and zero payoff for trying to raise the value of that variable unless it can be raised above the threshold. Second, seeking to increase the number mobilized or the average resource level in the network always increases the expected total contribution, but there is a limit above which increasing the average interest level adds nothing. The effects of increased interest are limited because interest functions as an on–off switch determining the individual's willingness to contribute. Once the average interest level is high enough that virtually everyone is willing to contribute, additional increments add nothing to the total level of action.

The models in Chapter 7 can be treated as static or dynamic. As static models, they imply that organizers may choose among recruitment strategies that reach different subgroups with different means. The models therefore provide a tool for comparing strategies. The models suggest that organizers target subgroups that meet the thresholds for all variables and, once those are met, focus on either larger or more resourceful subgroups. As dynamic models, they imply that organizers should seek to raise the values of a single subgroup on all three variables and thus suggest that, in the early phases of mobilization, they cannot concentrate on just one of the characteristics of the subgroup. In later phases organizers might focus on either numbers or resources, but probably not interest.

As our work on selectivity proceeds, it is clear that we are using the idea of the critical mass as a broad concept. It always refers to the insight of heterogeneity and difference among potential contributors. But in the organizer-centered model, it can refer both to the organizers and to those who are mobilized, as contrasted with noncontributors. Thus, we think it is important to stress that critical mass theory is about the role of large contributors in collective action, but that we do not use "the critical mass" in a rigorous way to denote one specific kind or role of large contributor.

The concept of selectivity is also being used broadly, but always refers to the organizer's ability to make choices about whom to organize. All of our mathematical models are imperfect representations of what organizers actually do, but we believe each contributes insights into some of the factors and processes that can affect the outcome of collective action campaigns.

Further issues

What kind of further analysis might prove most useful? We hope that others will contribute fresh perspectives and fresh ideas, but to help we suggest in this section two areas of inquiry that are important but that do not flow directly from what we have written here.

Organizing costs and incentive structures

Mancur Olson claimed to prove that collective action was irrational, that is, that it could not arise from selfish individuals' interest in collective goods. He could have concluded from this that collective action, when it occurred, must have arisen from unselfish or irrational motives, but he did not. Instead, he argued that collective action always required *selective incentives*, private (i.e., excludible) goods that would reward contributors and punish noncontributors. Olson believed that private incentives were necessary and sufficient for collective action. Subsequent analysts critiqued both necessity and sufficiency. Incentives were shown not to be necessary for collective action, because collective action is not always irrational. There are many critiques in this vein, which essentially shows that jointness of supply, interdependence, or other factors define broad classes of situations in which contributions are noticeable and individual benefits exceed individual costs. Incentives were also shown not to be sufficient for collective action, because the provision of an incentive system is, itself, a nonexcludible collective good that may be subject to the very dilemma of collective action described by Olson.

Although they are neither necessary nor sufficient for collective action, selective incentives are nevertheless a very important component of collective action in many situations. There is a great potential for future formal theorizing in analyzing them. Only a little of this work has been done.

Any analysis of selective incentives proceeds from Clark and Wilson's (1961) and James Wilson's (1973) typology of purposive, solidary, and material incentives. Material incentives are what Olson discussed: benefits of participation such as calendars, insurance, journals, job certification, and so forth. Paid activists also receive material incentives in the form of a salary. Physical coercion, monetary fines, and legal penalties such as jail can also be classed as material incentives.

Solidary incentives are those that arise from social ties to others. Wilson distinguishes between inclusive incentives, that is, the social reinforcement that all participants give to and receive from each other by virtue of their coparticipation, and exclusive incentives, the prestige and honor that only a few can be given for their special roles or contributions.

Purposive incentives are basically attitudes. They are feelings of self-worth and self-approval for doing the right thing (or self-reproach for doing the wrong thing). Since they are both attitudinal, it can be empirically difficult to distinguish between a subjective interest in a collective good and purposive incentive, but there is an analytic distinction. The subjective interest in the collective good is the value you attach to getting world peace or racial equality or whatever, while the purposive incentive is the value you attach to knowing that *you* helped to accomplish the goal, or at least gave outward expression to your concerns.

In an earlier work, one of us (Oliver 1980) provided some initial analysis of selective incentives and their cost structures. That work argued that attention must be paid to costs, and that rewards and punishments generally have very different cost structures because they are given to different people: rewards are given to cooperators and punishments to noncooperators. Incentive systems built on rewards should be most efficient for getting a small number of people do provide a collective good for a larger group, while incentive systems built on punishments are most efficient for getting a whole group to engage in unanimous action. This argument would imply a fit between rewards as incentives and decelerative production functions, and between punishments and accelerative production functions.

However, that older argument implicitly assumed that the production function for the incentive is linear with the person who receives it. This assumption is not quite right even for divisible material goods (every participant gets a clock radio), but it is certainly wrong for coercion and for solidary and purposive incentives. Once it is granted that the production function of the incentive is also problematic and not generally linear, it is clear that there can be great complexity in the second-order problem for deploying an incentive to motivate collective action.

We will have to write another book to treat this topic properly, but we would like to point to some of the crucial issues and how they relate to topics we have discussed here. First, it seems useful to treat incentive structures and organizing costs together as the overhead costs involved in generating collective action, at least when doing the kind of organizer-centered theory we have been doing. Thus, organizing costs include not only communication, but influence and enforcement. This is what we have typically assumed in this book. It seems particularly appropriate for purposive and solidary incentives, which are not things that have costs, but are individual attitudes and emotions that either produce fixed and immutable responses to communications from organizers or that can be affected by influence attempts from organizers. In our work so far, of course, we have oversimplified this whole problem by making organizing costs a linear function of the number of participants or contributors.

Second, it seems useful analytically to distinguish between what may be termed *intrinsic* incentives and *manipulable* incentives. Although all incentives influence individuals' participation, intrinsic incentives adhere to the act of participating itself. For example, some people enjoy being part of a group joined in a demonstration, others do it with clenched teeth. A person is either motivated by that incentive or not. Organizers cannot manipulate the incentive, but can only attempt to orient the whole collective action in ways that can evoke it. They can choose which populations to target or which kind of action or goal to pursue, but there is nothing specifically they can do to use or administer the incentive. Thus, any cost to the organizer of an intrinsic incentive is a lumpy cost incurred at the level of deciding what action to do, what strategy to pursue.

By contrast, manipulable incentives are administered or given to individual people on the basis of their participation. They are things like clock radios, punishment threats, letters of appreciation, and personal pressure. Their cost will vary with either the number of participants, the number of nonparticipants, or the total size of the interest group. Their cost functions will have some mixture of fixed and variable costs, and the production function for such incentives can take on any of the forms we discussed in Chapter 4. Positive and negative manipulable incentives will typically have very different cost structures. Individuals will often vary in the magnitude of incentive or the expenditure of effort required to recruit them to participation. Since individuals also typically vary in the amount they are likely to contribute, it can readily be seen that models for the effect of incentive systems and organizing costs can become quite complex.

We have also thus far considered only the organizers who are trying to promote collective action and have provided no models for repression or countermobilizations. We have repeatedly ducked the matter of competing interests within a population. There is doubtless a great deal to be learned from examining the joint effects of mixtures of negative and positive incentives being deployed by different agents for different ends.

Any discussion of incentive structures also needs to recognize that incentives have two sides: their effect on individuals deciding to participate and their cost to organizers. There is no simple relation between the cost borne by an organizer and the impact of an incentive on contribution decisions. This means that different kinds of incentives will affect the dynamics of collective action differently.

Only a small amount of work has been done on incentive systems, most of it by Douglas Heckathorn (1988, 1989, 1990, 1991, 1992). Heckathorn takes off from Oliver's (1980) discussion of the "second order collective action problem," the collective problem of paying for incentive systems to motivate collective action. Heckathorn shows that the possibility of within-group sanctioning can be used to enforce compliance with an external norm, sometimes when it benefits the group and sometimes when it does not or, when parameters are only slightly different, can be used to enforce resistance to an external norm that is harmful to the group. Although strictly applicable only to the narrow sets of conditions in the specific analyses, the processes he has identified are highly suggestive and likely to be of broad significance. It is clear from this work that there is an abundance of interesting theoretical results awaiting those who are willing to explore other dimensions of the second-order collective action problem.

Dynamic models

All of the models we have analyzed are essentially static, in that we take as givens the factors that affect individuals' decisions. This assumption is clearly false. It does not lead us to abandon our results, because we believe they provide us with useful baselines and insights. But we do feel that there is great promise in developing dynamic models that build on our work. Two directions for doing this appear feasible.

The first is to stay within the metatheory of decisions and to permit organizers' influence attempts, others' actions, or the outcomes of prior action sequences to affect resources, interests, or potential contribution sizes. It is also possible to take account of the fact that people in intact social groups jointly construct their understandings, and thus jointly and collectively change their interest levels, perceptions of the effects of action on outcomes, and even their "resource" levels, that is, the time, money, or skills they perceive themselves as having available for the action. We believe this has a great deal of potential. The computer technology already exists for building dynamic models with interrelated equations, and translating our models into simulations would be a straightforward, if cumbersome, task.

The second direction is to shift away from decision models to learning models, a project already begun by Macy (1989, 1990, 1991a). Learning metatheory posits that rewarded actions are repeated, and that unrewarded or punished actions are abandoned. Although learning and decision models are often posed as competing models for the truth about human behavior, it is more likely that each captures some of the empirical reality. Macy's work shows that a learning model generates different behavioral predictions from ours in response to the same production functions. The biggest difference is in the accelerative case. A decision model implies that small contributors will do nothing without some explicit organization or coordination of their efforts. By contrast, a learning model predicts that the unpleasantness of the baseline condition, with no collective action, increases the probability that small contributors will try contributing. Although most of these contributions go unrewarded, and the actors return to a pattern of inaction, the fact that attempts are made means that there is a nonzero probability that actors will "accidentally" contribute enough to overcome the start-up costs and shift to the steep part of the production function where contributing is rewarded. Again, we think there is great potential in exploring the implications of different assumptions about individual decisions.

In either extension, we believe the critical ingredient is not so much the computer technology, which is now widely available and sophisticated, but theoretical strategies for defining experiments and ranges of comparisons. It is not enough to set up an elaborate simulation with a lot of parameters and report how it behaves because we have little intrinsic interest in simulations as ends in themselves. It is almost never of interest to report that one's models produce high or low levels of collective action, or higher or lower levels than someone else reports. The overall mean outcomes of a simulation model simply reflect the effects of the fixed parameters and the ranges of the variables. The global outcome levels of collective action models are always determined by the chosen levels of resources and interests (or composite contribution sizes) relative to each other and to the cost of producing the collective good. The magnitude of any variable's effect is generally determined by its range within the simulation relative to the fixed parameters. Of course, if you change assumptions, you will change the results. What we need is a systematic strategy for identifying the effects of variables in interaction with the relevant means and an awareness that it is the effect coefficients, not the overall outcome, that are generally of interest in simulations.

It may be helpful in this concluding chapter to review our standards for theorizing with computer simulations, not because we always live up to these standards, but because we believe they are useful criteria for such work. Parameters and ranges of variables should be carefully defined and fixed. The constant factors and the ranges of variables are the scope conditions for the model, and all interpretations of results from the model should include references to the scope of the results. Because the results can apply only within the scope of these initial boundaries, the conditions that are selected should approximate some interesting type of collective action. Within these conditions, systematic experiments can be constructed to examine the ways variables affect outcomes, singly and in interaction with one another. It is important to go beyond just reporting a result to try to identify those aspects of the equations that made it happen. Once we understand how a particular model works, we can figure out what its results imply for collective action. It is the illumination of process and the recognition of how things might work, not global rates of "collective action," that are of interest. Of course, a detailed understanding of the model and its results inevitably leads us to recognize at least one initial condition that constrains our results more than we had anticipated, and at least one variable that behaves differently than expected. We gain knowledge in the process of exploring the deductive consequences of complex sets of assumptions. We reach understandings that lead us to pose new questions. And we try very hard to remember the difference between a deductive consequence of assumptions and an empirical finding.

One last exhortation

It is very important to stress that all our results depend on parameterizations and assumptions that permit the variables of interest to operate. *The most important determinants of collective action in our models are the interest and resource (or contribution size) levels relative to the cost of contributing.* Expensive actions that provide no noticeable benefit are predicted never to occur, no matter what the other variables are. Conversely, when individual benefits are greater than individual costs, we predict that people will act. We say little about these effects because we consider them to be obvious and, therefore, theoretically uninteresting. But if you imagine running a regression on the universe of possible collective action situations, the effect coefficients for the total or average levels of resources, benefits, and costs would dwarf any of the other factors we discuss. All of our results are net of these average levels, and all of our analyses hold these factors constant so that others may come into play.

Thus, contrary to some published citations to our work, there is nothing anywhere in our analysis that "solves" the collective dilemma, that explains away the problem of the relation between individual and group interests. What we do say is that the dilemma is not the same for everything denoted by the definition of collective goods or collective action, and that attempts to make sweeping generalizations about collective action are misguided. Instead, what we show is that the specifics of the problem and the nature of potential solutions can vary greatly depending on the nature of the collective good and the social structural situations within which people make interdependent choices.

Demonstrating the variability of collective action does have implications for the idea of a "solution" to collective dilemmas, of course, because our work points to the possibility that people can and do choose how to define their action choices, and they can choose to define things in ways that make collective action more rather than less possible. They can choose to solve a river-crossing problem by waiting for others spontaneously to contribute bits of a bridge, by opening a for-profit ferry service, by seeking to recruit people with the necessary skills to donate their labor and other people to donate materials to build the bridge, by launching a private-contribution campaign to raise enough money to pay a professional bridge-building firm, or by lobbying Congress for an appropriation for a bridge. They can choose to solve the dilemma of environmental pollution by trying to persuade every individual not to pollute or by trying to get antipollution laws passed and enforced by the government.

We make no general claim about the collective action terrain as a whole, except the claim that it is impossible to make such claims. Instead, we show that there are some very interesting patterns of relationships among variables within certain well-defined regions of the terrain. We find these results interesting in themselves, and we also hope that they can stimulate more explorations of other variables and regions.

References

Akers, R., M. Krohn, L. Lanza-Kaduce, and M. Radosevich. 1979. "Social Learning and Deviant Behavior: A Specific Test of a General Theory." *American Sociological Review* 44:636–55.

Alba, Richard D. 1981. "From Small Groups to Social Networks." *American Behavioral Scientist* 24:681–94.

Arabie, P. 1977. "Clustering Representations of Group Overlap." *Journal of Mathematical Sociology* 5:113–28.

Bator, Francis M. 1958. "The Anatomy of Market Failure." *Quarterly Journal of Economics* 72:351–79.

Berk, Richard. 1974, "A Gaming Approach to Crowd Behavior." *American Sociological Review* 39:355–73.

Bonacich, Philip, Gerald H. Shure, James P. Kahan, and Robert J. Meeker. 1976. "Cooperation and Group Size in the N-Person Prisoners' Dilemma." *Journal of Conflict Resolution* 20:687–706.

Brewer, M. B. 1985. "Experimental Research and Social Policy: Must it be Rigor Versus Relevance?" *Journal of Social Issues* 41:159–76.

Brubaker, E. R. 1982. "Sixty-eight Percent Free Revelation and Thirty-two Percent Free Ride? Demand Disclosures Under Varying Conditions on Exclusion." In *Research in Experimental Economics*, vol. 2, ed. V. L. Smith, pp. 151–66. Greenwich, Conn: JAI Press.

Burt, Ronald S. 1978. "Cohesion Versus Structural Equivalence as a Basis for Network Subgroups." *Sociological Methods and Research* 7:189–212.

——— 1980. "Models of Network Structure." In *Annual Review of Sociology*, vol. 6, ed. A. Inkeles, J. Coleman, and N. Smelser, pp. 79–141. Palo Alto, CA.: Annual Reviews.

Caldwell, M. D. 1976. "Communication and Sex Effects in a Five-Person Prisoner's Dilemma Game." *Journal of Personality and Social Psychology* 22:273–80.

Chamberlin, John. 1974. "Provisions of Collective Goods as a Function of Group Size." *American Political Science Review* 68:707–16.

Chong, Dennis. 1991. *Collective Action and the Civil Rights Movement*. Chicago: University of Chicago Press.

Clark, Peter B., and James Q. Wilson. 1961. "Incentive System: A Theory of Organizations." *Administrative Science Quarterly* 6:219–66.

Cohn, Samuel. 1985. *The Process of Occupational Sex-typing: The Feminization of Clerical Labor in Great Britain*. Philadelphia, Pa.: Temple University Press.

Coleman, James S. 1973. *The Mathematics of Collective Action*. Chicago: Aldine.

——— 1986. "Social Theory, Social Research, and a Theory of Action." *American Journal of Sociology* 91:1309–35.

——— 1988. "Free Riders and Zealots: The Role of Social Networks." *Sociological Theory* 6:52–57.

——— 1989. *Foundations of Social Theory*. Cambridge, Mass.: Harvard University Press.

Cornes, Richard, and Todd Sandler. 1983. "On Commons and Tragedies." *American Economic Review* 73:787–92.

——— 1984a. "The Theory of Public Goods: Non-Nash Behavior." *Journal of Public Economics* 23:367–79.

——— 1984b. "Easy Riders, Joint Production, and Public Goods." *Economic Journal* 94:580–98.

——— 1985. "On the Consistency of Conjectures with Public Good." *Journal of Public Economics* 27:125–9.

Dawes, R. M. 1980. "Social Dilemmas." *Annual Review of Psychology* 31:169–93.

Dawes, R. M., J. McTavish, and H. Shaklee. 1977. "Behavior, Communication, and Assumptions about Other People's Behavior in a Commons Dilemma Situation." *Journal of Personality and Social Psychology* 35:1–11.

Dawes, R. M., and J. M. Orbell. 1982. "Cooperation in Social Dilemma Situations: Thinking about It Doesn't Help." In *Research in Experimental Economics*, vol. 2, ed. V. L. Smith, pp. 167–73. Greenwich, Conn.: JAI Press.

Doreian, P. 1974. "On the Connectivity of Social Networks." *Journal of Mathematical Sociology* 3:245–58.

Fantasia, Rick. 1988. *Cultures of Solidarity: Consciousness, Action, and Contemporary American Workers*. Berkeley: University of California Press.

Fireman, Bruce, and William A. Gamson. 1979. "Utilitarian Logic in the Resource Mobilization Perspective." In *The Dynamics of Social Movements*, ed. Mayer N. Zald and John D. McCarthy, pp. 8–45. Cambridge, Mass.: Winthrop Publishers.

Fox, J., and M. Guyer. 1978. "Public Choice and Cooperation in N-Person Prisoner's Dilemma." *Journal of Conflict Resolution* 22:469–81.

Freeman, Jo. 1973. "The Origins of Women's Liberation Movements." *American Journal of Sociology* 78:792–811.

Freeman, L. C. 1979. "Centrality in Social Networks: Conceptual Clarification." *Social Networks* 1:215–39.

Frohlich, Norman, Thomas Hunt, Joe Oppenheimer, and R. Harrison Wagner. 1975. "Individual Contributions for Collective Goods: Alternative Models." *Journal of Conflict Resolution* 19:310–29.

Frohlich, Norman, and Joe Oppenheimer 1970. "I Get By With a Little Help From My Friends." *World Politics 23:*104–20.

Frohlich, Norman, Joe A. Oppenheimer, and Oran Young. 1971. *Political Leadership and Collective Goods.* Princeton, N.J.: Princeton University Press.

Gerlach, Luther P., and Virginia H. Hine. 1970. *People, Power, Change: Movements of Social Transformation.* Indianapolis, Ind.: Bobbs-Merrill.

Gitlin, Todd. 1987. *The Sixties: Years of Hope, Days of Rage.* New York: Bantam.

Granovetter, Mark. 1973. "The Strength of Weak Ties." *American Journal of Sociology 78:*1360–80.

——— 1978. "Threshold Models of Collective Behavior." *American Journal of Sociology 83:*1420–43.

——— 1980. "Threshold Models of Collective Behavior: Extensions and Applications." Paper presented at the meetings of the American Sociological Association, New York.

Hardin, Russell. 1971. "Collective Action as an Agreeable *N*-Prisoners' Dilemma." *Behavioral Science 16:*472–81.

——— 1982. *Collective Action.* Baltimore: Johns Hopkins University Press for Resources for the Future.

Head, John G. 1974. *Public Goods and Public Welfare.* Durham, N.C.: Duke University Press.

Heckathorn, Douglas D. 1988. "Collective Sanctions and the Emergence of Prisoner's Dilemma Norms." *American Journal of Sociology 94:*535–62.

——— 1989. "Collective Action and the Second Order Free Rider Problem." *Rationality and Society 1:*78–100.

——— 1990. "Collective Sanctions and Compliance Norms: A Formal Theory of Group-Mediated Social Control." *American Sociological Review 55:*366–84.

——— 1991. "Extensions of the Prisoner's Dilemma Paradigm: The Altruist's Dilemma and Group Solidarity." *Sociological Theory 9:*34–52.

——— 1992. "Collective Sanctions and Group Heterogeneity: Cohesion and Polarization in Normative Systems." In *Advances in Group Process Theory and Research,* Vol. 9, ed. Ed Lawler, pp. 41–63. Greenwich, Conn.: JAI Press.

Howard, N. 1971. *Paradoxes of Rationality: Theory of Metagames and Political Behavior.* Cambridge, Mass.: MIT Press.

Jenkins, J. Craig. 1982. "The Transformation of a Constituency into a Movement." In *The Social Movements of the 1960s and 1970s,* ed. J. Freeman, pp. 52–70. New York: Longmans.

——— 1987. "Interpreting the Stormy Sixties: Three Theories in Search of a Political Age." *Research in Political Sociology 3:*269–303.

Jenkins, J. Craig, and Craig M. Eckert. 1986. "Channeling Black Insurgency: Elite Patronage and Professional Social Movement Organizations in the Development of the Black Movement." *American Sociological Review 51:*812–29.

Kelley, H. H., and J. Grzelak. 1972. "Conflict Between Individual and Common Interest in an *N*-Person Relationship." *Journal of Personality and Social Psychology 21:*190–7.

Klandermans, Bert. 1984. "Mobilization and Participation: Social Psychological Expansions of Resource Mobilization Theory." *American Sociological Review* 49:583–600.

Latane, Bibb, and Steve Nida. 1981. "Ten Years of Research on Group Size and Helping." *Psychological Bulletin* 89:308–24.

Le Bon, Gustav. [1985] 1960. *The Crowd: A Study of the Popular Mind.* New York: Compass Books.

Macy, Michael W. 1989. "Walking out of Social Traps: A Stochastic Learning Model for Prisoner's Dilemma." *Rationality and Society* 1:197–219.

1990. "Learning Theory and the Logic of Critical Mass." *American Sociological Review* 55:809–26.

1991a. "Chains of Cooperation: Threshold Effects in Collective Action." *American Sociological Review* 56:730–47.

1991b. "Learning to Cooperate: Stochastic and Tacit Collusion in Social Exchange." *American Journal of Sociology* 97:808–43.

Marsden, Peter V. 1981. "Introducing Influence Processess into a System of Collective Decisions." *American Journal of Sociology* 86:1203–35.

1983. "Restricted Access in Networks and Models of Power." *American Journal of Sociology* 88:686–717.

Marwell, Gerald. 1970. "Comment on Scott and El-Assal." *American Sociological Review* 35:916.

Marwell, Gerald, and Ruth E. Ames. 1979. "Experiments on the Provision of Public Goods, I. Resources, Interest, Group Size and the Free-Rider Problem." *American Journal of Sociology* 84:1335–60.

1981. "Economists Free Ride, Does Anyone Else? Experiments on the Provision of Public Goods, IV." *Journal of Public Economics* 15:295–310.

Marwell, Gerald, and Pamela Oliver. 1984. "Collective Action Theory and Social Movements Research." *Research in Social Movements, Conflicts and Change* 7:1–27.

1991. "A Theory of the Critical Mass. VI. Cliques and Collective Action." In *Disziplin und kreativitat,* ed. Henrik Kreutz and Johann Becher, pp. 49–62. Opladen: Leshe und Burdich.

Marwell, Gerald, Pamela E. Oliver, and Ralph Prahl. 1988. "Social Networks and Collective Action: A Theory of the Critical Mass. III." *American Journal of Sociology* 94:502–34.

McAdam, Doug. 1982. *Political Process and the Development of Black Insurgency, 1930–1970.* Chicago: University of Chicago Press.

1986. "Recruitment to High-Risk Activism: The Case of Freedom Summer." *American Journal of Sociology* 92:64–90.

McCarthy, John, and Mayer Zald. 1973. *The Trend of Social Movements in America: Professionalization and Resource Mobilization.* Morristown, N.J.: General Learning Press.

1977. "Resource Mobilization in Social Movements: A Partial Theory." *American Journal of Sociology* 82:1212–39.

McGuire, Martin C. 1974. "Group Size, Group Homogeneity, and the Aggregate

Provision of a Pure Public Good Under Cournot Behavior." *Public Choice 18:*107–26.

McPhail, Clark. 1971. "Civil Disorder Participation: A Critical Examination of Recent Research." *American Sociological Review 36:*1058–73.

Messick, D. M., and C. L. McClelland. 1983. "Social Traps and Temporal Traps." *Personality and Social Psychology Bulletin 9:*105–10.

Messick, D. M., H. Wilke, M. B. Brewer, R. M. Kramer, P. E. Zemke, and L. Lui. 1983. "Individual Adaptations and Structural Changes as Solutions to Social Dilemmas." *Journal of Personality and Social Psychology 44:*294–309.

Michener, H. A., J. D. DeLamater, and S. A. Schwartz. 1986. *Social Psychology.* San Diego, Calif.: Harcourt Brace Jovanovich.

Mitchell, Robert Cameron. 1979. "National Environmental Lobbies and the Apparent Illogic of Collective Action." In *Collective Decision Making: Applications from Public Choice Theory,* ed. Clifford S. Russell, pp. 87–121. Baltimore: Johns Hopkins University Press for Resources for the Future.

Mizruchi, Mark. 1987. "Why do Corporations Stick Together? An Interorganizational Theory of Class Cohesion." In *Power Elites and Organizations,* ed. G. William Domhoff and Thomas Dye, pp. 204–18. Newbury Park, Calif.: Sage.

Moreno, J. L. 1934. *Who Shall Survive?* Washington, D.C.: Nervous and Mental Disease Publishing.

Morris, Aldon. 1981. "Black Southern Student Sit-In Movement: An Analysis of Internal Organization." *American Sociological Review 46:*744–67.

——— 1984. *The Origins of the Civil Rights Movement: Black Communities Organizing for Change.* New York: Free Press.

Oberschall, Anthony. 1973. *Social Conflict and Social Movements.* Englewood Cliffs, N.J.: Prentice-Hall.

——— 1979. "Protracted Conflict." In *The Dynamics of Social Movements,* ed. Mayer N. Zald and John D. McCarthy, pp. 45–70. Cambridge, Mass.: Winthrop Publishers.

——— 1980. "Loosely Structured Collective Conflicts: A Theory and an Application." In *Research in Social Movements, Conflict and Change,* vol. 3, ed. L. Kriesberg, pp. 45–68. Greenwich, Conn.: JAI Press.

Offe, Claus, and Hemut Weisenthal. 1980. "Two Logics of Collective Action." In *Political Power and Social Theory,* ed. Maurice Zeitlin, pp. 67–115. Greenwich, Conn.: JAI Press.

Oliver, Pamela. 1980. "Rewards and Punishments as Selective Incentives for Collective Action: Theoretical Investigations." *American Journal of Sociology 85:*1356–75.

——— 1984. "If You Don't Do It, Nobody Else Will: Active and Token Contributors to Local Collective Action." *American Sociological Review 49:*601–10.

Oliver, Pamela, and Mark Furman. 1989. "Contradictions Between National and Local Organizational Strength: The Case of the John Birch Society." In

Organizing For Change, ed. Bert Klandermans, pp. 45–70. Greenwich, Conn.: JAI Press.

Oliver, Pamela, and Gerald Marwell. 1988. "The Paradox of Group Size in Collective Action: Towards a Theory of the Critical Mass. II." *American Sociological Review* 53:1–18.

———. 1992. "Mobilizing Technologies for Collective Action." In *Frontiers in Social Movement Theory,* ed. Aldon D. Morris and Carol McClurg Mueller, pp. 251–72. New Haven, Conn.: Yale University Press.

Oliver, Pamela, Gerald Marwell, and Ruy Teixeira. 1985. "A Theory of the Critical Mass. I. Group Heterogeneity, Interdependence and the Production of Collective Goods." *American Journal of Sociology* 91:522–56.

Olson, Mancur. 1965. *The Logic of Collective Action.* Cambridge, Mass.: Harvard University Press.

Piliavin, Jane Allyn, John Dovidia, Sam Gaertner, and Russell Clark III. 1981. *Emergency Intervention.* New York: Academic Press.

Prahl, Ralph, Gerald Marwell, and Pamela Oliver. 1991. "Reach and Selectivity as Strategies of Recruitment for Collective Action: A Theory of the Critical Mass, V." *Journal of Mathematical Sociology* 16:137–64.

Samuelson, Paul A. 1954. "The Pure Theory of Public Expenditure." *Review of Economics and Statistics* 36:387–9.

Schelling, Thomas C. 1973. "Hockey Helmets, Concealed Weapons, and Daylight Saving: A Study of Binary Choices with Externalities." *Journal of Conflict Resolution* 17:381–428.

———. 1978. *Micromotives and Macrobehavior.* New York: Norton.

Schofield, Norman. 1975. "A Game Theoretic Analysis of Olson's Game of Collective Action." *Journal of Conflict Resolution* 19:441–61.

Scott, J. W., and M. El-Assal. 1969. "Multiversity, University Size, University Quality and Student Protest – An Empirical Study." *American Sociological Review* 34:702–9.

Smith, Jan. 1976. "Communities, Associations, and the Supply of Collective Goods." *American Journal of Sociology* 82:247–70.

Snow, David A., Louis A. Zurcher, Jr., and Sheldon Ekland-Olson. 1980. "Social Networks and Social Movements: A Microstructural Approach to Differential Recruitment." *American Sociological Review* 45:787–801.

Spilerman, Seymour. 1970. "The Causes of Racial Disturbances: A Comparison of Alternative Explanations." *American Sociological Review* 35:627–49.

Tilly, Charles. 1978. *From Mobilization to Revolution.* Reading, Mass.: Addison-Wesley.

Turner, Ralph H. 1981. "Collective Behavior and Resource Mobilization as Approach to Social Movements: Issues and Continuities." *Research in Social Movements, Conflicts and Change* 4:1–24.

Useem, Michael. 1975. *Protest Movements in America.* Indianapolis: Bobbs-Merrill.

Van de Kragt, A. J. C., J. M. Orbell, and R. M. Dawes. 1983. "The Minimal

Contributing Set as a Solution to Public Goods Problems." *American Political Science Review 77:*112–22.

Walsh, Edward, and Rex Warland. 1983. "Social Movement Involvement in the Wake of a Nuclear Accident: Activists and Free Riders in the TMI Area." *American Sociological Review 48:*764–80.

White, Harrison C., Scott A. Boorman, and Ronald L. Breiger. 1976. "Social Structure from Multiple Networks. I. Blockmodels of Roles and Positions." *American Journal of Sociology 81:*730–80.

Wilson, James Q. 1973. *Political Organizations.* New York: Basic.

Wilson, John. 1973. *Introduction to Social Movements.* New York: Basic.

Zald, Mayer N., and John D. McCarthy. 1979. *The Dynamics of Social Movements: Resource Mobilization, Social Control, and Tactics.* Cambridge, Mass.: Winthrop Publishers.

Name index

Subject index